Praise for This Book

"Everyone will enjoy reading *Red Wine For Dummies*. Its relaxed yet knowledgeable approach to a rather daunting topic will have novices and wine aficionados alike enjoying the book from cover to cover."

— Bruno Ceretto, Chairman, Ceretto Winery, one of the most influential wine producers in Piedmont, Italy

"Bravo! A complex subject taught clearly and comprehensibly with a touch of humor."

— Yves Durand, President, Sommelier Society of America, Inc.

"If you find red wine too intimidating to purchase, discuss or even drink, *Red Wine For Dummies* is a sure cure. Grape-by-grape, country-by-country, château-by-château, this book puts all the information at your fingertips and on the tip of your tongue. It's the next best thing to drinking red wine!"

— Alan H. Weitzman, Attorney and Wine Lover

"A fantastic book. Erudite and simple. Just what we need to navigate the maze of all the red wines in the world. It will help you appreciate and understand the basics of 'terroir' and the great pleasures that red wine can bring into your life."

— Jess Jackson, Proprietor, Kendall-Jackson, Artisans & Estates

"This book will keep you interested. I recommend it for every restaurant staff! It is a great way to learn about wine and share the knowledge with your customer. It's a 'full-blown' source of wine information that lingers on and on. . . ."

— Kevin Thompson, Wine Buyer, Mistral Restaurant, Redwood Shores, CA

Praise for Wine For Dummies

"[*Wine For Dummies*] is complete and done in an agreeably relaxed style."

— Frank J. Prial, *The New York Times*

Red Wine For Dummies™

Quick Reference Card

Guide to Red Wine Vintages

Like any wine vintage chart, you should consider this as only a rough guide.
Some wines are exceptions to the vintage's rating.

Wine Region	1985	1986	1987	1988	1989	1990	1991	1992	1993	1994
Bordeaux										
Médoc, Graves	90c	90a	75c	85a	90b	95a	75b	75b	80a	85a
Bordeaux										
Pomerol, St.-Emilion	85c	85a	75d	85a	90b	95a	65c	75b	80a	85a
Côte de Nuits										
Red Burgundy	85c	75d	85c	85b	85b	95a	85b	75b	85a	80a
Côte de Beaune										
Red Burgundy	85c	70d	80d	85b	85b	90b	70c	80b	85a	80a
Rioja (Spain)	80c	80c	80c	85b	90b	85b	75c	85b	85b	90a
Northern Rhône	90c	80b	75c	90c	95b	90a	90b	75c	65c	85a
Southern Rhône	80c	75c	60d	85c	95a	95b	70c	75c	80b	85a
Piedmont	95b	85c	80c	90a	95a	95a	80c	70c	85b	80a
Tuscany	95c	85c	75c	90a	70c	90b	75c	70c	75c	85a
California North Coast										
Cabernet Sauvignon	90b	80c	85c	75c	80b	95b	95a	90b	85a	95a

Key:
100	–	Outstanding	65	=	Poor
95	=	Excellent	50–60	=	Very poor
90	=	Very good	a	=	Too young to drink
85	=	Good	b	=	May be consumed
80	=	Fairly good			now, but will improve
75	=	Average			with time
70	=	Below average	c	=	Ready to drink
			d	=	May be too old

...For Dummies: Bestselling Book Series for Beginners

Red Wine For Dummies™

Quick Reference Card

BUSINESS AND
GENERAL
REFERENCE
BOOK SERIES
FROM IDG

Red Wine Style Finder

If You Want a...	Try...
Crisp, light-bodied red wine	Bardolino or Valpolicella Beaujolais Inexpensive U.S. Pinot Noir Inexpensive Chianti Loire Valley reds (Chinon, Bourgueil)
Medium-bodied, firm red wine	Less expensive Bordeaux wines Chianti Classico Rioja Cabernets or Syrahs from southern France Less expensive red Burgundies Beaujolais crus
Medium-bodied, soft red wine	Most U.S. Pinot Noirs Inexpensive California Cabernets and Merlots Inexpensive Zinfandels Many Australian Shiraz wines Australian Cabernets Most Côtes du Rhône reds Chilean Cabernets and Merlots
Full-bodied, intense red wine	Better California Cabernets, Merlots, and Zinfandels Better Bordeaux wines Barolo, Barbaresco, and Brunello di Montalcino Châteauneuf-du-Pape Hermitage and Côte Rôtie Better red Burgundy wines

Red Wines for Red Wine Novices

Many red wines can be quite austere and tannic — not easy drinking for the uninitiated. The following red wines are fairly low in tannin and/or soft and accessible. We recommend them particularly for those wine drinkers who are just beginning to enjoy red wine.

Wine	Country of Origin
Barbera	Italy
Bardolino	Italy
Beaujolais	France
Merlot	United States (California, Washington, Long Island)
Pinot Noir	United States (California, Oregon)
Shiraz	Australia
Valpolicella	Italy
Zinfandel	United States (California)

...For Dummies: Bestselling Book Series for Beginners

by Ed McCarthy and Mary Ewing-Mulligan MW

IDG Books Worldwide, Inc.
An International Data Group Company

Foster City, CA ✦ Chicago, IL ✦ Indianapolis, IN ✦ Southlake, TX

Red Wine For Dummies™

Published by
IDG Books Worldwide, Inc.
An International Data Group Company
919 E. Hillsdale Blvd.
Suite 400
Foster City, CA 94404
www.idgbooks.com (IDG Books Worldwide Web Site)
http://www.dummies.com (Dummies Press Web Site)

Library of Congress Catalog Card No.: 96-77705

ISBN: 0-7645-5012-8

Printed in the United States of America

10 9 8 7 6 5 4 3 2 1

Production: Please insert the following

1A/RT/QZ/ZW/IN

Distributed in the United States by IDG Books Worldwide, Inc.

Distributed by Macmillan Canada for Canada; by Contemporanea de Ediciones for Venezuela; by Distribuidora Cuspide for Argentina; by CITEC for Brazil; by Ediciones ZETA S.C.R. Ltda. for Peru; by Editorial Limusa SA for Mexico; by Transworld Publishers Limited in the United Kingdom and Europe; by Academic Bookshop for Egypt; by Levant Distributors S.A.R.L. for Lebanon; by Al Jassim for Saudi Arabia; by Simron Pty. Ltd. for South Africa; by Pustak Mahal for India; by The Computer Bookshop for India; by Toppan Company Ltd. for Japan; by Addison Wesley Publishing Company for Korea; by Longman Singapore Publishers Ltd. for Singapore, Malaysia, Thailand, and Indonesia; by Unalis Corporation for Taiwan; by WS Computer Publishing Company, Inc. for the Philippines; by WoodsLane Pty. Ltd. for Australia; by WoodsLane Enterprises Ltd. for New Zealand. Authorized Sales Agent: Anthony Rudkin Associates for the Middle East and North Africa.

For general information on IDG Books Worldwide's books in the U.S., please call our Consumer Customer Service department at 800-762-2974. For reseller information, including discounts and premium sales, please call our Reseller Customer Service department at 800-434-3422.

For information on where to purchase IDG Books Worldwide's books outside the U.S., please contact our International Sales department at 415-655-3172 or fax 415-655-3295.

For information on foreign language translations, please contact our Foreign & Subsidiary Rights department at 415-655-3021 or fax 415-655-3281.

For sales inquiries and special prices for bulk quantities, please contact our Sales department at 415-655-3200 or write to the address above.

For information on using IDG Books Worldwide's books in the classroom or for ordering examination copies, please contact our Educational Sales department at 800-434-2086 or fax 817-251-8174.

For authorization to photocopy items for corporate, personal, or educational use, please contact Copyright Clearance Center, 222 Rosewood Drive, Danvers, MA 01923, or fax 508-750-4470.

About the Authors

Ed McCarthy and Mary Ewing-Mulligan

Ed McCarthy and Mary Ewing-Mulligan are two wine lovers who met at an Italian wine tasting in New York's Chinatown in 1981 and formally merged their wine libraries and cellars when they married in 1983.

At the time of that fateful meeting, Mary had worked in the wine trade for ten years and had directed the Italian government's wine information bureau for the U.S. She grew up in Pennsylvania and studied English literature at the University of Pennsylvania.

Although employed full-time as an English teacher, Ed held part-time jobs in wine shops to satisfy his passion for wine and to subsidize his rapidly expanding wine collection. Born and raised in New York City, he earned a master's degree in psychology from City University of New York.

Today, Mary is co-owner and director of the International Wine Center, a wine school in Manhattan. She and Ed teach classes at the Center — solo and jointly — for wine lovers and for individuals employed in the wine trade. Retired from teaching English, Ed now devotes all of his time to wine, writing articles for *Wine Enthusiast* and *The Wine Journal*, consulting, and moonlighting at his favorite wine shop.

In 1993, Mary culminated five years of independent study in wine by becoming the only American woman who is a Master of Wine. She earned the title by passing a rigorous professional examination given by London's Institute of Masters of Wine. There are only 206 Masters of Wine in the world, including 14 in America.

In 1995, Mary and Ed coauthored *Wine For Dummies* (IDG Books Worldwide, Inc.).

When they are not teaching or writing about wine, Mary and Ed take busman's holidays to the wine regions of the world. They admit to living thoroughly unbalanced lives in which their only non-wine pursuits are hiking in the Italian Alps, running, unwinding to Neil Young music, and spending quiet time with Sherry, La Tache, Leoville, Pinot Grigio, Brunello, and Dolcetto — their cats.

Welcome to the world of IDG Books Worldwide.

ABOUT IDG BOOKS WORLDWIDE

Launched in 1990, IDG Books Worldwide, a subsidiary of International Data Group, is today the #1 publisher of best-selling computer books in the United States. We are proud to have received numerous awards from the Computer Press Association in recognition of editorial excellence and three awards from *Computer Currents'* First Annual Readers' Choice Awards. Our best-selling *...For Dummies* series has more than 30 million copies in print with translations in 30 languages.

Our mission is simple: Every one of our books is designed to bring extra value and knowledge-building instructions to the reader. Our books are written by experts who understand and care about our readers. The knowledge base of our editorial staff comes from years of experience in publishing, education, and journalism — experience that we use to produce books for the '90s. In short, we care about books, so we attract the best authors and editors. We devote special attention to details such as audience, interior design, use of icons, and illustrations. And because we use an efficient process of authoring, editing, and desktop publishing our books electronically, we can spend more time ensuring superior content and spend less time on the technicalities of making books.

One year after we started IDG Books Worldwide, Inc., our senior management team and friends traveled to Shafer Vineyards just north of our Bay Area offices to celebrate surviving our startup year. John and Doug Shafer graciously hosted a private tasting of their finest wines. We didn't know until that day that John Shafer had ventured into winemaking after spending over 20 years in book publishing! At the time, we remarked that "there is indeed life after book publishing," and we raised our glasses in a toast to John's success in making Shafer one of the premier wineries in the world. Since that fateful trip, we too launched a world-class venture, which established *Wine For Dummies* as a James Beard nominee in its debut year.

We want to thank John and Doug for having played a totally coincidental, yet memorable, role in our successful expansion into general reference publishing. Congratulations to John and Doug Shafer, two friends of IDG Books Worldwide and two world-class winemakers, on the debut of *Red Wine For Dummies* and *White Wine For Dummies*. May the best for both our operations be yet to come!

President and CEO
IDG Books Worldwide, Inc.

WINNER
*Eighth Annual
Computer Press
Awards ≥ 1992*

WINNER
*Ninth Annual
Computer Press
Awards ≥ 1993*

IDG Books Worldwide, Inc., is a subsidiary of International Data Group, the world's largest publisher of computer-related information and the leading global provider of information services on information technology. International Data Group publishes over 276 computer publications in over 75 countries. Ninety million people read one or more International Data Group publications each month. International Data Group's publications include: ARGENTINA: Annuario de Informatica, Computerworld Argentina, PC World Argentina; AUSTRALIA: Australian Macworld, Client/Server Journal, Computer Living, Computerworld, Computerworld 100, Digital News, IT Casebook, Network World, On-line World Australia, PC World, Publishing Essentials, Reseller, WebMaster; AUSTRIA: Computerwelt Österreich, Networks Austria, PC Tip; BELARUS: PC World Belarus; BELGIUM: Data News; BRAZIL: Annuário de Informática, Computerworld Brazil, Connections, Super Game Power, Macworld, PC Player, PC World Brazil, Publish Brazil, Reseller News; BULGARIA: Computerworld Bulgaria, Networkworld/Bulgaria, PC & MacWorld Bulgaria; CANADA: CIO Canada, Client/Server World, ComputerWorld Canada, InfoCanada, Network World Canada; CHILE: Computerworld Chile, PC World Chile; COLOMBIA: Computerworld Colombia, PC World Colombia; COSTA RICA: PC World Centro America; THE CZECH AND SLOVAK REPUBLICS: Computerworld Czechoslovakia, Elektronika Czechoslovakia, Macworld Czech Republic, PC World Czechoslovakia; DENMARK: Communications World, Computerworld Danmark, Macworld Danmark, PC Privat Danmark, PC World Danmark, PC World Danmark Supplements, TECH World; DOMINICAN REPUBLIC: PC World Republica Dominicana; ECUADOR: PC World Ecuador; EGYPT: Computerworld Middle East, PC World Middle East; EL SALVADOR: PC World Centro America; FINLAND: MikroPC, Tietoverkko, Tietoviikko; FRANCE: Distributique, Golden, Hebdo-Distributique, Info PC, Le Guide du Monde Informatique, Le Monde Informatique, Reseaux & Telecoms; GERMANY: Computer Partner, Computerwoche, Computerwoche Extra, Computerwoche Focus, I/M Information Management, Macwelt, PC Welt; GREECE: GamePro, Multimedia World; GUATEMALA: PC World Centro America; HONDURAS: PC World Centro America; HONG KONG: Computerworld Hong Kong, PCWorld Hong Kong, Publish in Asia; HUNGARY: ABCD CD-ROM, Computerworld Szamitastechnika, PC & Mac World Hungary, PC-X Magazine; ICELAND: Tolvuheimur/PC World Island; INDIA: Information Systems Computerworld, PC World India, Publish in Asia; INDONESIA: InfoKomputer PC World, Komputek Computerworld, Publish in Asia; IRELAND: ComputerScope, PC Live!; ISRAEL: People & Computers; ITALY: Computerworld Italia, Computerworld Italia Special Editions, Macworld Italia, Networking Italia, PC Shopping, PC World Italia, PC World/Walt Disney; JAPAN: DTP World, HP Open World Japan, Macworld Japan, Nikkei Personal Computing, Open World Japan, OS/2 World Japan, SunWorld Japan, Windows World Japan; KENYA: East African Computer News; KOREA: Hi-Tech Information/Computerworld, Macworld Korea, PC World Korea; MACEDONIA: PC World Macedonia; MALAYSIA: Computerworld Malaysia, PC World Malaysia, Publish in Asia; MEXICO: Computerworld Mexico, Macworld, PC World Mexico; MYANMAR: PC World Myanmar; NETHERLANDS: Computer! Totaal, LAN Magazine, LanWorld Buyers Guide, Macworld, Net Magazine, Totaal! Beursskrant; NEW ZEALAND: Absolute Beginner's Guide, Computer Buyer, Computer Industry Directory, Computerworld New Zealand, MTB, Network World, PC World New Zealand; NICARAGUA: PC World Centro America; NIGERIA: PC World Nigeria; NORWAY: Computerworld Norge, Computerworld Privat (Datamagasinet), CW Rapport Norge, IDG's KURSGUIDE, Macworld Norge, Multimediaworld, PC World Ekspress, PC World Nettverk, PC World Norge, PC World's Produktguide, Windows World Spesial; PAKISTAN: Computerworld Pakistan, PC World Pakistan; Panama: PC World Panama; P. R. OF CHINA: China Computer Users, China Computerworld, China Infoworld, China Telecom World Weekly, Computer & Communication, Electronic Design China, Electronics Today, Electronics Weekly, Game Camp, Game Soft, Network World China, PC World China, Popular Computer Weekly, Software Weekly, Software World, Telecom World; PERU: Computerworld Peru, PC World Profesional Peru, PC World Peru; PHILIPPINES: Computerworld Philippines, PC World Philippines, Publish in Asia; POLAND: Computerworld Poland, Computerworld Special Report, Macworld, Networld, PC World Komputer; PORTUGAL: Cerebro/PC World, Computerworld/Correio Informático, Dealer World Portugal, MacIn/PCIn, Multimedia World Portugal; PUERTO RICO: PC World Puerto Rico; ROMANIA: Computerworld Romania, PC World Romania, Telecom Romania; RUSSIA: Computerworld Russia, Mir PK, Sety; SINGAPORE: Computerworld Singapore, PC World Singapore, Publish in Asia; SLOVENIA: MONITOR; SOUTH AFRICA: Computing S.A., InfoWorld S.A., Network World S.A., Software World; SPAIN: Computerworld España, COMUNICACIONES WORLD, Dealer World, Macworld España, PC World España; SWEDEN: CAP&Design, Computer Sweden, Corporate Computing, MacWorld, Maxi Data, MikroDatorn, Nätverk & Kommunikation, PC/Aktiv, PC World, Windows World; SWITZERLAND: Computerworld Schweiz, Macworld Schweiz, PCtip; TAIWAN: Computerworld Taiwan, Macworld Taiwan, PC World Taiwan, Publish Taiwan, Windows World; THAILAND: Thai Computerworld, Publish in Asia; TURKEY: Computerworld Turkiye, MACWORLD Turkiye, PC WORLD Turkiye; UKRAINE: Computerworld Kiev, Computers & Software, Multimedia World Ukraine, PC World Ukraine; UNITED KINGDOM: Acorn User, Amiga Action, Amiga Computing, Appletalk, Computing, GamePro, Macworld, Network News, Parents and Computers, PC Advisor, PC Home, PSX Pro UK, The WEB; UNITED STATES: Cable in the Classroom, CD Review, CIO Magazine, Computerworld, Computerworld Client/Server Journal, Digital Video Magazine, DOS World, Federal Computer Week, GamePro, InfoWorld, I-Way, JavaWorld, Macworld, Multimedia World, Network World, Network World, PC Entertainment, PC World, Publish, SunWorld Online, SWATPro Magazine, Video Event, WebMaster; URUGUAY: PC World Uruguay; VENEZUELA: Computerworld Venezuela, PC World Venezuela; and VIETNAM: PC World Vietnam.   9/24/96

Dedication

To Bernie Fradin, proprietor of Quality House Liquors in New York, who introduced us many years ago to the pleasures of the red wines of Bordeaux, and taught us to love them.

Authors' Acknowledgments

What is most amazing about the publishers of *Red Wine For Dummies,* IDG Books Worldwide, is their ability to turn over our thoughts and manuscript into a book in what to us is record time. We acknowledge, with deep respect and gratitude, the guiding team responsible for this feat — President John Kilcullen, Milissa Koloski, Kathy Welton, Sarah Kennedy, Stacy Collins, and our project editor, Pam Mourouzis.We love the *...For Dummies* concept of taking difficult, technical subjects and turning them into readable prose that removes the intimidation factor from the subject. We're happy that we can be part of this concept.

We also acknowledge and thank all the winemakers of the world who have contributed to this book by providing inspiration through their wonderful red wines, which have given us countless hours of enjoyment and education.

On a more individual level, we thank Paul Hart and Jan Jacobsen of Rex Hill Vineyards for their unselfish hospitality at a crucial moment in the completion of this book.

We would also like to thank Margaret Stern of Stern Communications; Mario Cordero and Tricia Chimento of Remy Amerique, Inc.; Jeff Pogash of Schieffelin & Somerset Co.; David Wagner of Banfi Vintners; John W. Gay of Rosemount Estates; Barbara Scalera of Winebow Inc.; Jose Fernandez of Southcorp Wines, USA Inc.; Kimberly Charles of Kobrand Corporation; Bill Sciambi of Lauber Imports; Derry Golding of Jordan Winery; Brian Larky; Paula Ramsey of Valckenberg International, Inc.; Christine Deusen and Nina Brondmo of Clicquot, Inc.; Mary Marshall of Paterno Imports; J. Boutari and Son, S.A.; Miguel A. Torres, S.A of Torres Wines, Barcelona, Spain; Rainer Karl Lingenfelder; Lynn Penner-Ash of Rex Hill Vineyards; Kerry Godes of Kendall-Jackson (Cambria); John R. Shafer and Doug Shafer of Shafer Vineyards; Kathleen Talbert of Talbert Communications; and Marsha Palanci of Cornerstone Communications/Palace Brands Company for sending us labels for use in this book. We only wish we had room to use them all.

Publisher's Acknowledgments

We're proud of this book; please send us your comments about it by using the Reader Response Card at the back of the book or by e-mailing us at feedback/ dummies@idgbooks.com. Some of the people who helped bring this book to market include the following:

Acquisitions, Development, and Editorial

Senior Project Editor: Pamela Mourouzis

Executive Editor: Sarah Kennedy

Permissions Editor: Joyce Pepple

Copy Editor: Susan Diane Smith

General Reviewers: Norman Cox, Bill Hatcher, Tom Mathews

Editorial Manager: Kristin A. Cocks

Editorial Assistant: Ann Miller

Production

Project Coordinator: Debbie Sharpe

Layout and Graphics: Dominique DeFelice, Maridee Ennis, Patricia R. Reynolds, Michael Sullivan

Special Art: Shelley Lea

Proofreaders: Kathy McGuinness, Rachel Garvey, Carrie Voorhis, Karen York

Indexer: Sherry Massey

Special Help
Kathy Cox, Project Editor

General & Administrative

IDG Books Worldwide, Inc.: John Kilcullen, President and CEO; Steven Berkowitz, COO and Publisher

Dummies, Inc.: Milissa Koloski, Executive Vice President and Publisher

Dummies Technology Press and Dummies Editorial: Diane Graves Steele, Associate Publisher; Judith A. Taylor, Brand Manager

Dummies Trade Press: Kathleen A. Welton, Vice President and Publisher; Stacy S. Collins, Brand Manager

IDG Books Production for Dummies Press: Beth Jenkins, Production Director; Cindy L. Phipps, Supervisor of Project Coordination; Kathie S. Schutte, Supervisor of Page Layout; Shelley Lea, Supervisor of Graphics and Design; Debbie J. Gates, Production Systems Specialist

Dummies Packaging and Book Design: Patti Sandez, Packaging Assistant; Kavish+Kavish, Cover Design

♦

The publisher would like to give special thanks to Patrick J. McGovern, without whom this book would not have been possible.

♦

Contents at a Glance

Table of Contents

· ·

Chapter 11: The Other Great French Reds: Burgundy, Rhône, and Company 157

Chapter 12: Vino Rosso, Vino Tinto, Vinho Tinto 181

Part III: The Part of Tens 213

Chapter 13: Ten Little-Known Red Wines Worth Knowing 215

Chapter 14: Answers to Ten Frequently Asked Questions about Red Wine 221

The 5th Wave   By Rich Tennant

Introduction

. . . .

*R*ed wine used to be just a flavor of sorts — a particular version of the beverage called wine that people chose when they ate red meat or pizza for dinner. Then television programs and newspapers started reporting that alcohol is healthful. Did all those reports say *red wine* specifically, or did people just interpret the reports that way? Whatever. Red wine became medicine.

The interesting phenomenon is how eager people seem to be to take their medicine. (Back in the days when cod-liver oil was considered good for you, and then vitamin C, people didn't exactly go out of their way to incorporate those products into their entertaining.) Is everyone so health-conscious these days, we wonder, or was everyone just waiting for the right excuse to begin drinking red wine?

The fact of the matter is that red wine is much more than medicine. Red wine is a whole world — a fascinating and delicious world. Red wine has more flavors than you can count, and every flavor tastes a little different each time, depending on the particular brand and the foods you drink it with. Red wine is carefree like a picnic, friendly like a housewarming party, and serious like an investment portfolio. It mellows, it warms, it entertains, and it challenges. It is medicine for the spirit as well as for the heart. (And for once, medicine tastes good!)

Whether you're already a frequent traveler in the world of red wine or you're about to venture there for the first time, you're sure to love the scenery.

How to Use This Book

Red Wine For Dummies is small enough to carry with you when you go wine shopping and full of recommendations on what to buy. It is also a primer on red wine: You can read it to discover the fundamentals and become knowledgeable about red wine in general, even if you never have tasted red wine before.

Most red wines fall into the category of table wines — wines of the sort that you would drink with a meal — and those are the types of red wine that we cover in this book. We do not address *fortified* red wines (wines that have alcohol added to them), such as Port.

This book is divided into four parts. The following sections describe what you can find in each part.

Part I: A Course of Red Wine

The five chapters in this first part provide you with a foundation for understanding and enjoying red wine. They set the scene for your exploration and launch you on your journey.

Chapters 1 and **2** explain what red wine is and how it got that way: how the particular climate in different parts of the world affects the nature of red wine, and how winemaking techniques further affect the flavor and personality of the red wine in your glass. Both chapters offer advice on how to taste wine, and they establish the basic vocabulary of wine taste that we use throughout the book. Chapter 2 puts this vocabulary into a working context with a description of the four fundamental styles of red wine.

As **Chapter 3** explains, the taste of any red wine has one major influence besides climate and winemaking technique: the grape variety itself. We name the 11 most important types of grapes for making red wine, describe their flavor, tell you where in the world they grow, and name several wines that are made from each grape.

Role models of a red, liquid sort are the subject of **Chapter 4**. The red wines that we nominate as "the seven classic reds" are the prototypes for most other red wines, the inspiration for winemakers all over the world. Becoming familiar with these prototypical red wines is worth many years of wine-tasting experience.

Chapter 5 puts wine in its proper place — on the table, with food. Whether you're a carnivore or a vegetarian, the advice we offer about matching red wine with food is sure to enhance your enjoyment.

Part II: A World of Red Wine

Grab your passport and your wallet. The whole world of red wine awaits you!

In this part of the book, we discuss the major types of red wine from the major red wine regions of the world. We explain the style of wine for which each area is famous, what the wines cost, and when to drink them — young or with some age. Most important, we list our personal recommendations of specific wines you may want to try for yourself. You can find hundreds of recommendations in these chapters.

Many of the red wines we recommend are affordably priced wines that are widely available. Now and then, though, we get a little esoteric and mention extremely expensive wines or wines that are hard to find — just to round out the whole picture of red wine around the world.

We start our exploration on the home front, with the red wines of America. California Cabernet Sauvignons and Merlots fill the pages of **Chapter 6**. The other important red wines of California — Pinot Noir, Zinfandel, Rhône blends, and Cal-Ital renditions — are the subject of **Chapter 7**. The red wines of Oregon, Washington State, and New York provide a timely change of pace from California wines in **Chapter 8**.

Down Under, they make plenty of red wine — not just in Australia, but in Chile, Argentina, and South Africa, all of which are covered in **Chapter 9**.

In **Chapter 10**, we travel to the source — France, the home of the most famous, most classic red wines of all, Bordeaux. **Chapter 11** explores France's other great red wine, Burgundy, along with the other red wines of France. **Chapter 12** covers the rest of Europe: the unique red wines of Italy, Spain, and Portugal, and the wine values of the Eastern European countries.

Part III: The Part of Tens

In this part, we provide miscellaneous (and fun) information about red wines. **Chapter 13** names and describes "ten little-known reds" that deserve a shot at stardom. When you want to venture off the beaten track of already popular types of wine, turn here for inspiration.

Chapter 14 answers the ten most common (in our experience) questions about red wine; we hope that your questions are among them. **Chapter 15** gives you some wine-tasting exercises that you can do at home to improve your tasting skills and your general knowledge of red wine.

Part IV: Appendixes

If you ever run into Hannibal Lecter and he offers you a nice *key ANNN tee,* you can turn to our **Pronunciation Guide** to prove to him how *Chianti* really should be pronounced. The **Glossary** is the place to turn for definitions of technical terms, and we list **Addresses** for wineries whose wines are available only or primarily by mailing list. Finally, the **Vintage Chart** tells you which vintages are tops for the major types of red wine.

Icons Used in This Book

 So many wines, so little time! To narrow down the confusing array of wine brands and producers to a more manageable level, we indicate our favorite brands or producers of most of the red wines we discuss in this book — and we mark our recommendations with this symbol.

 Baloney (of the verbal sort) and red wine go hand in hand whenever wine snobs are around. This symbol indicates the subjects that particularly appeal to wine snobs; read these sections to get the straight scoop.

 Although we devote a whole chapter to pairing red wine with food, we also scatter food-and-wine suggestions throughout the other chapters. You can spot them quickly by looking for this icon.

 If you like to get to the bottom of things and enjoy knowing a few more details than the next person, be sure to read the paragraphs marked with this icon. On the other hand, if you *are* the next person, feel free to skip over these paragraphs.

 When we particularly want to drive a point home, we mark the paragraph with this symbol. Often, the point is something that we mentioned previously but that bears repeating.

 The space limitations of this book don't permit us to go into as much detail as we'd like on some aspects of red wine. When we know that we've already covered a particular subject in more detail in our full-sized book *Wine For Dummies,* also published by IDG Books Worldwide, Inc., we use this symbol to suggest that you turn there for more information.

 Although we try to make red wine as easy and confusion-free as possible, a few pitfalls and potholes are inevitable. Keep your eye out for the Caution sign so that you can steer clear of these danger areas.

 This symbol indicates tidbits of miscellaneous advice that we want to share with you.

Part I

A Course of Red Wine

In this part . . .

The world of red wine is as complex as a multicourse dinner — and in the eyes of some people, it's just as formal, elitist, and exclusive. But you don't need fancy clothes or perfect table manners to partake of the information that this part of the book offers. You don't even need to be a wine drinker already. All you need is interest, curiosity, and a hearty appetite for learning.

Oh — but there is one minor rite of admission. Before you begin reading, you must know the definition of the one technical word that we do not define in the following chapters: That's *red*.

Okay, then. Reddy . . . Set . . . GO.

Chapter 1

A Wine of a Different Color

In This Chapter

▶ Red stands for real

▶ Dress-for-success wines

▶ Why wines are red

▶ Flavor that's skin deep

*R*ed is the color of passion and royalty. It is also — in the opinion of many wine lovers — the color every wine would be, if only it could. In fact, nearly all the most celebrated, most legendary wines in the world are red wines.

Get serious wine lovers going on the topic of red wine versus white, and you'll probably hear that red wines are more important than white wines. Their arguments will be that red wines, generally speaking, have more flavor than white wines do, and that they offer a greater range of flavors, too. They'll certainly mention that red wines usually can age longer than white wines, and that they develop enticing characteristics in the process. Red wines are simply more complex than white wines, they'll conclude.

At the risk of alienating white wine loyalists, we confess some allegiance to these red-wing beliefs ourselves. If we ate only fish or lived in perpetual summer, maybe we'd think differently. As it is, though, red wine goes best with the foods we most like to eat, and it is red wine that feeds our never-ending fascination with wine.

What's So Special About Red

As stereotypes go, red wines are the wines to drink with meat. They are rich, "manly" wines that give an air of seriousness, maturity, and connoisseurship to all who imbibe them. Red wines dominate the innermost chambers of wine elitism: auction catalogs and collectors' cellars. They are the wines to drink when you have arrived or want to appear as if you've arrived — the liquid equivalent of dressing for success.

This stereotype involves *some* truth. Many wine drinkers begin drinking white wines and eventually acquire a taste for red wine. And male chauvinist winemakers from socially backward European countries swear that women prefer white wines.

Generally speaking, red wines are more collectible than white wines because they sustain the effects of time better than white wines (and often actually benefit from age). Anyone who buys wine for investment purposes rather than just for enjoyment usually owns far more red wine than white.

Red wines tend to be more popular than white wines during the colder months of the year. One reason may be that white wines are drunk colder than reds, and who wants a cold beverage in the midst of a blizzard? Another reason may be that the types of food that people tend to eat during the winter — roasts, stews, and other hearty dishes — taste better with red wines. (Turn to Chapter 5 for advice about red wine and food.)

Who's on top?

If anyone has undertaken a statistical analysis of the world's wines to determine the relative preponderance of white wine or red wine, we're not aware of it. In any such research, though, we bet that red wines would "win." Both France and Italy — which together make about 43 percent of the world's wine — produce more red wine than white. California, Germany, and Austria make more white wine than red, but their combined production is far less than either France's or Italy's alone.

The How and Why of Red Wine

If the only difference between red wines and white wines were what meets the eye — the color of the wine — wine drinkers wouldn't care whether they drank one or the other. In reality, the differences between white and red wine are far more than skin deep.

Thousands of different types of grapes in the world qualify as wine grapes. (Those people who like to go around muttering Latin botanical names know them as *vitis vinifera* grapes.) All these grapes fall into one of two categories, according to the color of their skins: *white grapes* or *black* (also known as *red*) *grapes*.

Red wines are red because they are made from so-called red grapes (they're actually blue or purple). During the winemaking process, the pigmentation of the grapeskins colors the grape juice — and consequently the wine from that juice. Only red grapes can make red wine.

In addition to being responsible for the color of red wines, red grapeskins contribute certain flavors and texture characteristics to red wines. Red wines therefore not only look completely different from white wines, but they also *taste* very different.

One substance that red wines take from their grapeskins is *tannin*. Tannin is a substance that exists in the skins of red grapes more so than in the skins of white grapes. (It's also in the seeds and stems.) If you were to taste grape tannin, you'd probably describe the flavor as dry or bitter. In red wine, the effect of tannin can be negative — too much of it can make a wine taste harsh and *astringent*. But the effect of tannin can also be very positive, making the wine feel thick and substantial in your mouth (more on the effect of tannin in Chapter 2).

The presence of tannin in red wines is the single most important difference between red wines and white wines. Some red wines are naturally lower in tannin than others. Without tannin, however, red wine would just be white wine of a different color.

Monkey in the middle

Pink-colored wines — called *rosé* wines or *blush* wines — fall precisely into the middle ground between red wine and white wine. Although they come from red grapes, they're made in such a way that they soak up less color and flavor from the grapeskins than red wines do. But they have more color and flavor than most white wines. So-called *White Zinfandel* (a pink wine made from the red Zinfandel grape) is the most common example of rosé wine in the United States. (This book does not include coverage of pink wines.)

The three stages of wine-tasting

 The differences between red wine and white wine become very evident when you taste each type of wine thoughtfully by using the three-step approach of professional wine-tasters:

- ✔ **See the wine:** Observe its color and the intensity of the color.

- ✔ **Smell the wine:** Rotate your glass on the table to swirl the wine and release the wine's aroma. Then take a good whiff of the wine (which should still be in your glass). Try to describe what you smell, drawing from your knowledge of what fruits, flowers, herbs, spices, and other things smell like.

- ✔ **Sip the wine:** Draw a little air into your mouth along with the wine and move the wine around in your mouth. Hold it in your mouth for several seconds — at least ten — so that all of its flavor can register, and think about how the wine feels and tastes (rough, smooth, full, light, sweet, tart, delicious, or yucky). After you swallow, notice how long the flavor lasts in your mouth. (If you like the wine, the longer the better!)

 For more discussion of how to taste wine, see Chapter 2 of *Wine For Dummies* (published by IDG Books Worldwide, Inc.).

Chapter 2

Red, Redder, Reddest

*W*ine professionals sometimes make a corny joke when they are handed a glass of red wine and asked to identify the wine. "Well," they say with mock bravado, "it's *red* wine!"

That line manages to draw a few laughs (along with quite a few groans) every time because its underlying premise — that all red wine is more or less alike — is ridiculous. Red wine collectively may be a distinct entity from white wine, but the resemblance among red wines stops there. The universe of red wines has all sorts of characters in it, from delicate lightweights to powerful brutes and everything in between. Some red wines, you could say, are a lot redder than others.

A Style Is Born

Because wine is an agricultural product, Mother Nature has a lot to say in creating the *style* of any wine: that is, the wine's combined attributes of color, aroma, flavor, and weight — the characteristics through which the wine manifests itself to you.

For a wine to be red in the first place, ripe red grapes are necessary — and red grapes can ripen only in vineyard locations that Nature blesses with warm-enough weather and enough sunshine during the summer and fall. Vineyards in cooler locations are destined to grow white grapes, which can survive in cooler growing conditions.

How climate affects style

Depending on how warm and how sunny the climate is, red grapes can become very ripe, very sweet, and very intensely flavored — or less so. The wine made from those grapes varies as a result. In fact, one of the main factors differentiating the taste of red wines from different parts of the world is the relative ripeness of the grapes. (Another big factor is the type of grape, but we get to that in Chapter 3.)

As red grapes ripen, they undergo several changes, just as any other fruit does. Here's some of what happens:

✔ They lose their raw, green color and take on a purple or blue color; the riper the grapes, the deeper their color.

✔ The grapes become sweeter and less tart, just as any other fruit does. (In technical terms, the *acidity* in the grapes falls and the natural sugar rises.)

✔ The *flavor compounds* of the grapes — molecules occupying a thin layer of pulp beneath the skin — change and "ripen."

✔ A substance in the grapes and stems called *tannin* slowly changes its molecular structure, becoming less bitter.

The amount of sugar and acid in red grapes at harvest time, and the extent to which the grapes' tannin and flavor have developed, determine what style of red wine those grapes give.

✔ Red wines from less-ripe grapes are generally lighter in color, lighter in *body* (the perceived weight of a wine in your mouth), have tart-fruit or herbal flavors, and can be slightly astringent.

✔ Red wines from very ripe grapes generally have deep color, full body, flavors of very ripe or cooked fruits, and are softer in texture.

How winemaking affects style

At the moment of perfect ripeness (a somewhat arbitrary occasion, rather like a perfect marriage), the sugar, acid, and tannin of the red grapes are within a suitable range to make good red wine of one style or another.

The juice of the red grapes turns into wine through a completely natural process called *fermentation*. As the crushed grapes — a concoction of juice, pulp, grapeskins, and seeds, or *pips* — sit in a tank, yeasts begin converting the sugar of the juice into alcohol. (Yeasts exist on the grapes, but the wine-maker can add his or her favorite yeast strain to the juice for good measure.) After all the sugar changes to alcohol, the grape juice is officially red wine.

Very ripe red grapes make a wine that is higher in alcohol than less-ripe grapes because they have more sugar for the yeasts to convert into alcohol. To some extent, the winemaker can simulate ripeness and increase the ultimate alcohol content slightly by adding sugar to the grape juice before it begins fermenting. The higher alcohol content causes the wine to taste fuller and more powerful.

While the juice is in the process of becoming wine, it absorbs color from the grapeskins and soaks up tannin from the skins and seeds of the grapes. (The grape stems, which have a lot of tannin, are usually discarded before fermentation begins.) Precisely *how much* color and tannin the juice absorbs depends on winemaking technique.

Temperature of the juice and *skin-contact time* — the length of time that the grapeskins mingle with the juice (or wine) — are two variables that determine the amount of color and tannin in a red wine. Generally speaking, a warm fermentation extracts more color and tannin from the grapes; long skin-contact time (also called *maceration*) before or after fermentation increases the amount of tannin in a wine — up to a point.

Although color is mainly an aesthetic issue, the amount of tannin in a wine directly affects the texture and flavor of the wine. Tannin brings richness and "character" to the wine. Professional wine-tasters use the word *amplitude* to describe the positive effect that tannin gives to the flavor of red wine; *breadth of flavor* is another way of describing tannin's contribution to red wine. Too much tannin, however, can make a wine tough and difficult to enjoy.

If a winemaker allows a red wine to age in new, small, 60-gallon oak barrels, the wood contributes its own tannin (called *wood tannin*) to the wine, supplementing the wine's natural grape tannin.

The wine's acidity — a vital consideration in white wines — is of secondary importance in red wines because tannin performs functions similar to acidity, such as making the wine taste firm and preserving the wine. High acidity in a red wine, in fact, can be detrimental to the wine's quality.

The Range of Red

When you open a bottle of red wine and pour the wine into a glass, what you see, smell, and taste varies from one wine to the next — sometimes only slightly and sometimes tremendously.

Shades of red

Red wines can be nearly purple in color, or they can be ruby, garnet, or brick colored. The color can vary in intensity from inky-opaque to pale. Although no correlation is guaranteed, deeper-colored red wines are generally intensely flavored and rich, and paler red wines tend to be lighter in body. And this bit of trivia may serve you well at your next dinner party: The younger the red wine, the more bluish tones its color is likely to have.

Smelling everything but the roses

The most common aromas of red wine are fruit aromas. These fruit aromas generally fall into two groups: red fruits, such as strawberries, cherries, raspberries, and red currants; and black fruits, such as blackberries, black currants, and plums. Fruit aromas in red wines can vary further, from fresh fruit scents to various cooked fruit aromas, such as jam, baked fruit, roasted fruit, or stewed fruit. (Just think: Learning to identify red wine aromas can give you a whole new excuse to order dessert!)

Other smells that you can find in red wines include

- **Spicy scents:** Cinnamon, cloves, black pepper, and so forth
- **Herbal scents:** Eucalyptus, mint, anise, fennel, fresh herbs in general, dried herbs
- **Vegetal scents:** Green beans, fresh tobacco, bell pepper
- **Earthy aromas:** Mushrooms, wet leaves, damp earth, dry leaves, dusty smells, mineral-like smells, tar, truffles
- **Animal-like aromas:** Leather, manure (politely referred to as *barnyard*), sweat, meaty scents
- **Wood-derived aromas:** Raw or charred wood, toast, smoke, vanilla, cedar

If you're not in the habit of paying attention to smells, you might have some difficulty recognizing these aromas in red wines, but practice helps. Even with experience, you'll be able to detect only one or two aromas in some wines. But the very best red wines dish out a stunning array of aromas that leave you so busy enumerating them that you might forget to *drink* the wine!

When you do drink the wine, you usually find that the wine's flavors are similar to its aromas — because flavor is simply aroma that you perceive through a nasal passage at the rear of your mouth. For more information about tasting wine, refer to Chapter 2 of our book *Wine For Dummies.*

The taste of red

Because red wines do have tannin and white wines generally don't, red wines are structurally more complex than white wines. In other words, a lot is happening in your mouth when you taste a red wine. The wine's acid and tannin give your tongue signals of firmness and solidity, and the alcohol suggests roundness and maybe a slight sweetness. Tannin may cause the wine to feel thick and velvety or sharp, depending on the wine. All the while, you are sensing flavors such as fruits, earthiness, and oak. No wonder no two red wines taste exactly the same!

Wine, plain and simple

Unlike chefs, winemakers don't have a whole pantry of ingredients available to make their product. All they have are grapes, yeasts, and a few natural chemical compounds that they use to clarify or stabilize the wine. Every aroma and flavor you find in wine, whether it's berries, mushrooms, or bell peppers, comes from the grapes and the chemical transformations that occur during fermentation and aging. The only exception is oaky character, which comes from the oak containers some winemakers use for their wines (see "How winemaking affects style," earlier in this chapter).

How wine tastes

The way any wine — red or white — tastes in your mouth is actually a combination of two forces:

✔ The *flavors* of the wine, which are really aromas that you "taste"

✔ The *structure* of the wine; that is, the combined effect of the wine's alcohol, sweetness (if any), acid, and tannin — all of which you sense tactilely on your tongue

Depending on how the four *structural components* interrelate in any particular wine, the wine may seem more or less full, more or less *dry* (that is, not sweet), and more or less smooth, sharp, or soft. The relationship of structural elements is called *balance* because the components balance each other out. Both acid and tannin create an impression of firmness in your mouth, which balances the wine's alcohol and sweetness (if any), the "softening" components of the wine.

A wine's *texture* — the way the wine feels in your mouth, such as velvety, silky, thick, or thin — is a reflection of its structure. (For more discussion of the taste of wine, see Chapters 2 and 18 of *Wine For Dummies*.)

Common Red Wine Styles

Although no two red wines are exactly alike, many red wines share common characteristics. Grouping wines according to their shared characteristics — their *style* — is a sensible way to approach red wine, because it simplifies into workable categories what is otherwise an impossibly vast and multifarious universe of individual wines.

You might think that people in the wine business would have figured that out already and created an official listing and description of various wine styles. But no such listing exists. People who make and sell wine prefer to emphasize the unique aspects of their wine ("We used ten different yeast strains to build complexity in our Cabernet") than to place their wine in a context of similar-style wines. Helping consumers to understand is a noble idea, but marketing drives sales.

In the absence of an industry-endorsed standard classification of red wines, we had to develop our own set of red wine styles. As we see it, two characteristics are pivotal determinants of style in red wine:

 ✔ The perceived weight of the wine (light bodied, medium bodied, or full bodied)

 ✔ The degree to which the wine is either crisp and firm on the palate or soft and smooth

Using these criteria, we offer the following breakdown of red wine styles. For more information about the specific wines that we use as examples of each style, peruse Chapters 6 through 11.

 ✔ **Light-bodied red wines, crisp:** These wines taste dry and crisp because their acidity and tannin (the firming or crisping components of the wine) have more to say than their alcohol (a softening component) does — even if their alcohol is in a perfectly normal range, such as 12.5 percent. Such wines are more or less flavorful, depending on the individual wine. Examples include Italian reds such as Bardolino, Valpolicella, and northeastern Italian Cabernets; inexpensive Pinot Noirs from the United States; some Cabernets from Chile; and many Beaujolais wines.

 ✔ **Medium-bodied red wines, firm:** These wines have more weight and substance than the first group but still balance out as firm rather than soft. Examples include many Bordeaux wines, most Chianti wines, Rioja from Spain, Loire Valley reds, and varietally labeled wines from the south of France. (See Chapter 3 for an explanation of varietal labeling.)

 ✔ **Medium-bodied red wines, soft:** Because of either their ripeness or their grape variety, you perceive these wines as fairly soft when you taste them. Examples include many U.S. Pinot Noirs, inexpensive Cabernets and Merlots, inexpensive Zinfandels, many Burgundy wines, many Shiraz wines from Australia, and wines from the Côtes du Rhône in southern France.

 ✔ **Full-bodied red wines, intense:** These wines are either very tannic, very high in alcohol, or intensely concentrated with flavors that come from the grape (sometimes all three at once!). Examples include the more expensive California Cabernets, Merlots, and Zinfandels; high-end Bordeaux wines from good vintages; Barolo, Barbaresco, and Brunello di Montalcino from Italy; northern Rhône reds; and the finest Burgundy wines.

The risk in any generalization — including our classification of red wine styles — is oversimplification. In reality, red wines follow a stylistic continuum from the simplest, lightest wines at one end to the "biggest," most intense wines at the other end. Don't be surprised if you find wines that you personally would describe as being on the cusp of two styles. We simply had to draw the line somewhere.

The stylistic continuum of red wines does correspond somewhat to price. The least expensive red wines (less than $8 or $10 a bottle) tend to be either light-bodied or fairly simple, quaffable wines. The most expensive red wines ($20 to $25 a bottle and up) tend to be the most intense wines. The wines in the middle price range ($10 to $20) either have more weight or flavor concentration coming from their grapes or are oaked more than the less-expensive wines.

The Bottom Line of Red Wine

In most fields, red is just a color. But in wine, the color red carries with it a whole array of flavors and textures, making red wine probably the most complex beverage on the planet.

Climate — and the grapes' growing conditions in general — determines how much "stuff" any batch of red grapes has to offer; the winemaker determines how much of that stuff finds its way into the wine. The combined variables of climate and winemaking technique interact to create an infinite number of unique red wines.

Is ageability a criterion of quality?

Because many great red wines are intense, full-bodied wines that improve with age, you might conclude that a red wine's capability to age implies high quality — and conversely, that red wines made to be drunk when young are lower in quality.

Actually, quality and ageability do not necessarily go hand in hand. Whether a wine will taste better after a few years of aging or is delicious when young is a matter of style, not quality. Depending on style, however, the wine's quality can be affected by age: fresh, charming red wines deteriorate with age because they lose their freshness; intense, full-bodied reds can improve with age because age can soften their harsh tannins and enrich the wines' flavors.

Chapter 3

What a Difference a Grape Makes

In This Chapter

▶ Beyond plain old chocolate

▶ How the grape makes the wine

▶ Major red grape varieties

▶ Purebreds, blends, and Bastardo

*I*f all the red wines in the world were made from the same grape variety, every red wine would still taste somewhat different from the next. Variations in the grape's flavor from vineyard to vineyard, and variations in winemaking technique from one winery to the next, would guarantee that. But all those wines would taste similar enough that you'd get bored pretty quickly. (Imagine if chocolate were the only flavor of ice cream!)

Luckily for those of us who enjoy wine, enough different types of red grapes exist to keep us entertained for a lifetime — especially considering that the same grape never makes exactly the same wine twice.

The Power behind the Throne

Grapes are the raw material of wine. Naturally, any difference in raw material creates a different wine. Some differences in the raw material of a wine are attributable to the grapes' ripeness level — how sweet and plump the grapes are when they are harvested. (See "How climate affects style" in Chapter 2.) Other fundamental differences come from the type of grape that constitutes the wine's raw material.

How many different red grape varieties exist in the world is anybody's guess. (If we say hundreds, we're probably underestimating the number.) Each variety is genetically distinct from the next, although some are closely related, like cousins. Many important red grape varieties (such as Cabernet Sauvignon and Merlot) grow in several different countries, and some obscure varieties grow only in isolated pockets of winedom.

Why finding out about grape varieties is great

Except for European wines, nearly all the wines of the world are named according to their grape variety; that's how fundamental the grape is. (Wines named for their grape variety are called *varietal wines.*) A California winery that makes three different red wines, for example, typically makes each wine from a different red grape variety and names each wine after the grape from which it is made.

Restaurant wine lists often divide wines into groups according to grape variety. *Cabernets* (wines made from, and usually named for, the Cabernet Sauvignon grape) may all be on one page, and *Merlots* or *Pinot Noirs* on another page. Your supermarket or wine shop may very well arrange the wines on its shelves the same way.

For anyone who buys wine in restaurants, supermarkets, or wine shops (or anyone who drinks wine, for that matter), the names of the major grapes are a key that unlocks one of the barriers between Those Who Know Wine and everyone else.

Why knowing grape varieties has a downside

We're sure that Ralph Waldo Emerson wasn't thinking about wine and grape varieties when he wrote, "A little knowledge is a dangerous thing." But his statement applies perfectly. The danger, in the case of wine and grape varieties, is oversimplification.

The fact that two wines are made from the same grape variety is no guarantee that those wines really resemble each other any more than two shirts, both made from cotton, resemble each other.

Following are just a few of the reasons:

> ✔ A wine ostensibly made from a specific, single grape —
> such as many wines labeled Merlot — may have been
> blended from as much as 25 percent of another grape,
> according to U.S. law. (Blending involves mixing together
> two or more different lots of grape juice or wine — in this
> case, juice or wine from different grape varieties.) Wines
> from Australia, Canada, and Europe can have a 15 percent
> fudge factor in their grape blends, generally speaking. (In

some circumstances, blending is forbidden.) Blending often improves the quality of the wine, but it decreases the accuracy of any assumptions you make about the wine based on what you believe its grape is.

✔ A big difference exists in flavor intensity and other crucial quality factors between grapes industrially farmed to produce a very large crop (called a *high yield*) and grapes grown at *low yields* with the specific intention of making the finest wine possible — even if both are the same variety.

✔ Two wines that have the same starting point — the very same grapes — can end up vastly different because of how the winemaker transforms the grape juice into wine.

✔ Such things as *clones* exist within any grape variety — that is, subvarieties whose grapes may taste subtly different from the norm for that grape.

If you look at grape varieties as just the starting point of wines, you won't fall into the trap of assuming that all red wines with the same name should taste the same, and you won't be disappointed when they don't. (Unfortunately, you also have fewer easy answers when you're trying to decide which wine to buy.)

Why individuality among grape varieties is important

Some of the ways in which red grape varieties differ from one another are irrelevant to wine drinkers — such as the shape and hairiness of the grape's leaves. The relevant differences from one variety to the next (in other words, the differences that you can taste) are simply that

✔ Each variety contributes its own set of aromas and flavors to wines made from it.

✔ Some varieties naturally have more (or less) tannin, acid, or sweetness.

Of these two factors, the aromas and flavors of each grape are more important in understanding the wines made from that grape. Because winemakers can manipulate all the other characteristics of a grape (and its juice) to some degree, a wine's tannin, acid, or alcohol level (which derives from the grape's sweetness) are less directly related to the nature of the grape variety or varieties from which the wine is made.

What variety where

In grape growing, as in any other agricultural pursuit, farmers have to plant the crop that grows best on the land they have. In grape terms, that means that Nature dictates which type of grape can grow in a vineyard. Even if the climate is generally warm enough for red grapes, it may not be warm enough to ripen Cabernet Sauvignon grapes completely. Or a vineyard may be too warm to grow good Pinot Noir grapes, which like slightly cooler weather than Cabernet grapes. In addition to temperature and amount of sunshine, the type of soil in a vineyard is a factor in determining which type of grape grows best there.

For more discussion of grapes and soil, refer to Chapter 9 of our book *Wine For Dummies*.

Major Red Grapes

Some red grape varieties are Major Players. Wine drinkers all over the world have heard of them, and the wines made from those varieties are so important that it's hard to imagine the world of wine without them. Each Major Player grape has spawned so many wines in so many different countries and wine regions that the grape's characteristics — known collectively as its *varietal character* — are easy to deduce.

Other red grape varieties are in the minor leagues in terms of global proliferation. But every such variety is important to certain wine regions, where the entire wine economy may revolve around the wines made from that grape. The characteristics of these grapes are closely linked to the climate, soil, and winemaking traditions of the particular region where the grapes are important — and knowing the grape's characteristics in the abstract is therefore difficult.

Most of the 11 red grape varieties we describe in the two following sections are Major Players, but those in the first section are particularly famous.

The Final Four

We don't want you to think that you must have just missed something, and we don't mean to suggest that we're starting at the end. The reason we call the four grapes described in the following sections "The Final Four" is that we can, somewhat cynically, imagine a world of the future where all red wine is made from one of these four grapes. Not only have these grapes adapted themselves well enough in far-flung corners of the wine world to make Darwin proud, but they also make wines that are popular enough to elbow out wines from "lesser" grapes in sales.

Cabernet Sauvignon

Nicknames: Cabernet, Cab

Origin: France

Where significant today: France's Bordeaux region; southern France; California, Washington State, Long Island, and many other U.S. wine regions; Australia; South Africa; Chile; Argentina; isolated parts of Spain and Portugal; parts of Italy; Romania; Bulgaria

Characteristics: Cabernet Sauvignon grapes are relatively small, their skin is relatively thick, and their seeds are large — all three factors contributing to a high solids-to-juice ratio. This ratio translates into deeply colored wines with a firm tannic structure (see "How wine tastes" in Chapter 2). Wines made entirely from Cabernet Sauvignon can be so tannic that winemakers often blend Merlot and sometimes Cabernet Franc (a related grape) with their Cabernet. In the Bordeaux region of France, in fact, where Cabernet became famous, such blending is the norm.

If the grapes have not ripened perfectly, Cabernet wine can have vegetal aromas and flavors, specifically raw green bell peppers. At full ripeness, Cabernet gives its wine the aroma and flavor of black currants or cassis. The best wines from Cabernet tend to age very well, developing fascinating aromas such as leather, tobacco, lead pencil, and cedar along the way. Figure 3-1 shows a label from a Cabernet Sauvignon wine.

Figure 3-1: Label from a Cabernet Sauvignon wine.

Merlot

Origin: France

Where significant today: France's Bordeaux region; southwestern France; southern France; California, Washington State, and Long Island; Argentina; Chile; northeastern Italy; Romania; Bulgaria; South Africa

Characteristics: Merlot's large, plump, thin-skinned berries provide winemakers with sweet juice from which they can make a dark, soft, low-tannin wine that is relatively high in alcohol. Because Merlot wine is softer and less tannic than Cabernet wine, many winemakers blend Merlot into their Cab; conversely, many winemakers blend some Cabernet into their Merlot to give the wine more intensity than the Merlot alone can provide. The aromas and flavors of Merlot tend toward plummy fruit and chocolate. Merlot wines are usually ready to drink at a younger age than Cabernet wines. Figure 3-2 shows a label from a Merlot wine.

Merlot wine is extremely popular with wine drinkers these days, and grapegrowers all over the world are growing the Merlot grape to capitalize on that popularity. Unfortunately, Merlot is more finicky than the Cabernet Sauvignon grape in terms of its growing conditions. Some of the places where Merlot is grown today are less than ideal because their climate is too warm or too cool, or their soil is too sandy. As a result, the range of quality levels that exists for Merlot wine is more dramatic than for Cabernet, with many thin, vegetal wines from underripe fruit and many overly alcoholic wines from overripe fruit. (For our recommendations of correct Merlot wines, turn to Chapter 6.)

Figure 3-2: Label from a Merlot wine made in Chile.

Pinot Noir

Origin: France

Where significant today: France's Burgundy region, the Alsace region of France, southern Germany (where this wine is called *Spätburgunder*), northeastern Italy (where it is called *Pinot Nero*), Switzerland, California and Oregon, New Zealand. Also important in the Champagne region of France, where it makes sparkling wines that are white, not red.

Characteristics: Pinot Noir is not a deeply pigmented grape; therefore its wines are usually not particularly dark in color. The grape is relatively low in tannin, and its wines are, too, unless the winemaker augments the tannin by aging the wine in new oak barrels (where it picks up the tannin of the oak) or by retaining some of the stems during fermentation.

The aromas and flavors of Pinot Noir vary tremendously according to where the grape is grown. The most common are a vivid fruity character — either red berries or black berries; a sweet, tomato-paste flavor (in parts of California); and earthy aromas reminiscent of dead leaves and underbrush. The aromas and flavors of this grape are so prized that Pinot Noir-based wines are almost always made entirely from the Pinot Noir grape without blending in other grapes. Except for the very finest (very expensive) examples, Pinot Noir wines are best when young, from one to six years of age. Figure 3-3 shows a label from a Pinot Noir wine.

Figure 3-3: Label from a Pinot Noir wine.

Syrah

Origin: France

Where significant today: France's Rhône region, southern France, Australia (where the wine is called *Shiraz*), Switzerland, South Africa (where it is called *Shiraz*), parts of California, Israel. Also grown in Italy and Washington.

Characteristics: Dark color and high levels of tannin character-ize Syrah grapes and most of the wines made from them. The aromas and flavors can be very complex, ranging from fruit flavors (strawberry, cherry, or raspberry) to vegetal flavors (roasted green peppers), meaty flavors (smoky bacon), spicy flavors (barbecue or black pepper), or even chemical aromas, such as burnt rubber.

The style of Syrah wines varies according to where the grapes are grown and the type of wine the winemaker intends to make. (Some winemakers intentionally extract very little color and/or tannin from their Syrah grapes, for example.) The least intense examples are very flavorful, easy-to-drink wines with candied fruit or fresh fruit flavors; the most intense examples are sturdy, concentrated, long-aging wines with vegetal and meaty flavors interwoven with fruit. Figure 3-4 shows a label from a Shiraz wine.

Figure 3-4: Label from a Shiraz (Syrah) wine.

The Contenders

Sociologists say that the world is shrinking: All cultures are blending into one. Fortunately for red wine lovers, global homogeneity of wines has not occurred — yet. Although Cabernet Sauvignon, Merlot, Pinot Noir, and Syrah are popping up in parts of the world where these grapes were unheard of as recently as ten years ago, most important native red grapes are still going strong.

Most of the red grapes we describe in the following sections come from Europe, and most of the wines made from them are European wines. Because European wines are usually named after the place where they are produced, and not their grape variety, you may never have heard of some of these grapes before — even if you have enjoyed the wine made from them. As winemakers in the rest of the world begin dabbling in these grapes and naming their wines after the grape itself, these grapes should become more familiar to wine drinkers.

That said, we start with an exception: a grape grown mainly in California whose name is no stranger to the lips of red wine (and pink wine) lovers.

Zinfandel

Nickname: Zin

Origin: Uncertain (we're not joking), but somewhere in Europe

Where grown: California

Important wines made from this grape: California Zinfandel (definitely a red wine), California "White Zinfandel" (a pink wine)

Characteristics: The Zinfandel grape gives good color to the red wines made from it, along with bramble-berry fruit flavors and aromas and a spicy character. The intensity of the wine varies according to where the grapes grew and how old the vines are; some very old (80 to 100 years) vineyards make wines that are full bodied and dense with flavor. More typically, Zinfandel makes wines that are medium bodied, with succulent fruit and medium tannin.

Gamay

Origin: France

Where grown: The Beaujolais district of France, France's Loire Valley wine region

Important wines made from this grape: Beaujolais, Anjou Gamay, Gamay de Touraine

Characteristics: "Grapey" is a descriptive term often associated with the Gamay grape because most of its wines, such as Beaujolais, are typically enjoyed when they are very youthful, fresh, and juicy tasting.

Gamay makes wines that are naturally low in alcohol and light in body (although winemakers can build in more alcohol by adding sugar to the juice), with high acidity and medium tannin. Sometimes Gamay-based wines have a slight floral fragrance, unusual for red wines, and they can have candied fruit flavors that are derived from a particular style of winemaking used for wines meant to be enjoyed young. California wines called Gamay Beaujolais and Napa Gamay are made from a different grape. Figure 3-5 shows a label from a wine made from the Gamay grape.

Figure 3-5: Label from a Beaujolais wine, which is made from the Gamay grape.

Sangiovese

Origin: Italy

Where grown: Central Italy, California, Argentina

Important wines made from this grape: Chianti, Rosso di Montalcino, Brunello di Montalcino, many so-called super-Tuscan wines (see Chapter 12)

Characteristics: Sangiovese makes wines that are relatively high in acidity for red wines, low to medium in tannin, and medium in color intensity. Cherry fruit and dusty aromas are typical. A few different subvarieties of Sangiovese are known to exist in Italy; the finest version, called *Sangiovese grosso,* makes Brunello di Montalcino and many of the more expensive, intensely flavored Chianti wines and super-Tuscan wines. Sangiovese wines are often unblended, but in traditional Chianti, Sangiovese is blended with some Canaiolo (a local red grape) and two white grapes. Nowadays, winemakers sometimes blend Sangiovese with Cabernet. Figure 3-6 shows a label from a wine made from the Sangiovese grape.

Nebbiolo

Origin: Italy

Where grown: Northwestern Italy (the regions of Piedmont and Lombardy), California

Important wines made from this grape: Barolo, Barbaresco, Nebbiolo d'Alba, Gattinara

Characteristics: When the Nebbiolo grape has just the right conditions to ripen, it makes wines that taste and smell of ripe strawberries mingled with a mélange of herbal and earthy aromas, such as eucalyptus, mint, tar, and the wonderfully smelly white truffles that grow in the same region as most Nebbiolo does. The finest Nebbiolo wines have high acidity, high tannin, and often a high alcohol content — monster wines that need many years to mature. Nebbiolo from certain vineyard areas makes a medium-bodied, less tannic wine that can be enjoyed young.

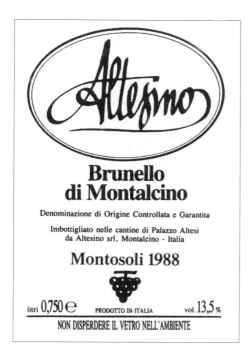

Brunello di Montalcino

Denominazione di Origine Controllata e Garantita

Imbottigliato nelle cantine di Palazzo Altesi
da Altesino srl, Montalcino - Italia

Montosoli 1988

litri 0,750 ℮   PRODOTTO IN ITALIA   vol. 13,5 %

NON DISPERDERE IL VETRO NELL'AMBIENTE

Figure 3-6: Label from a Brunello di Montalcino wine, made from the Sangiovese grape.

Barbera

Origin: Italy

Where grown: Northern Italy, California, Argentina, Brazil

Important wines made from this grape: Italian wines labeled Barbera followed by the name of a place, such as Barbera d'Alba or Barbera d'Asti; some California wines labeled Barbera

Characteristics: Wines made from the Barbera grape are usually deep in color, have high acidity and very low tannin, and show spicy and fruity flavors. Because the grape is low in tannin, the wine can be soft and very easy to drink. To compensate for this lack of tannin, some winemakers age Barbera wines in new oak casks so that the wine takes on tannin from the wood; these oak-aged wines are usually more expensive. Figure 3-7 shows a label from a wine made from the Barbera grape.

IMBOTTIGLIATO DA VIETTI CASTIGLIONE FALLETTO ITALIA

Vietti®

1990

BARBERA D'ALBA

DENOMINAZIONE DI ORIGINE CONTROLLATA

SCARRONE

ALCOHOL 13.50% BY VOL. - BOTTLED BY VIETTI - RED WINE - 750 ML
BOTTIGLIE PRODOTTE N. 8,000
PRODUCT OF ITALY

Figure 3-7: Label from a Barbera d'Alba wine.

Tempranillo

Origin: Spain

Where grown: Spain, Portugal, Argentina

Important wines made from this grape: Red Rioja wines, reds from Spain's Ribera del Duero region, Douro reds from Portugal (where the grape is called *Tinta Roriz*)

Characteristics: The thick-skinned Tempranillo grape gives wines deep color, moderate tannin, and low-to-moderate acidity. Tempranillo does not have a particularly marked aroma or taste that is all its own; in fact, most wine professionals recognize a Rioja wine not by the distinct flavor of the Tempranillo grape but by the aroma of the particular type of oak in which Rioja wine is aged (see Chapter 12). Another barrier to recognizing any distinct flavor of Tempranillo is that Tempranillo often appears as a blended wine, usually with Garnacha (Grenache) as its partner.

Grenache

Origin: Spain (where it is called *Garnacha*)

Where grown: Spain, France's Rhône Valley region, the south of France, California, Australia

Important wines made from this grape: Châteauneuf-du-Pape, Côtes du Rhône, Rioja, many Rhône-style wines from California

Characteristics: Grenache grapes ripen with a high level of sugar, thus making high-alcohol wines. Other characteristics of this grape vary according to how the grape is grown. When it is industrially farmed, for example, its color can be orangey and rather pale, and its flavors can be leathery and weak; grown more carefully, it can have intense red color and intense aromas and flavors of raspberry and black pepper. In neither case is it particularly tannic. Grenache is seldom seen on its own but is usually blended — with Tempranillo in Spain and with Syrah and other grapes in France and California.

Italy's wealth of grape varieties

Sangiovese, Nebbiolo, and Barbera represent just the tip of the iceberg among Italy's red grape varieties. Other important red wine grapes from Italy — to name just a few — include

- **Aglianico:** A high-quality grape from the south of Italy that makes intense red wines such as Taurasi and Aglianico del Vulture

- **Corvina:** The main, and finest, grape used to make the blended wines Valpolicella, Bardolino, and Amarone della Valpolicella

- **Dolcetto:** A grape used to make delicious everyday red wines in the Piedmont region, in northwestern Italy

- **Lambrusco:** The grape that makes the ever-popular wine of the same name, in the Emilia-Romagna region

- **Montepulciano:** A low-tannin grape responsible for huge quantities of easy-to-drink red wine in the south of Italy

Stranger than fiction

Some of the most obscure grapes of the world have the most colorful names. In Greece, for example, is a grape called *Xynomavro*, which means "bitter black" — probably not related to Italy's *Negro Amaro*, although both translate the same. The Portuguese have a red grape called *Bastardo*, which needs no translation, and a white grape called *Esgana Cão*, translated as "dog strangler." Italy boasts *Piedirosso* ("red feet") and white grapes called *Coda di Volpe* ("fox tail") and *Pagadebit* ("pays the bills"). Our favorite descriptive grape name, though, is *Dolcetto*, "little sweet thing," from the Piedmont region of Italy; we like that name so much that we borrowed it for one of our cats!

Chapter 4

The Seven Classic Types of Red Wine

• •

In This Chapter

▶ The most important types of red wines in the world

▶ The flavors of Beaujolais, Rioja, and California Cabs

▶ Wine names in Bordeaux, Burgundy, and Chianti

▶ Clues for deciphering wine labels

• •

*I*t's as true for wine as it is for literature, film, and art: Anyone who wants to be truly knowledgeable must study the classics. We spend this entire chapter describing and defining seven classic types of red wines because these wines form the comparative background against which nearly every other red wine can be understood. When you are familiar with these seven types of red wine, you become fluent in red wine.

What Becomes a Classic Most?

The classic red wines of the world are unique types of wine that owe their character to specific grapes (or combinations of grapes) grown in specific places. These wines are prototypes that inspire winemakers in other parts of the world and spawn admiring imitators.

Some of the classic red wines of the world — such as red Bordeaux and red Burgundy — have existed for a few hundred years, but others, such as California Cabernet Sauvignon, evolved more recently. Whether old or young, these classic types of wine are not static; their styles change gradually as times and tastes change. But each type of wine remains a distinct idiom.

Style, more than quality, is at issue in our discussion of the classic red wine types. True, many individual examples of these classic wines achieve such heights of quality that they can very well be nominated as Greatest Red Wine in the World. But we believe that the seven types of wine we call classic reds are even more important for their individual expression of grape variety and growing conditions than for their quality. In fact, we believe that each classic type of red wine is so individual that it is entitled to make its own rules and be judged by its own standards, not measured impersonally against external criteria of quality.

A fancy term for "Everything that makes a wine what it is"

 The quality and style of every wine are the result of a complex bundle of influences that prevail upon the wine from the moment of its conception as a bud on a grapevine. These influences include (but are by no means limited to)

- The grape variety itself

- The fixed characteristics of the place where the grapes grew (soil, slope, altitude, and directional facing of the vineyard; typical climatic pattern of the region; how densely the vineyard is planted; and so on)

- The variable characteristics of the place where the grapes grew (the weather in a particular year, how much crop the vines bear in a particular year, how the vines are maintained, how and when the grapes are harvested, and so on)

- The winemaking (the list of winemaking variables is almost endless)

Fortunately, a single word exists for this whole bundle of influences. (Of course, it's a French word.) That word is *terroir* (pronounced *terr wahr*).

Unfortunately, not everyone who talks or writes about wine agrees on the beginning and ending point of the influences encompassed in the concept of *terroir*. Some people use the word *terroir* to represent the entirety of developmental influences on a wine; other people use the word as a synonym for growing conditions (both fixed and variable) of the grapes. In this book, we use the term *terroir* in the latter, more limited sense: the growing conditions of grapes that influence the wine made from those grapes.

Bordeaux, Toujours Bordeaux

The reasons that red Bordeaux is a classic type of wine are quite understandable. The best wines from Bordeaux are long-lived wines (20 to 40 years of life is typical) that just seem to get better and better with age. These wines are the ultimate collectibles. What's more, they have been famous and beloved among wine connoisseurs for more than two centuries. (Thomas Jefferson made his first purchase of Bordeaux wine while visiting France in 1784.)

Bordeaux wines come from the Bordeaux region in western France — France's largest official wine region (see *Wine For Dummies,* Chapter 10). In this region, wineries call themselves *châteaux* (the singular is *château),* and the brand names of the wines are, therefore, usually Château This or Château That (with a few exceptions, especially among less expensive wines). See Figure 4-1 for an example.

The large Bordeaux region is subdivided into districts and villages (also known as *communes);* in addition to its brand name, each Bordeaux wine carries the name of either the village where the grapes grew (such as St.-Julien or Pomerol), or the district where the grapes grew (such as Médoc or Haut-Médoc) or the name of the large region itself: Bordeaux. (The smaller the geographic location, the finer the wine is presumed to be, generally speaking.)

Multiplicity of grapes, terrains, and wines

Through trial and error over the centuries, the winemakers of Bordeaux have narrowed the red grape varieties in their vineyards down to five, three of which are the most important. These five grapes, in approximate order of importance, are

- ✔ Cabernet Sauvignon
- ✔ Merlot
- ✔ Cabernet Franc
- ✔ Petit Verdot
- ✔ Malbec

All red Bordeaux wines are blends of wine from at least two, and commonly three, of the grapes in the preceding list.

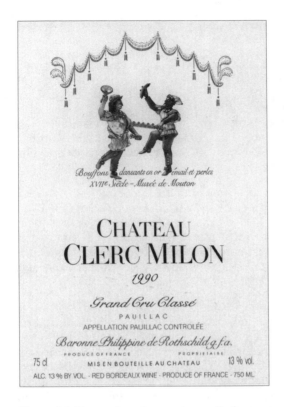

Figure 4-1: The producer's name is usually the most prominent name on a red Bordeaux label.

Because the Bordeaux region is situated on the Atlantic coast of France and subject to unpredictable maritime weather (such as rain in the middle of the summer or at harvest time and cool, damp ocean winds), the grapes ripen very differently from year to year. Occasionally, a warm, sunny summer and a dry autumn bring perfect ripeness and richer, fuller-bodied wines than Bordeaux customarily makes. The norm, however, is temperate weather and moderate ripeness, resulting in medium-bodied red wines.

Because Cabernet Sauvignon is one of the main grape varieties of many red Bordeaux wines, the wines can be tannic (see Chapter 2). The amount of tannin varies a great deal, though, according to the ripeness of the grapes and the specific blend of grapes in any one wine. (Merlot is less tannic; more Merlot in the blend makes a softer wine.)

Because Bordeaux is a large area, the soil and other precise details of the *terroir* (growing conditions) vary from one district or village (and even one property) to the next. In the best vineyards, the grapes are able to ripen better, and the wines tend to be richer and more intense than wines from other areas. That's the main reason that the price of red Bordeaux wines is so variable: from about $6 a bottle to more than $90 a bottle when the wines are first released. (The best wines increase in price as they get older.)

The range of Bordeaux styles

All this variability in weather, grape blend, *terroir* character, quality, and price makes it a little difficult to pin down the style of red Bordeaux wine as an absolute. In fact, red Bordeaux is a *range* of wines encompassing many different quality, intensity, and price levels. The extremes of the range set the stylistic parameters of red Bordeaux.

At one end of the spectrum are dark, concentrated, fully dry wines with ripe fruit but just as much rich tannin and plenty of new oak. When these wines are young, they have aromas and flavors of black currants, plums, cassis, spice, and herbs; with age, they develop cedar, tobacco, and leather notes. At the other end of the spectrum are light-bodied, supple, smooth, dry red wines with subdued aromas and flavors that can be fruity, spicy, herbal, or vegetal.

The middle ground of this range — the typical red Bordeaux wine — is a dry, medium-bodied, firm, and somewhat austere red wine with complex, but only moderately intense, aromas and flavors of black currants, plums, herbs, vegetation, and cedar. Speaking more creatively, we can describe red Bordeaux as a polished and refined wine that is somewhat reserved and ungiving, especially when it is young, but harbors subtle complexities that can intrigue and fascinate wine drinkers who give it adequate attention. (Our favorite anthropomorphic comparison is a well-mannered, intelligent, but politely re served lad who just finished boarding school.)

For specific recommendations of red Bordeaux wines to try, turn to Chapter 10.

Red Bordeaux wine at a glance

Where from: The Bordeaux region in western France

Grape variety: A blend of Cabernet Sauvignon and Merlot, with Cabernet Franc and sometimes one or two minor grapes (Petit Verdot and Malbec)

Style of wine: Medium-bodied, dry, fairly tannic, and austere with moderately intense, complex aromas and flavors of black currants, plums, herbs, vegetation, and cedar

Price range: $6 to more than $100 a bottle

Recent good vintages (the finest vintages appear in bold type): 1994, **1990**, **1989**, 1988, **1986**, **1985**, **1982**

Where to turn for more specific information: The section "Bordeaux, the Red Wine King of France" in Chapter 10

Burgundy the Beautiful

Along with Bordeaux, red Burgundy wine is a pillar that upholds the image and reputation of French red wine around the world. But Burgundy is a very different kind of wine from Bordeaux. If Bordeaux is a well-mannered, reserved sort of fellow, Burgundy is a sensual, earthy, but capricious beauty that, at its best, can exert a bewitching power over those who taste it.

Red Burgundy wine comes from the Burgundy region of eastern France. The vineyard properties in that area are much smaller than in Bordeaux, and the wineries are more modest. Instead of Château Anything emblazoned on the label of a Burgundy wine, winemakers give the wine name the most prominence and list their own names (the brand name) in smaller print, often at the bottom of the label as if it is an afterthought. (*Domaine* is the word they use for winery.) For example, a wine name such as Musigny might appear front-and-center on the label in 24-point type, and then low on the label the producer's name, Domaine Whatever, appears in 12-point type.

Place-names, place character

The name of a red Burgundy wine is the name of the place
where the grapes grew. That place is sometimes just the region
itself, Burgundy (or its French translation, *Bourgogne,* pronounced *bor guh nyeh)* — but in many cases, the place (and the
name of the wine) is a district, a village, or even a specific
vineyard. About 380 possible place-names probably exist for
red Burgundy wines. Any one producer might make five or ten
(or more) different red Burgundies, each named after the
specific place where the grapes grew.

The Burgundians make such a big deal about the grapes'
location because the location seriously affects the taste of the
grapes and, therefore, the final wine. Of course, vineyard
location (and the soil and microclimate specific to that location) always affects the taste of grapes everywhere — but in
Burgundy, all the more so.

Differences from one vineyard to the next are particularly
evident because only one red grape is grown in all 380 individual red Burgundy locations. That grape is Pinot Noir (see
Chapter 3).

The style of red Burgundy wines

Because Pinot Noir is not a tannic grape, most red Burgundies
are only moderately tannic unless the winemaker uses some
technique to purposely increase the wine's tannin level. (Aging
the wine in new oak barrels is an example of this kind of
technique, as is letting the grape stems remain with the juice
during fermentation.) Besides being low in tannin, most red
Burgundies tend to be fairly high in alcohol, have firming
acidity, and have much less color than Bordeaux wines.

The *intensity* of aroma and flavor in red Burgundy wines varies
with the vintage, the vineyard location, and the age and quality
of the wine. The *nature* of the aromas and flavors also varies.
Some wines exude a fresh, fruity character that suggests
berries (all sorts of berries, from raspberries, cherries, and
wild strawberries to blackberries). Other wines have a more
subdued berry character along with earthiness, such as
woodsy or autumnal aromas, smoky character, or mineral notes.

The composite style of red Burgundy wine is (as generalizations go) that of a fairly full-bodied, generous wine with moderately intense flavors of berries and earthiness.

Although red Burgundy in concept is fairly straightforward — one grape, one region, and, for the most part, one traditional way of making wine — individual wines show great differences in quality and style (within the stylistic range of red Burgundy). Besides varying according to where the grapes grew, Burgundy varies a great deal from producer to producer, according to how much care the producer takes in growing the grapes and translating the grapes into wine, and according to the producer's personal stylistic preferences. The wine of a great producer, from a great vineyard, in a great year, can be one of the most memorable wines you ever enjoy; an ordinary *Bourgogne,* from an ordinary producer, in an average year, on the other hand, can be disappointing.

Our discussion of red Burgundy in Chapter 11 explains how you can recognize the better vineyards and lists some good producers.

Red Burgundy wine at a glance

Where from: The Burgundy region of eastern France

Grape variety: Pinot Noir

Style of wine: Fairly full-bodied, ample and generous, with moderately high alcohol, low to moderate tannin, and moderately intense aromas and flavors of berries and earth

Price range: $10 to well more than $100 a bottle

Recent good vintages (the finest vintages appear in bold type)**: 1993**, 1991, **1990**, **1989**, 1988, 1985

Where to turn for more specific information: The section "The Magic of Red Burgundy" in Chapter 11

Il Magnifico Chianti

Chianti *(key AHN tee)* is Italy's most famous type of wine by far. Six hundred years of history and sporadic periods of enormous popularity in export markets all over the world have made Chianti the very symbol of Italian wine for most people.

We first knew Chianti many years ago as a pizza wine, light-bodied and oh, so easy to drink. Chianti is still that. But the serious side of Chianti is evident more and more these days in many first-rate, concentrated wines that are worth every penny of their $20-and-up price tags.

Chianti wine comes from the Chianti district of central Italy. The large area where grapes for Chianti legally grow is divided into several subzones. The label of each Chianti wine indicates which subzone grew the grapes for that wine; the least expensive wines are usually labeled just Chianti; better wines indicate a specific subzone, such as Chianti Classico or Chianti Rufina *(ROO fee nah)*, on their labels.

Chianti is a DOCG wine, meaning that it is officially ranked at the highest level possible among Italian wines. (DOCG stands for *Denominazione di Origine Controllata e Garantita,* translated as "Regulated and Guaranteed Place Name.") See Chapter 8 of *Wine For Dummies* for a complete explanation of wine-ranking systems in Italy and the rest of Europe.

Of producers and grapes

A winery in Chianti often goes by the name *castello* or *villa;* the brand name of a Chianti is, therefore, often Castello Something or Villa Something Else — although many famous Chiantis carry only a family name, such as Antinori or Ruffino, as their brand. Most producers make at least two different Chianti wines:

- ✔ A lighter Chianti wine to drink when it is young
- ✔ A more serious Chianti wine that is labeled with the word *riserva* (see Figure 4-2)

Some producers also bottle a *single-vineyard* Chianti made only from the grapes of a specific vineyard they own — as opposed to their other Chiantis, which are made from the grapes of several vineyards.

VILLA
ANTINORI

CHIANTI CLASSICO RISERVA

DENOMINAZIONE DI ORIGINE CONTROLLATA E GARANTITA

1993

A N T I N O R I

ITALIA

750 ml ℮   IMBOTTIGLIATO IN SAN CASCIANO V.P. DA MARCHESI ANTINORI S.R.L. - FIRENZE - ITALIA   12.5% vol.

Figure 4-2: A riserva is a more serious Chianti wine.

Chianti is traditionally a blended wine, made primarily from the Sangiovese grape (pronounced *san joe VAY say;* described in Chapter 3), along with the local red grape called Canaiolo *(can eye OH loh)* and small amounts of two local white grapes, Trebbiano *(treb bee AH noh)* and Malvasia *(mahl vah SEE ah).* But the best Chianti wines these days, especially in the Chianti Classico subzone, contain little or no wine from white grapes, and some are made entirely from the noble Sangiovese. (Some of these top wines have a little Cabernet Sauvignon blended in.) The wines with no white grapes in their blend are naturally richer and fuller than those containing white grapes.

Dry, crisp, and harmonious

Like most Italian red wines, Chianti is high in acidity — a real virtue with food. It is usually medium bodied (although the less expensive wines can be light bodied), and it doesn't have much tannin or a very dark color unless the winemaker uses Cabernet Sauvignon in the blend or ages the wine in new oak barrels (a high price is often a tip-off to that style).

Chianti wine is always dry. In fact, Chianti is one of the driest types of red wines you can find; nothing about Chianti gives the slightest impression of sweetness or juiciness (again, a virtue with many foods). The best wines deliver a wonderful sense of gracefulness and harmony when you taste them.

The aromas and flavors of Chianti are subtle and fine rather than intense. A hint of cherry is common, as well as a nutty character and what we call a dusty smell, suggestive of dry earth. The Italians claim that Chianti smells of violets, but we have never been able to capture that scent.

Chianti wines vary a great deal because the Chianti district is large, the climate and soil vary from one subzone to another, and many winemakers disagree on the exact style of Chianti they like to make. Chiantis range from pale, light-bodied, quaffing wines that cost as little as $6 a bottle to concentrated, medium-bodied, riserva-style or single-vineyard wines that cost as much as $25. The better Chiantis from a good producer and a good vintage benefit from a few years of bottle-age. But most Chianti wines can, and should, be enjoyed young, while they are fresh, vibrant, pretty, refreshing, so easy to drink, and . . . wait, we feel a corkscrew emergency coming on!

If you're eager to open a bottle of Chianti yourself, turn first to Chapter 12, where we list our favorite producers.

Chianti wine at a glance

Where from: The Chianti district in the region of Tuscany in central Italy

Grape variety: Primarily Sangiovese, used alone or with Canaiolo or other red grapes in small amounts, and/or two kinds of white grapes in very small amounts

Style of wine: Light-bodied to medium-bodied, with crisp acidity, low to moderate tannin, very dry texture, and subdued aromas and flavors of cherry and nuts

Price range: $6 to $25 a bottle

Recent good vintages (the finest vintages appear in bold type): 1994, 1993, **1990, 1988, 1985**

Where to turn for more specific information: The section "Tuscany: The home of Chianti" in Chapter 12

Rioja, Spain's Own Classic

Rioja *(ree OH hah)* is Spain's answer to Chianti: It is the best-known and best-loved type of Spanish red wine, the one red wine type from Spain that has found a home for itself on restaurant wine lists and retail shelves all over the world.

Rioja wine comes from the Rioja wine region of northeastern Spain. Three subzones exist there, and the climate and soil profile of each zone influences the quality and character of its grapes. Most Rioja wines are blends of grapes or wines from more than one subzone, although some *bodegas* (as Spanish wineries are called) make their wine entirely from the grapes of a single area — but the name of that area is usually not identified on the label of the wine.

Rioja is a blended wine not only in its geography but also in its grape content. The grape most often associated with red Rioja is Spain's great Tempranillo *(tem prah NEE yoh)* grape, which forms the base of most of the finest Rioja reds. But Tempranillo is usually blended with Grenache (known in Spain as *Garnacha*) and two other local red grapes, Mazuelo (known elsewhere as *Carignan*) and Graciano. Some Rioja reds are made almost entirely from Grenache (see Chapter 3 for descriptions of Tempranillo and Grenache).

Depending on which grapes go into a Rioja red blend and where in the region those grapes have grown, the style of red Rioja wine varies. Those wines with a high percentage of Grenache, for example, usually are higher in alcohol, less tannic, and less fruity than those wines with less Grenache.

Rioja wines also vary considerably in style according to how long they age at the winery, in oak barrels and in bottles, before they are released. Although you usually can't know the grape blend and the subzone(s) by studying the label of a red Rioja, at least you can figure out the age-style of the wine.

- ✔ Rioja wines with at least two years of aging at the winery are labeled *crianza* (often you see this word not on the main label but on a colorful sticker on the back of the bottle).
- ✔ Wines with at least three years of aging are labeled *reserva*.
- ✔ Wines with at least five years of aging are labeled *gran reserva*.

The longer a wine ages at the winery, the less fresh and fruity its aromas and flavors are; with age, the wines develop increasing complexity and subtlety, with aromas and flavors of leather and tobacco and other nonfruity characteristics.

The producers of red Rioja aren't precisely in agreement (to say the least) about how to make the wine of their region, and their disparate beliefs result in distinctly different styles of wine under the name Rioja — even within wines of the same age classification. At one extreme, the wines are deeply colored and show concentrated fruit flavor along with an oaky character; at the other extreme are wines that have lost their adolescent fruitiness in favor of a complex, silky dimension.

Red Rioja wine in its most classic manifestation is a medium-bodied, soft, and mellow type of wine with only moderate levels of tannin. This wine has wonderful vanilla aroma and flavor that comes from the barrels in which the wine ages and, depending on how mature the wine is, it can have aged aromas such as leather or decaying leaves or more youthful aromas and flavors of dried red fruits. Nuance is the hallmark of classic red Rioja wine.

Chapter 12 contains a listing of several Rioja producers whose wines we recommend.

Red Rioja wine at a glance

Where from: The Rioja region of northeastern Spain

Grape variety: Tempranillo, often blended with Grenache and, less so, with Mazuelo (Carignan) and Graciano — all considered native Spanish varieties

Style of wine: Medium-bodied, soft, and silky with low tannin; its aromas and flavors (vanilla and spice) usually derive as much from wood-aging as they do from the grapes themselves

Price range: $6 to $25

Recent good vintages (the finest vintages appear in bold type): **1994**, 1993, 1992, 1990, **1989**, 1988, **1982**, 1981

Where to turn for more specific information: The section "The Red Wines of Spain" in Chapter 12

Beaujolais, the Carefree Wine

Light-hearted. Approachable. Friendly. Unpretentious. Easy to like.

If Beaujolais were a person, he would be the perfect next-door neighbor (especially if he were handy with tools). As a type of wine, Beaujolais *(boh jhoe lay)* is as close to all-purpose, down-to-earth enjoyment as it comes.

Beaujolais wine hails from the Beaujolais district of eastern France. Technically, this area is part of the Burgundy region, but Beaujolais is a distinctly different type of wine from what we call red Burgundy. For one thing, it's made from a totally different grape variety, Gamay (see Chapter 3). Elsewhere in the world, the Gamay grape isn't high on winemakers' lists of grapes to try growing, but in the Beaujolais area, it shines.

Although all (red) Beaujolais wine comes entirely from the Gamay grape, Beaujolais actually comes in three different versions, according to the soil in which the grapes grow and the winemaking technique.

Grapes grown on rich, clay soil that makes a lighter-bodied wine are usually destined either for basic Beaujolais wine or for Beaujolais Nouveau, an extremely young wine that's released each year in late November, just weeks after the harvest. Beaujolais Nouveau is the lightest, freshest, and least serious style of Beaujolais. Special winemaking techniques make the wine drinkable and delicious at such a young age.

Grapes from specific areas in the northern part of the Beaujolais district, where granite and schist soil builds more intensity and concentration into the wine, become Beaujolais-Villages wines. These are medium-weight Beaujolais wines, with more character than basic Beaujolais or the Nouveau style.

The finest Beaujolais wines come from ten vineyard areas surrounding specific villages in the northern part of the Beaujolais district. These wines don't even say Beaujolais on them, because they are named for a more specific geography — the village in which the grapes grew, such as Fleurie (pronounced *fluh ree;* see Figure 4-3) or Chiroubles *(sheh roob'l).* These cru Beaujolais, as they are collectively called, are the fullest, most concentrated, and most intense version of Beaujolais. (For a complete listing of the ten crus and general information on enjoying Beaujolais, see the Beaujolais section of Chapter 11; for a description of each of the ten Beaujolais crus, see our book *Wine For Dummies,* Chapter 10.)

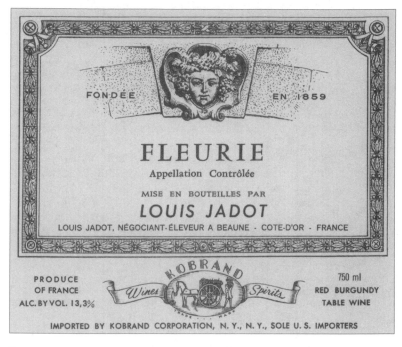

Figure 4-3: Label from a Beaujolais wine that is named for Fleurie, the village in which its grapes grew.

Beaujolais wine at a glance

Where from: The Beaujolais district in the southern part of the Burgundy region in eastern France

Grape variety: Gamay

Style of wine: Light- to medium-bodied dry wines with crisp acidity and low to moderate amounts of tannin; aromas and flavors are pronounced and fruity; usually unoaked

Price range: $6 to $15 a bottle

Recent good vintages: 1994, 1990, 1989

Where to turn for more specific information: The section "Beaujolais: Easy-drinking and affordable" in Chapter 11.

Even at its most intense, however, Beaujolais is not a big, full-bodied type of wine. Beaujolais wines are light- to medium-bodied with crisp acidity and moderate tannin; their pronounced aromas and flavors are fresh and grapey, unmarked by oakiness (except in an occasional cru Beaujolais). Although Beaujolais wine is fruity and easy to drink, it is also dry.

California Cabernet Sauvignon Wine

Considering that most wineries in California are barely 20 years old, you might think that we're premature in including California Cabernet wine among the classic types of red wine in the world. But in the short modern history of California winemaking, the state has managed to make a type of wine that is stylistically unique — and so good that winemakers from all over the world have been influenced by its style.

Technically speaking, any wine made from Cabernet Sauvignon grapes (see Chapter 3) and grown in the state of California is a California Cabernet Sauvignon wine. That's a huge amount of wine, and not all of it is particularly good. What we refer to as classic are the better California Cabernet wines — roughly speaking, those priced at $12 a bottle and up.

U.S. law permits winemakers to make Cabernet wine with as little as 75 percent Cabernet juice. The usual blending partner in Cabernet Sauvignon wines is Merlot (and — surprise, surprise! — the usual blending partner in Merlot wines is Cabernet Sauvignon). As the winemakers of France's Bordeaux region discovered many decades ago, Merlot and Cabernet complement each other beautifully.

Top regions and districts

California is a big place (30 percent bigger than the entire country of Italy) with a big variety of microclimates and soil types. The best Cabernet Sauvignon grapes grow in areas that are warm but not too warm, where climatic idiosyncrasies such as morning fog or cool, high-altitude nights enable the grapes to ripen fully but not so quickly that they lose their fresh flavor.

Napa Valley is such an area — or maybe we should say areas, because several distinct *terroirs* that are ideal for Cabernet grapes exist there. These areas include the following:

✔ The Stags Leap District in eastern Napa (see Figure 4-4)

✔ The Rutherford and Oakville areas on the valley floor

✔ Howell Mountain in the east

✔ Spring Mountain and Diamond Mountain in the west

Sonoma Valley's two ideal areas for Cabernet are Sonoma Mountain and Alexander Valley. The Santa Cruz Mountain vineyards (south of San Francisco) are another important source for high-quality California Cabernet grapes.

Good Cabernet Sauvignon wine also comes from grapes grown in the warm inland section of Mendocino County and the Paso Robles area of Santa Barbara County.

Figure 4-4: The Stags Leap District is one area in Napa Valley that has ideal *terroir* for growing Cabernet Sauvignon grapes.

California Cabernet wine varies in style according to exactly where the grapes grow. The wines from some areas (such as the Stags Leap district) have very soft tannins, for example. The wines from other areas (such as the mountain vineyards) are toughened by firm tannins.

The common chord

Most good California Cabernet wines have these characteristics in common: deep, dark color; intense aromas (usually of ripe black currant fruit); intense, fresh flavors of ripe berry and plum fruit (usually spiced with oakiness); full body derived from high alcohol and tannin; and rich, velvety texture.

Many of California's best Cabernet wines are so richly fruity that they are delicious when they are young, even if wine critics and winemakers advise that the wines need more age to reach their peak of enjoyment. The hallmark of California Cabernet wine, in fact, is its irresistible, delicious fruitiness. That intensely fruity character is exactly what has caused winemakers from elsewhere in the world to rethink their own wines — and what has already made California Cabernet a classic type of red wine.

For practical advice in buying California Cabs, don't miss our list of recommended wines in Chapter 6.

California Cabernet wine at a glance

Where from: The state of California

Grape variety: Cabernet Sauvignon, often blended with Merlot or sometimes with Cabernet Franc

Style of wine: Full-bodied, with intense fruity aroma and flavor, and thick, velvety texture

Price range: $4 to $45 a bottle (although the more classic wines generally cost $12 and up)

Recent good vintages (the finest vintages appear in bold type): **1994**, 1992, **1991**, **1990**, 1987, **1985**, 1984

Where to turn for more specific information: Chapter 6

Hermitage and Côte Rôtie

If you have never tasted either of these classic types of red wines, we're not surprised. Unlike all our other classic reds, Hermitage *(er mee tahj)* and Côte Rôtie *(coat ro tee)* are very specific types, of small production. They don't encompass a range of quality levels or price levels as Bordeaux, Burgundy, and Chianti do; they represent only two quality levels — very good and even better — and two price levels, expensive and more expensive.

Hermitage wine and Côte Rôtie wine are each named after a specific growing area in the northern part of the Rhône Valley wine region of France. Côte Rôtie is the bigger area of the two, but, even so, its vineyard acreage is 133 times smaller than that of Beaujolais.

The northern Rhône Valley is a long, narrow wine region along the banks of the Rhône River in southeastern France, south of Beaujolais and Burgundy. Vineyards cover steep hills of poor soil, where reflected heat from the soil and the severe angle of the sun's rays help ripen the grapes. The sole red grape in these vineyards is Syrah (see Chapter 3).

In these circumstances, the Syrah grape produces very tannic, robust wines with aromas and flavors dictated by the particular soil and sun exposure of the vineyards where the grapes grow. Not only does Côte Rôtie's Syrah taste different from Hermitage's, but specific parts of Côte Rôtie (and of Hermitage) grow Syrah that tastes different from that grown in other parts of the Côte Rôtie area (or the Hermitage area).

Although both Côte Rôtie and Hermitage wines are based on the Syrah grape, some producers of Côte Rôtie traditionally blend up to 10 percent Viognier *(vee oh nyay,* a white grape) with their Syrah to soften and perfume the wine. For that reason, and because of the separate growing areas, Côte Rôtie and Hermitage are two distinct types of wine.

Hermitage is the darker, fuller bodied, more tannic and concentrated of the two, and Côte Rôtie is somewhat softer and more elegant (although still a full-bodied wine). Both types often have grilled-vegetal, black-pepper, and bacon-like aromas typical of Syrah, but Côte Rôtie often sports a unique green olive aroma and flavor. Both types of wine are very complex and can improve with age for decades.

Chapter 11 features a listing of recommended producers of Côte Rôtie and Hermitage.

Côte Rôtie and Hermitage wines at a glance

Where from: The small Côte Rôtie and Hermitage vineyard areas in France's Northern Rhône wine region, in southeastern France

Grape variety: Syrah (Côte Rôtie wine may contain as much as 20 percent Viognier, a white grape, although it seldom does)

Style of wine: Deeply colored, full-bodied, and tannic, with concentrated aromas and flavors of a vegetal, slightly burnt, bacon-like sort; capable of very long aging

Price range: $25 to $55 a bottle

Recent good vintages: 1994, **1991** (for Côte Rôtie), **1990, 1989, 1988**

Where to turn for more specific information: The section "The Majestic Northern Rhône Reds" in Chapter 11

Chapter 5
Red Wine with Meat — and More

> *Jack Sprat could eat no fat,*
> *His wife could eat no lean.*
> *But with a glass of good red wine,*
> *They licked their platters clean.*

You might not remember the nursery rhyme exactly like that, but we're convinced that our version accurately describes how Mr. and Mrs. Sprat managed to survive mealtimes together. Although the Sprats didn't have the same taste in food, we know that they loved red wine with all their food, fatty and lean, because red wine made the food taste richer (in Jack's case) and less greasy (in the case of the Mrs.).

If you have your own food idiosyncrasies, read on. We see a glass of red wine in your dinner's future.

Fundamental Principles of Food and Wine Pairing

When people choose a wine to drink with a particular meal or create a meal to complement a particular wine, their hope is that the food and wine together taste better than either one does alone. Sometimes that perfect synergy happens. More frequently, what occurs is that the food and wine taste acceptable together and don't clash with each other, but the match falls short of spectacular.

Matching food and wine is an extremely imprecise business. Wine alone is a very complex food with many different flavors. And every meal is complex, too, with flavors of sauces and seasonings in addition to the flavors of the foods themselves. Perhaps the most difficult part of wine and food pairing is that you usually have to make all your decisions in your imagination before you actually taste the food or sip the wine. No wonder that peaceful coexistence between wine and food is considered a successful marriage!

Two strategies guide wine and food pairings. The first is to choose a wine of similar character to the food so that the wine and food complement each other; the second is to choose a wine with a character that contrasts in a favorable way with the food. The characteristics of a wine that can either resemble or contrast with the characteristics of a dish are

- ✔ **The wine's flavors:** Earthy, herbal, fruity, vegetal, and so on
- ✔ **The intensity of flavor in the wine:** Weak flavor intensity, moderately flavorful, or very flavorful
- ✔ **The wine's texture:** Crisp and firm, or soft and supple
- ✔ **The weight of the wine:** Light bodied, medium bodied, or full bodied

Every dish has its own flavors, intensity of flavor, texture, and weight, just as every wine does. If the characteristics of a food and a wine are in the same ballpark, or if they contrast agreeably with each other (for example, if a crisp wine is paired with a dish that's soft and creamy), the food and wine are likely to go well together.

The Particulars of Red

Because so many different red wines exist in the world (and on your wine shop's shelves), red wines cover the whole gamut of food-friendly characteristics. Red wines come in all weights, flavor intensities, and textures. The only bases that red wines don't cover are certain flavors common in white wines — specifically citrus, tropical fruit, butter, and butterscotch.

Table 5-1 suggests specific types of red wine that fall into various weight, texture, flavor, and flavor-intensity categories. In the interest of suggesting as many different types of wine as possible (to allow for individual preferences), we list each type in only one category, even if it can appear in as many as four categories. For example, we list Bardolino under "light-bodied"; we could have repeated it under "weak flavor intensity" and "crisp," but we chose not to, in order to list additional wines. For information about any wine, you can refer to our descriptions of red wines and our suggested wine and food pairings all through Chapters 6 through 12.

Table 5-1	How Red Wines Measure Up in Weight, Flavor Intensity, Texture, and Flavor		
Weight:	*Light*	*Medium*	*Full*
	Bardolino	Rioja	Barolo/ Barbaresco
	Beaujolais	Cru Beaujolais	Better California Cabernets
	Valpolicella	California Pinot Noir	
Flavor Intensity:	*Weak*	*Moderately Flavorful*	*Very Flavorful*
	Inexpensive Chianti	Bordeaux	Zinfandel
	Valpolicella	Chianti Classico	Australian reds
	Inexpensive Bordeaux		
Texture:	*Crisp*	*Moderately Soft*	*Very Soft*
	Italian Barbera	Burgundy	California Merlot
	Chinon	Chilean Cabernets and Merlots	Most Zinfandels
		Portuguese reds	Australian Shiraz
Flavors:	*Fruity*	*Spicy*	*Earthy*
	California Cabernet	Northern Rhône reds	Southern Rhône reds
	Beaujolais	California Syrah	Southern Italian reds
			Pinotage

To decant or not to decant — that is the question

One of the most intimidating rituals in the whole world of wine, decanting, is the nearly exclusive domaine of red wine aficionados. If you drink good red wine, sooner or later you will encounter a decanter (the vessel), a decanter (the person who performs the action, maybe you), or a wine that needs decanting.

Decanting is the process of pouring wine from one container (usually its bottle) into another (a carafe, pitcher, or fine crystal decanter). You decant a red wine for one of two reasons:

- The wine is young and tannic, and the aeration it receives when you decant it softens its harsh tannins to some degree.

- The wine is an older wine (more than eight years old), and the act of decanting it separates the sediment (solid particles that fall to the bottom of the bottle) from the wine.

Many red wines do not have to be decanted, but some red wines benefit from decanting. In general, young, inexpensive (under $10) red wines and/or lighter-colored, light-bodied red wines do not have to be decanted because they have no sediment and do not particularly benefit from aeration. Young, dark-colored red wines — such as red Bordeaux, the better (over $15) Rhône wines, the better (over $15) California Cabernet Sauvignons, and all Petite Sirahs — probably don't have sediment yet but can benefit from the aeration that occurs with decanting. Sometimes these wines even benefit from *double-decanting:* pouring the wine back and forth a few times from one decanter to another.

If your red wine is more than eight years old and the type of wine that develops sediment — Bordeaux is especially prone, but Barolo, Rhône wines, and some California Cabernets are other examples — you probably want to decant it to remove the wine's sediment.

Here's how:

- ✔ Stand the wine up for a couple of days before you plan to drink it so that all the sediment can fall to the bottom of the bottle.

- ✔ When you are about to decant the wine, stand a powerful flashlight upright on a table or counter, its beam pointing toward the ceiling. (A candle, which is more in keeping with the tone of the ritual, will do, also, but a flashlight is more practical.) Have another container handy to pour the wine in.

- ✔ Hold the neck of the open bottle over the beam of the flashlight so that you can see the light through the glass and the clear wine inside, and slowly begin pouring the wine into the decanter.

- ✔ When you see dark particles or cloudy, unclear wine in the neck of the bottle, stop pouring. Voilà! You have successfully decanted your wine.

Within any type of red wine — Chianti, for example, or Beaujolais or California Cabernet — individual brands can vary in style according to the specific source of grapes and the winemaking techniques used. (See "How climate affects style" and "How winemaking affects style" in Chapter 2.) If you're uncertain about the style of a specific wine, ask your retailer.

We wish we could say that our chart can solve every red-wine-with-food dilemma you'll ever face. The fact is that it's just a blueprint — and a blueprint of only half the equation (the wine half). You still have to decide where your food falls within each category and decide which characteristics to match or contrast with the wine. Fortunately, the fun lies in the experimentation.

As a shortcut in wine and food pairing, or to trigger your imagination, you can always fall back on certain classic wine and food combinations. Refer to "The wisdom of the ages" in Chapter 19 of our book *Wine For Dummies,* for a listing of those classic matches.

The tannin issue

The presence of tannin in most red wines presents issues in wine and food pairing that go beyond the simple principles of complementary or contrasting characteristics. Some foods have an M.B.A. in tannin management, but others are distinctly unfriendly to tannin. (See Chapter 2 for more information about tannin.)

Simple foods that are rich in protein — such as rare steak or prime rib (or hamburger, for that matter) — and hard cheeses, such as cheddar or Gruyère, soften the tannin in red wines and actually seem to wipe it away from the wine. That effect can be very pleasant, especially if the wine is too tannic to drink alone (if it is too young, for example, and its tannins haven't softened yet, as they would over time).

On a molecular level, protein and tannin have quite an attraction for each other (protein molecules have a positive electrical charge, and tannin has a negative charge — and you know what they say about opposites!). If you eat protein with a very tannic red wine, such as a young Cabernet-based wine or a Barolo, the protein binds with the wine's tannin in such a way that the tannin is no longer perceptible. If a wine is overly tannic — if it has picked up too much tannin from oak casks, for example, or if it is way too young — the only conditions in which that wine may taste drinkable is with steak or cheese. (When professional wine-tasters judge tannic young reds, they often nibble rare roast beef between sets of wines to cleanse their mouths of the wines' tannic residue.)

Here are additional predictable food interactions with tannin:

- ✔ If a dish is slightly sweet — if it has sweet barbecue sauce as an ingredient, for example, or even tomato ketchup — the tannin in wine diminishes the impression of sweetness in the food. This effect can be positive or not, depending on your own taste for sweetness in food.
- ✔ Salty dishes taste unpleasant with tannic wines.
- ✔ Tannic foods, such as walnuts, taste terrible with tannic wines unless the wine is sweet (such as the dessert wine, Port, which we do not cover in this book) or other elements in the dish offset the tannin.
- ✔ Highly acidic foods, such as tomatoes, usually make a tannic red wine taste astringent. Often, however, dishes with acidic foods contain other ingredients to balance the acid. (Chefs frequently add a little sugar when preparing a tomato sauce to cut the tomatoes' acidity, for example.)

Following are several red wines that are relatively low in tannin:

- ✔ Barbera
- ✔ Simple Beaujolais
- ✔ Pinot Noir
- ✔ Inexpensive Burgundies
- ✔ Bardolino and Valpolicella
- ✔ Inexpensive Merlots

And here are several red wines that are high in tannin:

- ✔ Better Cabernet Sauvignon-based wines
- ✔ More expensive Zinfandels
- ✔ Hermitage and Côte Rôtie
- ✔ Barolo and Barbaresco
- ✔ Super-Tuscan reds
- ✔ Chianti Classico Riservas

The tanninless wonder

One red wine that can be a real miracle worker in wine and food pairings is Italian Barbera (see Chapter 10). The Barbera grape contains almost no tannin. Unless the winemaker ages the Barbera wine in new oak barrels, the wine has very little tannin, too. (You can identify oak-aged wines because they cost much more than other Barberas: $20 to $40, compared to $6 to $16 for unoaked Barbera.) Structurally, Barbera resembles a white wine more than a red because its firmness comes from high acidity, not tannin. It's our favorite wine to drink with any dish that has tomatoes in it, and it should work well in any other situation when you want a red wine but not tannin.

Red wine with fish

Despite the adage that proclaims "Red with meat, white with fish," you *can* drink red wine with fish. The success of any pairing of red wine and fish depends on which fish and which wine.

Salmon with Pinot Noir wine is a delicious combination that succeeds because salmon is a fatty and flavorful fish and Pinot Noir is low in tannin. Try Pinot Noir with a simple, broiled filet of sole, and you will probably be disappointed because the wine overpowers the fish. Try salmon with a full-bodied, tannic Cabernet, and the fish can make the wine taste metallic.

Fish that are likely to complement red wine include salmon, fresh tuna, swordfish, and bluefish. Red wines can accompany lighter fish also, provided that the fish is part of a fairly flavorful dish with a sauce or other ingredients that are friendly to red wine (such as a red wine sauce!) — and provided that the wine is not very heavy or tannic.

We find it difficult to imagine shrimp ever tasting good with red wine, however — likewise for lobster, raw oysters, and scallops.

A handy guideline for pairing red wine with fish is to choose richer, more flavorful types of fish or preparations, and to select light-bodied or medium-bodied wines that are not very tannic. (See Table 5-1 for suggestions of lighter-bodied wines, and the section "The tannin issue" for suggestions of low-tannin wines.)

Vegetarian delight

Ironically, red wine — so ideal with rare meat — is wonderful with vegetarian dishes as well. Beans, cheese, risotto, and meaty vegetables such as eggplant and portobello mushrooms are right up there among our favorite red wine foods.

If your meal is light and delicate in flavor — say a pasta primavera — the best red wine matches are very light-bodied, crisp red wines, such as Bardolino, a very light Chianti wine, or a light Pinot Noir or Burgundy wine. Heartier dishes like winter vegetable stew can stand up to fuller-bodied reds, such as Rhône Valley reds and southern Italian reds.

The one element of vegetarian dishes that's likely to conflict with many red wines (but not all of them) is bitter green vegetables, such as spinach, kale, collard greens, escarole, and broccoli rabe. The bitterness of these greens is likely to bring out bitter flavors in a red wine.

If these bitter flavors form the dominant taste in your meal, try a red wine that's very fruity and not very tannic — such as a Zinfandel that's made in a ripe, rich style (not a *claret-style* Zin; see Chapter 7), or an under-$8 California Cabernet. (Even though Cabernet should be a tannic wine, the least expensive examples from California tend to be low in tannin and slightly sweet.) Or try a Barbera (see the sidebar "The tanninless wonder" in this chapter). Or buy our book *White Wine For Dummies* and read about all the wonderful white wines that you can enjoy with your greens.

In reality, however, these bitter flavors probably don't dominate your meal. If your vegetarian lasagna contains cheese, for example, the cheese can offset the bitter flavor of the greens. If carrots (which are sweet) are anywhere in your food, they help to balance out the bitterness. If you consider the whole meal and not just one element of it, most red wines accompany the food well. Just save your very tannic reds for the cheese course.

The burning issue

People frequently ask us which wines we drink with very spicy foods such as Tex-Mex, southwestern cuisine, or spicy Asian dishes. Unfortunately, we don't have a ready answer because most dishes in these cuisines are quite complex, boasting an array of flavors and textures. Even if a dish has fiery flavors, for example, it often has sweet flavors, too.

Frankly, we like sparkling white wine with Asian food, and we're not averse to drinking beer with Tex-Mex! But red wine can work, too.

To put out the fire of a very spicy dish, we suggest you try a full-flavored, very fruity red wine that may even have a little sweetness to it, such as a full-blown style of Zinfandel. An alternative is a fruity, fairly low-tannin red such as a simple Beaujolais that you can chill a great deal (because it's low in tannin); the cool wine makes a nice contrast with the spicy food.

Refer to the section "The tannin issue" for ideas about low-tannin red wines.

Cool is cool

"We need an ice bucket for our red wine, please." Does this statement represent the words of A) a wine snob, B) a savvy wine lover, or C) someone who's got it all backwards? Unless you answered B, read on.

Many restaurants and many wine drinkers serve red wine too warm. If red wine is warmer than it should be, it tastes higher in alcohol than it should, and it is less enjoyable to drink. A bottle of red wine should feel quite cool to your hand when you open it and pour it into a wine glass. In numbers, it should be about 62° to 65° F — that is, cooler than your home in the winter months.

If your bottle of red is warmer than that, put it in the refrigerator for 15 to 20 minutes or into a bucket filled with ice and water for about 5 to 10 minutes. In a restaurant, ask for an ice bucket to cool down an overheated red wine — and keep the ice bucket within your reach so that the wine doesn't get *too* cold.

 For detailed information about serving temperatures and storage temperatures for wine, read Chapter 6 of *Wine For Dummies.*

Part II
A World of
Red Wine

In this part . . .

*T*he theory and concept of red wine are nice, but practical advice and easy answers are even nicer. At least they're a little handier when you walk into the supermarket or wine shop and need to choose this wine or that one for tomorrow's dinner. You'll find plenty of recommendations and practical advice in the chapters that follow, in which we describe the major red wine regions of the world.

Taste is personal, of course, and we can give you no guarantee that the wines we like and recommend will be to your liking. But taking our advice on which wines to try is at least a little more logical than pointing at wine bottles and muttering, "Eenie, meenie, minie, mo. . . ."

Chapter 6

Cab and Merlot Lead the Way in California

* *

In This Chapter

▶ Spanish missionaries planted the seeds

▶ The name of the grape

▶ California Cabs still driving

▶ Merlot: America's new redheaded darling

* *

*J*ust as the people in Paris or Madrid are markedly different from New Yorkers, Chicagoans, or San Franciscans, the red wines of Europe and America are — literally and figuratively — thousands of miles apart.

We don't believe that it's just a question of growing conditions such as climate, soil, and terrain — although these factors obviously play a large role. American culture has developed differently from European culture over a shorter period of time. American wines, like American people, are more up-front and less subtle. In fact, American wines, particularly California's, have more in common with Australian wines than they have with the wines of France, Italy, Portugal, or Spain.

Made in the U.S.

In general, Americans drink their homegrown American wines. (This is particularly true beyond the East Coast of the United States; the East Coast's relative proximity to Europe seems to create more acceptance for European wines than we find elsewhere in America.) Nearly 85 percent of all the wine consumed in the United States is made in the United States.

These days, Americans buy and make more wine than ever before; in fact, the United States ranks fifth in the world in wine production — well behind Italy and France, but close to Spain and Argentina. In terms of red wine production, however, the United States ranks behind all four countries.

A short history of American wine

Spanish missionaries planted the seeds for winemaking in what is now California (but was then part of Mexico) in 1779 at the San Juan Capistrano Mission. Later, in the second half of the 19th century, immigrant farmers — many Italians, but also French, Germans, and Hungarians — moved to California and began growing grapes to make wine. (Given the Spanish, French, and Italian preference for red wines, most of these early American wines were probably red.) Many adventurers who had come to California to find gold stayed on to become farmers, and they, too, planted grapes for wine.

Some of the vineyards that were planted more than 100 years ago still exist; fine wine shops commonly carry red Zinfandels and other red wines from California that contain grapes from prized, old vineyards.

But the wine industry in the United States was practically wiped out by Prohibition, which occurred from 1920 to 1933. The Great Depression and World War II also hindered the industry's growth. The wine industry in the United States, as we know it today, began to take off only in the early 1970s. Before 1970, only a sprinkling of wineries existed in the U.S.; today, California alone boasts almost 800 *bonded* (legally licensed) wineries — and the number is still growing.

Although 47 of the 50 states produce wine, wine is a really important agricultural product in only four states: California, New York, Washington, and Oregon. We concentrate on the wines from these states in this chapter and the following two chapters.

In the U.S., grapes name the wine

European tradition names wines after their place of origin; red wines named Bordeaux, Burgundy, Chianti, and so on all come from actual places of the same name, where people live and make wine. Lacking tradition of their own, early American winemakers borrowed these famous European names for their own wines — although the wines were quite dissimilar to their namesakes. The American versions were generally not made from the classic grape varieties of the famous European wine regions but were made from the easiest-to-grow, most prolific grape varieties available. (These grapes — such as Carignane, Grenache, Barbera, and Zinfandel — were wine grapes of European origin, but they were not always Europe's best grapes, nor were they grown in the best sites.)

Some Americans had the idea that the classic European grape varieties could do a better job of producing fine wine in America. One such person was Frank Schoonmaker, a pioneer in the American wine industry in the 1940s to 1960s; he was also a wine writer (one of the very few in the United States at that time).

A few California wineries blazed the trail by making wines from the better European grape varieties:

- ✔ Beaulieu Vineyards (BV) has made a highly regarded Cabernet Sauvignon wine named Georges de Latour Private Reserve (after the winery's founder, a Frenchman) since 1936; the winery also made a Pinot Noir wine in some vintages.

- ✔ Inglenook Vineyards and Simi Winery, two other important pioneers, produced very good Cabernet Sauvignon-based wines in the 1930s and early 1940s. (Inglenook's 1941 Cabernet Sauvignon is still a noteworthy wine.)

- ✔ Charles Krug and Louis M. Martini wineries made Cabernet Sauvignon-based wines and other single-variety wines in the 1940s and '50s.

During the 1960s, a few more wineries, such as Heitz, Ridge, and Hanzell, started making wines from one predominant grape variety, such as Cabernet Sauvignon, Pinot Noir, or Chardonnay (a white grape). In 1966, Robert Mondavi left his family's winery (Charles Krug) to produce his own wines, each made from a predominant, classic grape variety and named for its grape. Mondavi was so successful not only in making fine wine but also in promoting his wines that other wineries quickly followed suit. A baby-boom of new wineries making premium, grape-named wines began in the early 1970s. The trend of making *varietal* wines (wines that are named after their principal or sole grape variety) is still going strong today.

Today, red and white wines all over the world (with the exception of most of Europe) are named after their principal grape variety — Cabernet Sauvignon, Merlot, Pinot Noir, Chardonnay, and so on.

Grape-named American wines have become so popular that many Americans don't realize that the same grapes are grown in Europe to make the classic European wines. People are surprised to learn that red Bordeaux wine is predominantly Cabernet Sauvignon or Merlot (see Chapter 10), that red Burgundy wine is 100 percent Pinot Noir (see Chapter 11), that Chianti is predominantly Sangiovese (see Chapter 12), and that white wines such as Pouilly-Fuissé, Chablis, Mâcon-Villages, and other white Burgundies (see our book, *White Wine For Dummies*) are 100 percent Chardonnay.

The 75 percent rule

Most red American varietal wines — wines named after a grape variety — are actually blends made from two or more grape varieties; for example, using some Merlot wine in making a Cabernet Sauvignon, and vice versa, is very common. As long as at least 75 percent of the blend comes from the grape whose name appears on the label, the wine can go by that grape name. This 75 percent rule is U.S. federal law; a few states — such as Oregon, but not California — supersede this law by requiring an even higher minimum percentage.

California Red Wines by Flavor

Nowadays, the easiest way to categorize and discuss California wines is by the grape variety on the label — and that's exactly what we do in discussing that state's red wines. The four most popular red varietal, or grape-named, wines made in California are

- ✔ Cabernet Sauvignon
- ✔ Merlot
- ✔ Zinfandel (Yes, Zinfandel wine is red, although the red Zinfandel grape also makes a popular pink wine called "white Zinfandel.")
- ✔ Pinot Noir

California's wine monopoly

Californian wine is synonymous with American wine. No wonder: This one state produces a whopping 88.8 percent of all the wine produced in the United States. Much of that huge quantity, of course, is made on an industrial level by large producers.

Other less-well-known red varietal wines are Syrah, Cabernet Franc, Petite Sirah, and Sangiovese. (See Chapter 3 for information about the grape varieties that make some of these wines.) Quite a few premium red wines in California are made up of a blend of two, three, or even more grape varieties. These wines often use the fanciful name *Meritage* (a name shared by several producers) when their predominant variety is Cabernet Sauvignon or Merlot.

The California story: Cabernet Sauvignon

Cabernet Sauvignon is the most popular red wine in California — and, in the opinion of many wine critics, it's the wine California does best (although red Zinfandel fanatics give those critics an argument!). Napa Valley has always been the most important location for growing fine Cabernet Sauvignon, but good and even great Cabs originate throughout California's other wine regions. For more information about California Cabernet wine, turn to the section "California Cabernet Sauvignon Wine" in Chapter 4, where we describe them among the classic red wine types of the world.

In this section on California Cabs (as their friends call them), we include premium red wine blends in which Cabernet Sauvignon is the dominant variety but might or might not be 75 percent of the wine, and that have no named variety on the label. (The blending wines are usually Merlot and/or Cabernet Franc.) One such example, Opus One, actually does contain more than 90 percent Cabernet Sauvignon in most vintages, but it does not have a varietal name. Figure 6-1 shows another example.

Cabernet Sauvignon-based wines should be your wines of choice if you want a dry, fairly tannic, full-flavored, typically full-bodied red wine. They are excellent companions with steak, lamb, pot roast, veal, duck, game birds, or hard cheeses.

Figure 6-1: Label from a premium red wine blend.

Recommended California Cabernet Sauvignons and Cab blends

We have divided our recommended California Cabernet Sauvignons and Cab blends into three categories:

✔ **Light- to medium-bodied, low-tannin wines:** Wines in this group range from $4 to $12. You can drink them when you buy them; they are not made for aging.

✔ **Medium-bodied, medium-concentration wines:** Wines in this group fall into the $12 to $25 price range. You can usually enjoy them within a few years of the vintage, about the time when they are sold, but they hold their quality or even improve for a few more years.

✔ **Full-bodied, intensely concentrated, long-lived wines:** Wines in this category cost over $25 a bottle, and they often need several years from the vintage date to reach their peak drinkability.

For each category, we name what we believe to be the best wines. We list these wines alphabetically according to the name of the producer, and we indicate the geographic location that corresponds to the grape source. We mark our personal favorites with a ♀ symbol — and wines that are really good values with a ¢ symbol. Wines marked with a ✉ symbol are difficult to purchase except directly from the winery; see Appendix C for addresses of those wineries.

The following tables — and all the tables and lists of recommended wines and wine producers in this book — are not all-encompassing. As long as our lists are, they represent only a small fraction of California's wines. We believe the wines listed are some of California's best; please forgive us if we have left out one of your favorites.

Second labels

Some wineries have come up with a perfect solution for their less-than-perfect grapes (grapes grown in vineyards that are not the winery's best sites, or grapes from young vines). The solution is to create a second label for the wines made from such grapes and to sell that second label wine at a lower price than their prestigious, primary brand. The winery's high image lends value to the second-label wine. For example, knowing that Stag's Leap Wine Cellars is one of the established stars among Napa Valley wineries, you would expect that winery's second-label wine, Hawk Crest, to be a reliable, inexpensive alternative to the pricier Stag's Leap wines. And you would be right (as long as your expectations are not too high!).

The Cabernet wines listed in Table 6-1 range from $4 to $12. You can drink them when you buy them; they are not made for aging.

Table 6-1 Light- to Medium-Bodied, Low-Tannin Cabernets

Producer	Wine	Vineyard Location
Arrowood	Domaine du Grand Archer Cabernet Sauvignon	Sonoma County
Bandiera Winery	Cabernet Sauvignon	Napa Valley
Lawrence J. Bargetto	"Cypress" Cabernet Sauvignon	Central Coast
Beaulieu (bo l'yuh) Vineyards (BV)	"Beautour" Cabernet Sauvignon	Napa Valley
🍷 ¢ Château Souverain	Cabernet Sauvignon	Alexander Valley
Corbett Canyon Vineyards	Cabernet Sauvignon Reserve	Napa Valley
Creston Vineyards	Cabernet Sauvignon	Paso Robles
¢ Estancia (eh STAHN see ah)	Cabernet Sauvignon	Alexander Valley
Fetzer Vineyards	"Valley Oaks" Cabernet Sauvignon	California
Foppiano Vineyards	Cabernet Sauvignon	Russian River Valley
¢ Geyser Peak	Cabernet Sauvignon	Sonoma
¢ Glen Ellen	"Proprietor's Reserve" Cabernet Sauvignon	California
¢ Guenoc Winery	Cabernet Sauvignon	North Coast
Hawk Crest (Stag's Leap Wine Cellars' 2nd label)	Cabernet Sauvignon	California
Hess Select (The Hess Collection's 2nd label)	Cabernet Sauvignon	California
Husch Vineyards	Cabernet Sauvignon, La Ribera Ranch	Mendocino
Indian Springs Vineyards	Cabernet Sauvignon	Nevada County
🍷 ¢ Laurel Glen Vineyard	"Terra Rosa" Cabernet Sauvignon	Napa Valley

Producer	Wine	Vineyard Location
Liberty School (Caymus Vineyards' 2nd label)	Cabernet Sauvignon	California
J. Lohr	"Seven Oaks" Cabernet Sauvignon	Paso Robles
The Meeker Vineyard	Cabernet Sauvignon	Dry Creek Valley
Meridian Vineyards	Cabernet Sauvignon	Paso Robles
Mill Creek Vineyards	Cabernet Sauvignon	Dry Creek Valley
Robert Mondavi Woodbridge	Cabernet Sauvignon	California
The Monterey Vineyard	Cabernet Sauvignon "Classic"	Monterey County
	Limited Release Cabernet Sauvignon	Monterey County
🍷 ¢ Napa Ridge	Cabernet Sauvignon	Central Coast
	Cabernet Sauvignon	North Coast
	Cabernet Sauvignon Reserve	Central Coast
	Cabernet Sauvignon Reserve	North Coast
R. H. Phillips Vineyard	Cabernet Sauvignon	California
Raymond Vineyard	"Amberhill" Cabernet Sauvignon	California
Rodney Strong Vineyards	Cabernet Sauvignon	Sonoma County
St. Francis Winery	Cabernet Sauvignon	Sonoma County
St. Supéry Vineyard	Cabernet Sauvignon	Napa Valley
Sebastiani Vineyards	Cabernet Sauvignon	Sonoma County
Seghesio *(seh GAY see oh)* Winery	Cabernet Sauvignon	Sonoma County
Shenandoah Vineyards	Cabernet Sauvignon	Amador County
Sutter Home Winery	Cabernet Sauvignon	California
	Cabernet Sauvignon Reserve	Napa Valley
Trefethen Vineyards	"Eshcol" Cabernet Sauvignon	Napa Valley

(continued)

Table 6-1 *(continued)*

Producer	Wine	Vineyard Location
Vichon Winery	"Coastal Selection" Cabernet Sauvignon	California
Villa Mt. Eden	"Cellar Select" Cabernet Sauvignon	California
Wente Bros.	Cabernet Sauvignon	Livermore Valley

Vintage Cabernet Sauvignon and Merlot

Although vintages do not vary nearly as much in California as they do in Europe, the following vintages (from 1980 on) are very good for Cabernet Sauvignons and Merlots in California (those in bold type are especially good): **1992**, **1991**, **1990**, 1987, 1986, **1985**, and 1984. Also, both **1994** and **1995**, judging by our preliminary tasting notes, look super; the finer wines from these two vintages will be generally available in 1997 and 1998, respectively.

The Cabernet wines in Table 6-2 fall into the $12 to $25 price range. You can usually enjoy them within a few years of the vintage, about the time when they are sold, but they hold their quality or even improve for a few more years.

Table 6-2 Medium-Bodied, Medium-Concentration Cabernets

Producer	Wine	Vineyard Location
Arrowood Vineyards	Cabernet Sauvignon	Sonoma County
Atlas Peak Vineyards	Cabernet Sauvignon	Napa Valley
Beaulieu *(bo l'yuh)* Vineyard (BV)	"Rutherford" Cabernet Sauvignon	Napa Valley
	"Tapestry Reserve"	Napa Valley
Beringer Vineyards	Cabernet Sauvignon	Knights Valley
Burgess Cellars	"Vintage Selection" Cabernet Sauvignon	Napa Valley

Producer	***Wine***	***Vineyard Location***
Cakebread Cellars	Cabernet Sauvignon	Napa Valley
¢ Carmenet *(car meh nay)* Vineyard	"Meritage"	Sonoma Valley
Caymus Vineyards	Cabernet Sauvignon	Napa Valley
Chateau Montelena	"Calistoga Cuvée" Cabernet Sauvignon	Napa Valley
Cinnabar Vineyard	Cabernet Sauvignon	Santa Cruz Mountains
Clos du Val *(clo dew val)*	Cabernet Sauvignon Cabernet Sauvignon	Napa Valley Stags Leap District
Corison Wines	Cabernet Sauvignon	Napa Valley
Dry Creek Vineyard	Cabernet Sauvignon Reserve "Meritage"	Dry Creek Valley Dry Creek Valley
Duckhorn Vineyards	Cabernet Sauvignon	Napa Valley
Étude *(ae tood)* Wines	Cabernet Sauvignon	Napa Valley
Ferrari-Carano Winery	Cabernet Sauvignon	Sonoma County
Fisher Vineyards	"Coach Insignia" Cabernet Sauvignon	Napa Valley
Franciscan Vineyards	"Oakville Estate" Cabernet Sauvignon "Meritage"	Napa Valley Napa Valley
🍷 ¢ Freemark Abbey	Cabernet Sauvignon, Bosché *(bo shay)* Vineyard Cabernet Sauvignon, Sycamore Vineyard	Napa Valley Napa Valley
Frog's Leap Winery	Cabernet Sauvignon	Napa Valley
¢ Geyser Peak	"Meritage" "Estate Reserve" Cabernet Sauvignon	Alexander Valley Alexander Valley
Groth Vineyards	Cabernet Sauvignon	Napa Valley
¢ Guenoc Winery	Cabernet Sauvignon "Langtry Estate Meritage"	Lake County Lake County
Hanna Winery	Cabernet Sauvignon	Alexander Valley
Heitz Wine Cellars	Cabernet Sauvignon	Napa Valley

(continued)

Table 6-2 *(continued)*

Producer	Wine	Vineyard Location
♟ The Hess Collection Winery	Cabernet Sauvignon	Mount Veeder
♟ Jordan Vineyard	Cabernet Sauvignon	Alexander Valley
Justin Vineyards	"Society" Cabernet Sauvignon Reserve "Isosceles" Cabernet Sauvignon Reserve	San Luis Obispo County San Luis Obispo County
La Jota *(lah HO tah)* Vineyard	Cabernet Sauvignon	Howell Mountain
¢ Laurel Glen Vineyard	"Counterpoint" Cabernet Sauvignon	Sonoma Mountain
Lockwood Vineyard	Cabernet Sauvignon	Monterey County
Markham Vineyards	Cabernet Sauvignon	Napa Valley
Louis M. Martini	Cabernet Sauvignon, Monte Rosso Vineyard Selection	Sonoma Valley
Robert Mondavi Winery	Cabernet Sauvignon Cabernet Sauvignon	Napa Valley Oakville
Monticello Cellars	"Corley Reserve" Cabernet Sauvignon "Jefferson Cuvée" Cabernet Sauvignon	Napa Valley Napa Valley
Newton Vineyard	Cabernet Sauvignon	Napa Valley
Oakville Ranch Vineyards	Cabernet Sauvignon	Napa Valley
Robert Pecota Winery	Cabernet Sauvignon, Kara's Vineyard	Napa Valley
Joseph Phelps Vineyards	Cabernet Sauvignon	Napa Valley
¢ A. Rafanelli Winery	Cabernet Sauvignon	Dry Creek Valley
Raymond Vineyard	Cabernet Sauvignon	Napa Valley
♟ Renaissance Vineyard	Reserve Cabernet Sauvignon	North Yuba

Producer	Wine	Vineyard Location
♥ ¢ Ridge Vineyards	Cabernet Sauvignon	Santa Cruz Mountains
Saddleback Cellars	Cabernet Sauvignon	Napa Valley
St. Clement Vineyards	"Orappas" Cabernet Sauvignon	Napa Valley
	Cabernet Sauvignon	Napa Valley
St. Francis Winery	Cabernet Sauvignon Reserve	Sonoma Valley
Santa Cruz Mountain Vineyard	Cabernet Sauvignon, Bates Ranch	Santa Cruz Mountains
Shafer Vineyards	Cabernet Sauvignon	Stags Leap District
Silverado Vineyards	Cabernet Sauvignon	Stags Leap District
♥ Simi Winery	Cabernet Sauvignon	Alexander Valley
Stag's Leap Wine Cellars	Cabernet Sauvignon	Napa Valley
Sterling Vineyards	"Diamond Mountain Ranch" Cabernet Sauvignon	Napa Valley
Stonestreet	Cabernet Sauvignon	Alexander Valley
Swanson Vineyards	Cabernet Sauvignon	Napa Valley
Trefethen Vineyards	Cabernet Sauvignon	Napa Valley
Turnbull Wine Cellars	Cabernet Sauvignon	Napa Valley
Vichon	Cabernet Sauvignon	Stags Leap District
Whitehall Lane Winery	Cabernet Sauvignon	Napa Valley
	Cabernet Sauvignon Reserve	Napa Valley
Wild Horse Winery	Cabernet Sauvignon	Paso Robles *(ROH blays)*
ZD Wines	Cabernet Sauvignon	Napa Valley

Wines listed in Table 6-3 cost over $25 a bottle, and they often need several years from the vintage date to reach their peak drinkability.

Table 6-3 Full-Bodied, Intensely Concentrated, Long-Lived Cabernets

Producer	Wine	Vineyard Location
Anderson's Conn Valley	Estate Cabernet Sauvignon Reserve	Napa Valley
♟ Araujo *(ah RAU ho)* Estate	Cabernet Sauvignon, Eisele *(EYE seh lee)* Vineyard	Napa Valley
♟ Beaulieu *(bo l'yuh)* Vineyard	Cabernet Sauvignon, Georges de Latour Private Reserve	Napa Valley
♟ Beringer Vineyards	"Private Reserve" Cabernet Sauvignon	Napa Valley
Cain Cellars	"Cain Five"	Napa Valley
♟ ¢ Cakebread Cellars	Cabernet Sauvignon Reserve	Napa Valley
Caymus Vineyards	"Special Selection" Cabernet Sauvignon	Napa Valley
♟ Chateau Montelena	"Estate" Cabernet Sauvignon	Napa Valley
Dalla Valle Vineyards	"Estate" Cabernet Sauvignon	Napa Valley
	"Maya"	Napa Valley
Dominus Estate	"Dominus"	Napa Valley
Dunn Vineyards	Cabernet Sauvignon	Howell Mountain
	Cabernet Sauvignon	Napa Valley
Far Niente *(nee EN tay)*	Cabernet Sauvignon	Napa Valley
Flora Springs	Cabernet Sauvignon Reserve	Napa Valley
	"Trilogy"	Napa Valley
Forman Vineyard	Cabernet Sauvignon	Napa Valley
✉ Grace Family Vineyards	Cabernet Sauvignon	Napa Valley
Groth Vineyards	Reserve Cabernet Sauvignon	Napa Valley
Harrison Vineyards	Cabernet Sauvignon	Napa Valley

Producer	Wine	Vineyard Location
Heitz Wine Cellars	Cabernet Sauvignon, Martha's Vineyard	Napa Valley
♀ The Hess Collection Winery	Cabernet Sauvignon Reserve	Mount Veeder
Kendall-Jackson	♀ "Cardinale" ♀ "Grand Reserve" Cabernet Sauvignon	California California
♀ Laurel Glen Vineyard	Cabernet Sauvignon	Sonoma Mountain
Livingston Wines	Cabernet Sauvignon, Moffett Vineyard	Napa Valley
♀ Robert Mondavi Winery	Cabernet Sauvignon Reserve	Napa Valley
Mount Eden Vineyards	"Old Vine Reserve" Cabernet Sauvignon	Santa Cruz Mountains
♀ Niebaum-Coppola *(NEE baum COPE poh lah)*	"Rubicon"	Napa Valley
Opus One	Opus One (1985, 1990, 1991 ♀)	Napa Valley
Pahlmeyer	Cabernet Sauvignon	Napa Valley
Joseph Phelps Vineyards	"Insignia" Cabernet Sauvignon, Backus Vineyard	Napa Valley Napa Valley
♀ Ravenswood Winery	Cabernet Sauvignon, Pickberry Vineyard	Sonoma Mountain
♀ Ridge Vineyards	"Monte Bello" Cabernet Sauvignon	Santa Cruz Mountains
♀ Shafer Vineyards	"Hillside Select" Cabernet Sauvignon	Stags Leap District
Silver Oak Cellars	Cabernet Sauvignon Cabernet Sauvignon	Napa Valley Alexander Valley
Silverado Vineyards	"Limited Reserve" Cabernet Sauvignon	Stags Leap District
Simi Winery	Cabernet Sauvignon Reserve	Alexander Valley
Spottswoode Winery	Cabernet Sauvignon	Napa Valley

(continued)

Table 6-3 *(continued)*

Producer	Wine	Vineyard Location
Stag's Leap Wine Cellars	♀ "Cask 23" Cabernet Sauvignon	Stags Leap District
	Cabernet Sauvignon, Fay Vineyard	Stags Leap District
	Cabernet Sauvignon, SLV Vineyards	Stags Leap District
Philip Togni Vineyards	Cabernet Sauvignon	Napa Valley
Villa Mt. Eden	"Signature Series" Cabernet Sauvignon	Mendocino County

California Merlot: The understudy becomes the star

Merlot is not new to California; the Merlot grape has been around for several decades. But until recently, Merlot mainly played a supporting role to Cabernet Sauvignon as an anonymous blending wine. (California winemakers often add a little Merlot to their Cabernets — just as winemakers do in Bordeaux, France — to make their Cabernets a bit softer and more accessible.)

Since the early 1990s, however, Merlot as a wine has been catching up quickly to Cab in popularity in the United States. Suddenly, Merlot is fashionable and in the spotlight. In fact, a 1996 U.S. restaurant survey showed that nowadays, diners order Merlot just as frequently as they do Cabernet Sauvignon. At the moment, American wineries can't get their hands on enough Merlot grapes to make enough Merlot wine to fill the demand.

One of the reasons for the popularity of Merlot-based wines is that the Merlot grape has less tannin than the thicker-skinned Cabernet Sauvignon grape. (See Chapter 3 for a description of both grapes.) As a result, you can usually enjoy Merlot wines as soon as they are released by the wineries; they are not austere and tannic as young Cabernet Sauvignons frequently are.

Backstage in Merlot's ascendancy

The timing of Merlot's sudden fame is not accidental. Red wine in general has gained popularity in the United States, and Merlot is a beneficiary of that trend. Ten or 15 years ago, white wine outsold red wine by more than three to one; now, red wine sells just as much as white wine in restaurants and has almost caught up in retail sales, too. As wine consumption in America increases, wine-drinking patterns seem to be emulating the traditional wine-drinking countries in Europe, where red wine has always been more popular than white wine. Two big surges in red wine sales came as the result of two reports on the healthful properties of wine that aired on the popular television show *60 Minutes* in 1991 and 1995; both reports suggested that red wine might be especially beneficial to one's health.

For wine drinkers trying red wine for the first time, soft Merlot has proven to be an easy and friendly wine.

Merlot goes well with chicken, duck, and other poultry dishes; lamb; and any foods that can accompany Cabernet Sauvignon. But because it is normally less tannic, softer, and rounder than Cabernet Sauvignon, Merlot is more versatile. For example, meat with fruit sauces, which could clash with a Cab, may be just fine with a Merlot. (For more advice on pairing red wine with food, see Chapter 5.)

Different wineries produce different styles of wines. Some California wineries, such as Duckhorn and Newton, make a quite full-bodied, tannic Merlot — you might say a Merlot made in the Cabernet Sauvignon style. But the tendency for California winemakers lately has been to produce a softer, rounder, more velvety wine — whatever the grape variety — that you can drink as soon as it is released from the winery. Ask your wine retailer or restaurateur if you're not sure of a particular Merlot's style.

Recommended California Merlots

As with Cabernet Sauvignons, we have divided our recommended Merlots into three categories, according to their style and price. You'll notice one small difference from our Cabernet tables, however: We have raised the lower end of the first category to $6, as it is extremely difficult to find a decent Merlot for less. Our categories are

✓ **Light- to medium-bodied, soft, fruity Merlots:** Wines in this group are generally fairly uncomplicated, easy-drinking, inexpensive ($6 to $12) wines. You can drink them immediately; they are not made for aging.

✓ **Medium-bodied, medium-concentration Merlots:** Wines in this group have more character and intensity. You can usually enjoy them soon after they become available. They range from $12 to $25.

✓ **Full-bodied, intensely concentrated, long-lived Merlots:** Wines in this category are the fullest, richest, and most expensive Merlots, costing over $25 a bottle. They often need a few years from the vintage date to mature to prime drinkability.

Tables 6-4, 6-5 and 6-6 list only what we consider to be the finest Merlot wines — not every single Merlot in California (and being human, we may have overlooked one or two that deserve mention). We list these wines alphabetically according to the name of the winery. We mark our personal favorites with a 𝕐 symbol, and wines that are really good values with a ¢.

Wines in the first group, listed in Table 6-4, range from $6 to $12. You can drink them immediately; they are not made for aging.

Table 6-4   Light- to Medium-Bodied, Low-Tannin Merlots

Producer	Wine	Vineyard Location
Beaulieu *(bo l'yuh)* Vineyard (BV)	"Beautour" Merlot	Napa Valley
𝕐 ¢ Château Julien	"Private Reserve" Merlot	Monterey County
¢ Château Souverain	Merlot	Alexander Valley
𝕐 ¢ Estancia *(eh STAHN see ah)*	Merlot	Alexander Valley
Foppiano Vineyards	Merlot	Russian River Valley
Hahn Estates	Merlot	Monterey County
J. Lohr Winery	"Cypress" Merlot	California
Mirassou Vineyards	"Family Selection" Merlot	Central Coast

Producer	Wine	Vineyard Location
♟ ¢ Napa Ridge	Merlot	North Coast
	Merlot	Central Coast
Poppy Hill	"Founder's Selection" Merlot	Napa Valley
Vichon *(VEE shon)* Winery	"Coastal Selection" Merlot	California

Wines listed in Table 6-5 are in the $12 to $25 price range; you usually can enjoy them soon after they become available.

Table 6-5   Medium-Bodied, Medium-Concentration Merlots

Producer	Wine	Vineyard Location
Beringer Vineyards	"Meritage"	Knights Valley
Clos du Bois	Merlot	Sonoma County
♟ Clos du Val	Merlot	Stags Leap District
Cuvaison Winery	Merlot	Carneros
Duckhorn Vineyards	Merlot	Napa Valley
Ferrari-Carano Winery	Merlot	Alexander Valley
Franciscan Vineyards	"Oakville Estate" Merlot	Napa Valley
Havens Wine Cellars	Merlot	Napa Valley
	Merlot Reserve	Carneros
Kenwood Vineyards	Merlot, Jack London Vineyard	Sonoma Valley
Markham Vineyards	Merlot	Napa Valley
Robert Mondavi Winery	Merlot	Napa Valley
Peachy Canyon Winery	Merlot	Paso Robles
Robert Pecota Winery	Merlot, Steven Andre Vineyard	Napa Valley
Joseph Phelps Vineyards	Merlot	Napa Valley
Pride Mountain Vineyards	Merlot	Napa Valley
Richardson Vineyards	Merlot	Carneros
Ravenswood Winery	Merlot	Sonoma County

(continued)

Table 6-5 *(continued)*

Producer	Wine	Vineyard Location
St. Clement Vineyards	Merlot	Napa Valley
St. Francis Vineyard	Merlot Merlot Reserve	Sonoma Valley Sonoma Valley
Santa Cruz Mountain Vineyard	Merlot	Santa Cruz Mountains
♈ Selene Wines	Merlot	Napa Valley
♈ Shafer Vineyards	Merlot	Stags Leap District
Silverado Vineyards	Merlot	Stags Leap District
Stag's Leap Wine Cellars	Merlot	Napa Valley
Sterling Vineyards	Merlot, Three Palms Vineyard	Napa Valley
Swanson Vineyards	Merlot	Napa Valley
Villa Mt. Eden	"Napa Grand Reserve" Merlot	Napa Valley
Whitehall Lane Winery	Merlot	Napa Valley
Wild Horse Winery	Merlot	Central Coast

Wines in the final category, listed in Table 6-6, cost over $25 a bottle; they often need a few years from the vintage date to mature to prime drinkability.

Table 6-6   Full-Bodied, Intensely Concentrated, Long-Lived Merlots

Producer	Wine	Vineyard Location
Arrowood Vineyards	Merlot	Sonoma County
Beringer Vineyards	Merlot, Bancroft Ranch	Howell Mountain
♈ Duckhorn	Merlot, Three Palms Vineyard	Napa Valley
	Merlot, Vine Hill Ranch	Napa Valley
Fisher Vineyards	Merlot, RCF Vineyard	Napa Valley

Producer	Wine	Vineyard Location
Kendall-Jackson	"Grand Reserve" Merlot	California
¶ ¢ Matanzas Creek Winery	Merlot	Sonoma Valley
Newton Vineyard	Merlot	Napa Valley
Pahlmeyer	Merlot	Napa Valley
¶ Ravenswood Winery	Merlot, Sangiacomo Vineyard	Carneros

Chapter 7

California Pinot Noir, Zinfandel, and Company

* *

In This Chapter

▶ A red wine for all seasons

▶ California's own wine

▶ Que Syrah Syrah

▶ Cal goes Ital

* *

*L*ife would be pretty boring if the only red wines you could drink were Cabernet Sauvignons and Merlots — even as good as those wines are. Fortunately, California makes some other really fine red wines, with Pinot Noir and Zinfandel — two completely unique wines — being the most popular. But the variety of California red wines runs even deeper. Why not try an S wine tonight: a Petite Sirah, a Syrah (they're quite different), or a Sangiovese?

California Pinot Noir: The Coming Star

Pinot Noir wine is the young American debutante about to go public. Not that she hasn't been around in the United States for a while. But American winemakers have needed a couple of decades to figure out this extremely difficult grape variety.

No other major grape variety in the world (and perhaps we can include all the lesser varieties, too) is as fussy about its *terroir* as Pinot Noir is. Like Goldilocks, it needs just the right temperature (on the cool side, with a long growing season), just the right soil (preferably poor and well drained — limestone is nice), some sunshine, and very little rain. Cabernet Sauvignon grows successfully in most temperate localities on the planet, but Pinot Noir, until recently, has been a failure just about everywhere except for a small region in Burgundy, France.

Early attempts to make a decent wine from Pinot Noir in California were quite disastrous — with a few notable (lucky?) exceptions. But, by trial and error, viticulturists and winemakers managed to identify three regions in California (and one region in Oregon — see Chapter 8) where Pinot Noir grapes make fine wines:

- The Santa Barbara region of California's South-Central Coast

- The Carneros region, which covers southern Napa and Sonoma Counties

- The Russian River Valley, near the coast of northern Sonoma County

A fourth region is a serious contender: the Anderson Valley in Mendocino County. What all these regions have in common is a relatively cool climate, a long growing season with plenty of sunshine, and fairly poor soil. A few other successful Pinot Noirs are being made in isolated, mountainous areas near the coastline in California, but that's about it.

Why do grown men and women deliberately complicate their lives by growing this difficult grape?

Anyone who has ever tasted a great red Burgundy from France can understand winemakers' fascination with Pinot Noir. Under the right circumstances, the Pinot Noir grape can make the most delectable red wines in the world. Supple, low in tannin, with delicious, tart berry fruit and — at its best — a long, velvety finish, good Pinot Noir wine redefines red wine. California Pinot Noir (and, of course, its French relative, red Burgundy; see Chapter 11) has become the red wine of choice for many of the world's discriminating wine lovers. We think that Pinot Noir may just become the next in-vogue red wine in the United States. Figure 7-1 shows a label from a California Pinot Noir wine.

The red wine for all seasons

Pinot Noir is the ideal red wine to order in restaurants. You can enjoy it when it is young or when it has some age. It is also versatile with different foods — equally at home with salmon and seafood as with chicken, veal, pork, duck, and game birds. Fuller-bodied, more concentrated Pinot Noirs are excellent with roast beef.

Figure 7-1: Label from a California Pinot Noir.

Because of the grape's fickle nature, Pinot Noir wines do not experience many great vintages, even in sunny California. But of recent vintages, **1990**, 1991, and 1992 are all good, and **1994** may be the best Pinot Noir vintage yet in California.

Recommended California Pinot Noirs

We have divided California Pinot Noirs into three categories, according to the style of the wine and its price:

- ✓ **Light- to medium-bodied, very fruity, low-tannin Pinot Noirs:** Wines in this group range from $6 to $12. You can drink them immediately; they are not made for aging.

- ✓ **Medium-bodied, medium-concentration Pinot Noirs:** Wines in this group cost $12 to $25 retail. You can usually enjoy them soon after they become available.

- ✓ **Full-bodied, concentrated, long-lived Pinot Noirs:** Wines in this category cost over $25 a bottle. They often need a few years from the vintage to mature fully.

In Tables 7-1, 7-2, and 7-3, we name what we believe to be California's best Pinot Noir wines, listed alphabetically within each category. The location mentioned for each wine indicates the origin of the grapes. We mark our personal favorites with a ♈ symbol, and wines that are really good values with a ¢ symbol. Wines that are difficult to find outside the winery itself are marked with a ✉ symbol; consult Appendix C for addresses of those wineries.

Generally, California producers of Pinot Noir make a basic Pinot Noir wine as well as a special bottling that is either called a *reserve* or named for a specific vineyard from which the grapes for that wine come. Some of our recommended wines are single-vineyard or reserve wines and are indicated accordingly; if we don't mention any vineyard for a particular wine, that wine is made using the grapes of two or more vineyards or is the producer's basic wine.

The following tables are *not* all-encompassing. As long as our lists are, they represent only a small fraction of California's Pinot Noir wines. We believe that the wines listed are some of California's best; please forgive us if we have left out one of your favorites.

Light- to medium-bodied, low-tannin Pinot Noir wines, listed in Table 7-1, range from $6 to $12. You can drink them immediately; they are not made for aging.

Table 7-1   Light- to Medium-Bodied, Low-Tannin Pinot Noirs

Producer	Wine	Vineyard Location
¢ Aries (2nd label, Robert Sinskey Vineyards)	Carneros Pinot Noir	Carneros
Carneros Creek Winery	"Fleur de Carneros"	Carneros
¢ Christophe	Pinot Noir	Carneros
Corbett Canyon Vineyards	Pinot Noir Reserve	Santa Barbara County
Creston Vineyards	Pinot Noir	Paso Robles
¢ Estancia	Pinot Noir	Monterey County
Fetzer Vineyards	Pinot Noir Reserve	California
Charles Krug Winery	Pinot Noir	Carneros
Louis M. Martini Winery	Pinot Noir	Carneros
Mont St. John Cellars	Pinot Noir	Carneros

Producer	Wine	Vineyard Location
♀ ¢ Napa Ridge	Pinot Noir	North Coast
Pepperwood Grove (2nd label, Cecchetti Sebastiani Cellars)	Pinot Noir	California
Q. C. Fly (2nd label, Bouchaine Vineyards)	Pinot Noir	California
♀ ¢ Saintsbury	"Garnet"	Carneros
Shooting Star (2nd label, Steele Wines)	Pinot Noir	Mendocino County
¢ Villa Mt. Eden	"Cellar Select" Pinot Noir	California

Medium-bodied, medium-concentration Pinot Noirs, listed in Table 7-2, cost $12 to $25 retail. You can usually enjoy them soon after they become available.

Table 7-2   Medium-Bodied, Medium-Concentration Pinot Noirs

Producer	Wine	Vineyard Location
Au Bon Climat *(oh bahn klee maht)*	Pinot Noir	Santa Maria Valley
Bernardus Vineyards	Pinot Noir, Bien Nacido Vineyard	Santa Barbara
Bouchaine Vineyards	"Carneros Reserve" Pinot Noir	Carneros
David Bruce Winery	Pinot Noir Estate Pinot Noir	Russian River Valley Santa Cruz Mountain
Buena Vista Winery	"Grand Reserve" Pinot Noir	Carneros
Byron Vineyards	Pinot Noir Reserve	Santa Barbara County
♀ Cambria Winery	Pinot Noir, Julia's Vineyard	Santa Maria Valley
Carneros Creek Winery	Pinot Noir	Carneros
Chimere Winery	Pinot Noir	Edna Valley

(continued)

Table 7-2 (continued)

Producer	Wine	Vineyard Location
Cuvaison Winery (coo vay sohn)	Pinot Noir	Carneros
🍷 Dehlinger Winery	Pinot Noir Pinot Noir Reserve	Russian River Valley Russian River Valley
Edmeades Winery	Pinot Noir, Dennison Vineyard	Anderson Valley
Étude Wines	Pinot Noir	Carneros
Gary Farrell Wines	Pinot Noir	Russian River Valley
Fiddlehead Cellars	Pinot Noir	Santa Maria Valley
Foxen Vineyard	Pinot Noir	Santa Maria Valley
Gainey Vineyard	Pinot Noir, Santa Maria Vineyard Pinot Noir, Sanford & Benedict Vineyard	Santa Barbara Santa Barbara
Greenwood Ridge Vineyards	Pinot Noir, Roederer Estate Vineyard	Anderson Valley
Handley Cellars	Pinot Noir	Anderson Valley
Hanzell Vineyards	Pinot Noir	Sonoma Valley
Husch Vineyards	Pinot Noir	Anderson Valley
Lazy Creek Vineyards	Pinot Noir	Anderson Valley
Mahoney Estate (2nd label, Carneros Creek Winery)	Pinot Noir, Las Piedras Vineyard	Carneros
Robert Mondavi Winery	Pinot Noir Pinot Noir	Carneros Napa Valley
Morgan Winery	Pinot Noir Reserve Pinot Noir Reserve	Carneros Monterey County
Navarro Vineyards	Pinot Noir	Anderson Valley
Ojai (OH hi) Vineyard	Pinot Noir	Santa Barbara County
Page Mill Winery	Pinot Noir, Bien Nacido Vineyard	Santa Barbara County
Fess Parker Winery	"American Tradition Reserve" Pinot Noir	Santa Barbara

Producer	Wine	Vineyard Location
Kent Rasmussen Winery	Pinot Noir	Carneros
J. Rochioli Vineyard	Pinot Noir	Russian River Valley
¢ Saintsbury	Pinot Noir	Carneros
Sanford Winery	Pinot Noir	Santa Barbara County
Santa Cruz Mountains	"Estate" Pinot Noir Pinot Noir, Matteson Vineyard	Santa Cruz Mountains Santa Cruz Mountains
Steele Wines	Pinot Noir	Carneros
¢ Stonestreet	Pinot Noir	Sonoma County
Joseph Swan Vineyards	Pinot Noir, Steiner Vineyard	Sonoma Mountain
Talley Vineyards	Pinot Noir, Rosemary's Vineyard	Arroyo Grande
Lane Tanner	Pinot Noir, Bien Nacido Vineyard Pinot Noir, Sierra Madre Vineyard	Santa Barbara Santa Barbara
Wild Horse Winery	Pinot Noir	Central Coast

The full-bodied, concentrated, long-lived wines listed in Table 7-3 cost over $25 a bottle. They often need a few years from the vintage to mature fully.

Table 7-3　Full-Bodied, Concentrated, Long-Lived Pinot Noirs

Producer	Wine	Vineyard Location
🍷 Au Bon Climat *(oh bahn klee maht)*	Pinot Noir (all single-vineyard bottlings)	Santa Barbara
Babcock Vineyards	"Estate" Pinot Noir	Santa Ynez Valley
David Bruce Winery	"Estate" Pinot Noir "30th Anniversary Reserve" Pinot Noir	Santa Cruz Mountains Santa Cruz Mountains

(continued)

Table 7-3 *(continued)*

Producer	Wine	Vineyard Location
♟ Calera Wine Company	Pinot Noir (all single-vineyard bottlings)	San Benito County
El Molino	Pinot Noir	Napa Valley
♟ Gary Farrell Wines	Pinot Noir, Allen Vineyard	Russian River Valley
Foxen Vineyard	Pinot Noir, Sanford & Benedict Vineyard	Santa Ynez Valley
Kendall-Jackson	"Grand Reserve" Pinot Noir	California
Kistler Vineyards	Pinot Noir (all single-vineyard bottlings)	Sonoma
Robert Mondavi Winery	Pinot Noir Reserve	Napa Valley
Mount Eden Vineyards	"Estate" Pinot Noir	Santa Cruz Mountains
♟ J. Rochioli Vineyard	Pinot Noir (all reserve bottlings)	Russian River Valley
♟ Saintsbury	Pinot Noir Reserve	Carneros
♟ Sanford Winery	Pinot Noir, Sanford & Benedict Vineyard	Santa Barbara County
Lane Tanner	Pinot Noir, Sanford & Benedict Vineyard	Santa Ynez Valley
♟ ✉ Williams & Selyem Winery	Pinot Noir (all single-vineyard bottlings, especially Pinot Noir, Rochioli Vineyard; Pinot Noir, Allen Vineyard)	Russian River Valley

Gallo power

E. & J. Gallo Winery of Modesto, California, is by far the largest winery in the world. So awesome is the marketing power of this colossus that only six months after launching one of its many second labels, Turning Leaf, Gallo had sold 1 million cases of Turning Leaf wines! Perhaps even more amazing, Turning Leaf is already the largest-selling Pinot Noir in the United States and the second-largest-selling Zinfandel (red and "white" combined) in the 750 ml category (in plain English, that's regular wine bottle size), behind Sutter Home Winery.

Zinfandelity: California's Own Craze

Although the Zinfandel grape variety does have European origins (of a rather obscure nature), today it is grown almost nowhere in the world outside California. And it's been in California for about 150 years. In fact, many of the oldest vineyards in the United States produce Zinfandel grapes.

Red Zinfandel wine usually has a dark ruby color. It is typically dry and full bodied — although it can be made in a lighter-bodied style. Red Zin often exhibits exuberant, wild berry fruit, and peppery or spicy flavors, and it normally has a good amount of tannin and acidity.

Ironically, many wine drinkers know Zinfandel through its popular, fruity, fairly sweet version: white Zinfandel (which is pink). Zinfandel's metamorphosis from dark, spicy red to sweet pink is a story of ingenuity and survival. Back in the early 1970s, red Zinfandel wine was not selling well. (In general, the wine's quality wasn't as high as it is today. Besides, wine drinkers in America were just discovering another red wine called Cabernet Sauvignon, as well as falling head over heels for a new white wine called Chardonnay.)

In 1972, Bob Trinchero of Sutter Home Winery — known for its good Zinfandel — hit upon a brilliant concept: Make a pink, slightly sweet, easy-drinking, inexpensive wine out of some of the many Zinfandel grapes available. To put it mildly, the experiment worked. The rest, as they say, is history. Millions of Americans, brought up on Coke and Pepsi, graduated to "white

Zinfandel," and Sutter Home became one of the largest, most successful wineries in the United States. (Sutter Home continues to make red Zinfandel, too.)

Despite the enormous popularity of "white Zinfandel," red Zinfandel has made a strong comeback in the past few years.

Enjoying Zinfandel

Red Zinfandel is a natural in restaurants — it goes beautifully with many different foods and cuisines, and it is not expensive. Zin is truly one of the most versatile red wines around. Try it with grilled meats, barbecue, pizza, spicy foods — you name it.

Many of the best Zinfandels being made today come from Sonoma County, especially the Dry Creek, Alexander, and Russian River Valleys. Still one of the best bargains among "serious" red wines, Zinfandel is priced in the $10 to $20 range in retail stores, with a few exceptions. And a number of fine red Zinfandels are available for less than $10. In terms of quality-price ratio, red Zinfandel is a thrifty shopper's delight.

Like Cabernet Sauvignon, Zinfandel has had a string of really good vintages in California lately: 1993, **1992**, **1991**, and **1990**, with **1994** looking promising. Among the older vintages, 1987, **1985**, and 1984 are quite fine.

What's your style?

Zinfandel comes in all different styles, ranging from lean, lighter-bodied, *claret-style* Zins (*claret* is a synonym for red Bordeaux wine; claret-style wines are not very full and not extremely fruity) to full-bodied, tannic, lusty blockbusters. Zinfandel is especially delicious when it's young — in the first five or six years from its vintage date — when it shows its exuberant berry fruit flavor, but Zin also ages well.

Recommended red Zinfandels

Because few expensive Zinfandels are available, we have divided our recommended wines into only two price categories:

> ✔ **Under $10 Zinfandels:** These wines tend to be lighter bodied, fairly low in tannin, and ready to drink immediately; they typically do not benefit from further aging. You can find them for less than $10 a bottle.

✔ **$10 to $20 Zinfandels:** Wines in this category *tend* to be fuller bodied, tannic, and concentrated. (*Some* wines in this category are made in a lighter style; ask your wine merchant if you're not certain.) They often benefit from two or three years of aging. (We lump the occasional Zin that sells for more than $20 into the $10 to $20 category and indicate that it is more expensive with a $ $ symbol.)

Within each category, we name what *we* believe to be the best wines, listed alphabetically. The location mentioned for each wine indicates the origin of the grapes. We mark our personal favorites with a ⍦ symbol, and wines that are really good values with a ¢ symbol. The ✉ symbol indicates wines that are difficult to find outside the winery; consult Appendix C for addresses of those wineries.

Zinfandel producers often make several different red Zinfandel wines: For example, they might make a basic bottling, a special bottling called a *reserve*, and/or a special bottling (or several special bottlings) named for the specific vineyard from which the grapes for that wine come. Some of our recommended wines are single-vineyard or reserve wines and are indicated accordingly; if we don't mention any vineyard for a particular wine, that wine is made using the grapes of two or more vineyards or is the producer's basic wine.

The wines in Table 7-4 tend to be light- to medium-bodied, fairly low in tannin, and ready to drink immediately after they are released. They typically do not benefit from further aging, and might even suffer from it, because they lose their fruity, youthful charm. You can expect to find these wines for less than $10 a bottle.

Table 7-4	Lighter-Bodied, Low-Tannin, Easy-Drinking Zinfandels	
Producer	**Wine**	**Vineyard Location**
Beringer Vineyards	Zinfandel	Napa Valley
¢ Boeger Winery	Zinfandel, Walker Vineyard	El Dorado County
¢ Bogle Vineyards	Zinfandel	California
Davis Bynum Winery	Zinfandel	Russian River Valley
Castoro Cellars	Zinfandel	Paso Robles

(continued)

Table 7-4 *(continued)*

Producer	Wine	Vineyard Location
¢ Chateau Souverain	Zinfandel	Dry Creek Valley
Cline Cellars	Zinfandel	Contra Costa County
Fetzer Vineyards	"Barrel Select" Zinfandel	Mendocino County
	Zinfandel Reserve	Mendocino County
E. & J. Gallo Winery	Zinfandel	Northern Sonoma
Gundlach-Bundschu Winery	Zinfandel	Sonoma Valley
Hop Kiln Winery	"Marty Griffin's Big Red" (Zinfandel blend)	Sonoma County
Karly Wines	Zinfandel	Amador County
Lolonis Winery	Zinfandel	Mendocino County
♆ ¢ Marietta Cellars	"Old Vine Red" (Zinfandel blend)	Sonoma County
Milano Winery	Zinfandel, Sanel Valley Vineyard	Mendocino County
Mirassou Vineyards	"Family Selection" Zinfandel	Central Coast
Monteviña Wines	Zinfandel, Brioso Vineyard	Amador County
	Zinfandel	Amador County
Parducci Wine Cellars	Zinfandel	Mendocino County
J. Pedroncelli Winery	Zinfandel	Dry Creek Valley
Pelligrini Winery	"Old Vines" Zinfandel	Sonoma County
Ravenswood	"Vintner's Blend" Zinfandel	North Coast
Rosenblum Cellars	"Vintner's Cuvée" Zinfandel	California
Santa Barbara Winery	Zinfandel, Lafond Vineyard	Santa Ynez Valley
♆ ¢ Sausal Winery	Zinfandel	Alexander Valley

Producer	Wine	Vineyard Location
🍷 ¢ Seghesio Winery	Zinfandel	Sonoma County
Shenandoah Vineyards	Zinfandel	Amador County
Shooting Star (2nd label, Steele Wines)	Zinfandel	Lake County
Sutter Home Winery	Zinfandel Zinfandel	Amador County California
🍷 ¢ Trentadue Winery	Zinfandel	Sonoma County
Villa Mt. Eden	"Cellar Select" Zinfandel	California
Wellington Vineyards	"Casa Santinamaria" Zinfandel	Sonoma Valley
Wildhurst Vineyards	Zinfandel	Clear Lake

Wines in Table 7-5 *tend* to be fuller bodied, tannic, and concentrated — but some of these wines are made in a lighter style. (Ask your wine merchant for guidance.) These Zins often benefit from two or three years of aging. Most of the wines listed sell for $10 to $20, but some wines that are indicated with a $ $ cost slightly more.

Zinfully fun

Zinfandel is not only delicious to drink, but it's also fun to talk about. Zinfandel lovers have all sorts of pet descriptions and slogans for their favorite wine, from the wine's nickname, *Zin,* to expressions that describe how the wine tastes, like *zinfully good, zinsational,* and *zintillating.* Many Zinfandel fans belong to a club called *ZAP* (Zinfandel Advocates and Producers, telephone 415-851-2319 or fax 415-851-5579). One producer has named his wine *Original Zin.* We joined the fun ourselves once when we organized a tasting of Zinfandels and wrote on the invitations *Commit Zinfandelity with someone you love.* Hey, fun wine deserves a fan club!

Table 7-5 Fuller-Bodied, Tannic, Concentrated Zins

Producer	Wine	Vineyard Location
Adelaida Cellars	Zinfandel	San Luis Obispo County
Alderbrook Winery	Zinfandel	Dry Creek Valley
Bannister Winery	Zinfandel	Russian River Valley
Benziger Family Winery	Zinfandel	Sonoma County
Beringer Vineyards	Zinfandel	Napa Valley
Robert Biale Vineyards	Zinfandel, Aldo's Vineyard	Napa Valley
David Bruce Winery	Zinfandel	San Luis Obispo County
Brutocao Cellars	Zinfandel, Hopland Ranch	Mendocino County
Burgess Cellars	Zinfandel	Napa Valley
Chateau Montelena	Zinfandel	Napa Valley
$ $ Château Potelle	V.G.S.	Mount Veeder
Cline Cellars	Zinfandel (all single-vineyard bottlings)	Contra Costa County
	Zinfandel Reserve	Contra Costa County
Clos du Bois Winery	Zinfandel	Sonoma County
Clos du Val	Zinfandel	Stags Leap District
Cosentino Winery	"The Zin"	Sonoma County
H. Coturri and Sons	Zinfandel	Sonoma Valley
De Loach Vineyards	"O.F.S." Zinfandel	Russian River Valley
	Zinfandel (all single-vineyard bottlings)	Russian River Valley
Dry Creek Vineyard	"Old Vines" Zinfandel	Dry Creek Valley
	Zinfandel Reserve	Dry Creek Valley
Eberle Winery	Zinfandel, Sauret Vineyard	Paso Robles
Edmeades Vineyard	Zinfandel, Ciapusci Vineyard	Mendocino County
	Zinfandel, Zeni Vineyard	Mendocino County

Producer	Wine	Vineyard Location
Edmunds St. John	Zinfandel Zinfandel Zinfandel	Mount Veeder Howell Mountain California
Elyse Vineyards	Zinfandel Zinfandel, Morisoli Vineyard	Howell Mountain Napa Valley
Gary Farrell Wines	Zinfandel, Collins Vineyard	Russian River Valley
Ferrari-Carano Winery	Zinfandel	Dry Creek Valley
Franciscan Vineyards	"Oakville Estate" Zinfandel	Napa Valley
♟ Franus Winery	Zinfandel, Brandlin Ranch Zinfandel, George Hendry Vineyard	Mount Veeder Napa Valley
Frog's Leap Winery	Zinfandel	Napa Valley
E. & J. Gallo Winery	Zinfandel, Frei Ranch Vineyard	Dry Creek Valley
♟ Green & Red Vineyard	Zinfandel, Chiles Mill Vineyard	Napa Valley
Greenwood Ridge Vineyards	Zinfandel, Scherrer Vineyard	Sonoma County
Grgich Hills Cellar	Zinfandel	Sonoma County
Gundlach-Bundschu Winery	Zinfandel, Rhinefarm Vineyard	Sonoma Valley
Haywood Winery	Zinfandel, Los Chamizal Vineyard Zinfandel, Rocky Terrace Vineyard	Sonoma Valley Sonoma Valley
Hidden Cellars	Zinfandel, McAdams Vineyard Zinfandel, Pacini Vineyard	Mendocino Mendocino
Homewood Winery	"110-Year-Old Vines" Zinfandel	Sonoma Valley

(continued)

Table 7-5 *(continued)*

Producer	Wine	Vineyard Location
Hop Kiln Winery	Primitivo Reserve	Russian River Valley
	Zinfandel	Russian River Valley
Kendall-Jackson	"Grand Reserve" Zinfandel	California
	Zinfandel, Dupratt Vineyard	Anderson Valley
Kenwood Vineyards	Zinfandel (all single-vineyard bottlings)	Sonoma Valley
Lamborn Family Vineyards	Zinfandel	Howell Mountain
Limerick Lane	Zinfandel, Collins Vineyard	Russian River Valley
Lytton Springs Winery	Zinfandel	Sonoma County
Marietta Cellars	Zinfandel	Sonoma County
Martinelli Winery	Zinfandel, Jackass Vineyard	Russian River Valley
Robert Mondavi Winery	Zinfandel	Napa Valley
Murrieta's Well	Zinfandel	Livermore Valley
Nalle Winery	Zinfandel	Dry Creek Valley
Newlan Vineyards	Zinfandel	Napa Valley
♒ Niebaum-Coppola Estate	"Edizione Pennino" Zinfandel	Napa Valley
Peachy Canyon Winery	Zinfandel (all single-vineyard bottlings)	Paso Robles
Peterson Winery	Zinfandel	Dry Creek Valley
Joseph Phelps Vineyards	Zinfandel	Alexander Valley
Preston Vineyards	Zinfandel	Dry Creek Valley
Quivera Vineyards	Zinfandel	Dry Creek Valley
Rabbit Ridge Vineyards	Zinfandel	Dry Creek Valley
	Zinfandel Reserve, San Lorenzo Vineyard	Dry Creek Valley

Producer	Wine	Vineyard Location
🍷✉ A. Rafanelli Winery	Zinfandel	Dry Creek Valley
🍷 Ravenswood	Zinfandel	Sonoma County
	$ $ ✉ Zinfandel (all single-vineyard bottlings)	Sonoma County
	$ $ ✉ Zinfandel, Dickerson Vineyard	Napa Valley
Renwood Winery	Zinfandel (all single-vineyard bottlings)	Amador County
Richardson Vineyards	Zinfandel, Nora's Vineyard	Sonoma Valley
🍷 Ridge Vineyards	Zinfandel	Sonoma County
	$ $ Zinfandel (all single-vineyard bottlings)	Sonoma County
🍷 J. Rochioli Vineyard	Zinfandel, Sodini Vineyard	Russian River Valley
Rombauer Vineyards	Zinfandel	Napa Valley
🍷 Rosenblum Cellars	Zinfandel (all single-vineyard bottlings)	Sonoma County
	Zinfandel (all single-vineyard bottlings)	Napa Valley
St. Francis Winery	"Old Vines" Zinfandel	Sonoma Valley
Saucelito Canyon Vineyard	Zinfandel	Arroyo Grande Valley
Scherrer Vineyard	"Old Vines" Zinfandel	Alexander Valley
Sky Vineyards	Zinfandel	Mount Veeder
Steele Wines	Zinfandel, Catfish Vineyard	Clear Lake
	Zinfandel, Pacini Vineyard	Mendocino County

(continued)

Table 7-5 *(continued)*

Producer	Wine	Vineyard Location
Storybook Mountain Vineyards	Zinfandel $ $ Zinfandel Reserve	Napa Valley Napa Valley
Rodney Strong Vineyards	Zinfandel, River West Vineyard	Russian River Valley
Joseph Swan Vineyards	Zinfandel, Frati Ranch	Russian River Valley
The Terraces	Zinfandel	Napa Valley
$ $ ✉ Turley Wine Cellars	Zinfandel (all single-vineyard bottlings)	Napa Valley
Wellington Vineyards	"100-Year-Old Vines" Zinfandel	Sonoma Valley
Whaler Vineyard	"Flagship" Zinfandel Zinfandel	Mendocino County Mendocino County
Wild Horse Winery	Zinfandel	Paso Robles
✉ $ $ Williams & Selyem Winery	Zinfandel	Russian River Valley

Petite Sirah Is Not Petite!

One of the heartiest, most rustic red wines in California is the totally misnamed Petite Sirah. Petite? Hello? This wine is for confirmed red wine drinkers who think that lusty red Zinfandel is wimpy.

The Petite Sirah grape produces one of the most full-bodied, tannic wines in the world. It is frequently used as a blending grape to "beef up" or add complexity to red Zinfandel, and it is also made as a varietal wine. Petite Sirah is perfectly suited for a hearty winter meal, such as beef stew or cassoulet. In fact, it demands substantial food to tame down its tannin.

Like the Zinfandel grape, Petite Sirah is a California specialty (it is *not* related to the Syrah grape from France's Rhône Valley). And, like Zinfandel wine, the not-quite-fashionable Petite Sirah has the advantage of being inexpensive (under $15); in fact, many Petite Sirah wines are under $10.

The wines listed in Table 7-6 are some of the best Petite Sirahs in California (which, in real terms, means the world, in the case of this wine).

Table 7-6	Outstanding California Petite Sirahs	
Producer	**Wine**	**Vineyard Location**
Bogle Vineyards	Petite Sirah	California
♀ Concannon Vineyard	Petite Sirah	Livermore Valley
Field Stone Winery	Petite Sirah	Alexander Valley
♀ Foppiano Vineyards	Petite Sirah	Russian River Valley
	Petite Sirah	Sonoma County
	Petite Sirah	Napa Valley
Guenoc Winery	Petite Sirah	North Coast
Hop Kiln Winery	Petite Sirah, M. Griffin Vineyards	Russian River Valley
Mirassou Vineyards	"Family Selection" Petite Sirah	Monterey County
Parducci Wine Cellars	Petite Sirah	Mendocino County
♀ Ridge Vineyards	Petite Sirah, York Creek	Napa County
♀ Trentadue Winery	Petite Sirah	Alexander Valley
	Petite Sirah	Sonoma County

And then there's Preston Vineyards' unique wine, Sirah-Syrah. We didn't know where to place this interesting blend of two grape varieties, so we put it square in the middle, between Petite Sirah and Syrah (which follows).

Syrah and Other "Rhône Ranger" Reds

For a while, wines made from the principal red grape varieties of the Rhône Valley in France — such as Syrah, Mourvèdre, and Grenache (the latter two grapes originally from Spain) — seemed to be becoming the new wave of red wines in California. But the California Rhône phenomenon really hasn't happened in a big way — at least not yet.

Nevertheless, several producers are making provocative wines based on Rhône grape varieties, led by the colorful Randall Grahm of Bonny Doon Vineyard in the Santa Cruz Mountains. Grahm gives his wines some wacky names, often satirizing wines or events from the Rhône. His Le Cigare Volant (a Rhône blend) pokes fun at the fact that the good burghers of Châteauneuf-du-Pape *(shah toe nuf doo pahp),* a town in France's Rhône Valley, passed a law during the 1950s prohibiting flying saucers (which the French call *flying cigars*) from landing in their region. Other Bonny Doon wines include Old Telegram (a Mourvèdre wine, satirizing the Châteauneuf-du-Pape wine called *Vieux Telegraphe,* or "Old Telegraph") and Clos de Gilroy (a Grenache-based wine).

Not to be outdone, Stillman Brown of Jory Winery in the Santa Clara Valley has an engaging wine called Red Zeppelin (a blend of Carignane — another variety used in the southern Rhône and southern France — Zinfandel, and Cabernet Franc). Jory also makes a Mourvèdre-Syrah blend named Black Zeppelin.

Other leading wineries making wines based on Rhône varieties include those listed in Table 7-7.

Table 7-7 More Wineries That Make Rhône-Based Wines

Winery	Winery Location	Wine
Cline Cellars	Contra Costa County	"Oakley Cuvée" (Rhône blend) Mourvèdre Syrah Carignane
Edmunds St. John	Alameda County	"Les Côtes Sauvages" (Rhône blend) Syrah Grenache
Jade Mountain Winery	Mount Veeder	Syrah Mourvèdre "La Provencale" (Rhône blend) "Les Jumeaux" (Rhône blend with Cabernet Sauvignon)
McDowell Valley Vineyards	Mendocino	"Les Vieux Cépages" (Rhône blend) Syrah
The Ojai Vineyard	Santa Barbara	Syrah

Winery	Winery Location	Wine
Joseph Phelps	Napa Valley	"Le Mistral" (Rhône blend) Syrah
R.H. Phillips Vineyard	Central Valley	Syrah "Alliance" (Rhône blend) Mourvèdre
Preston Vineyards	Dry Creek Valley	Syrah "Faux" (Rhône blend)
Quivera Vineyards	Dry Creek Valley	"Dry Creek Cuvée" (Rhône blend)
Qupé Cellars	Santa Maria Valley	Syrah "Los Olivos Cuvée" (Syrah-Mourvèdre blend)
Ridge Vineyards	Santa Cruz Mountains	Mátaro (Mourvèdre)
Sobon Estate	Shenandoah Valley	"Rhône Rouge" (Rhône blend) Syrah
Swanson Vineyards	Napa Valley	Syrah
Sean Thackeray & Co.	Napa Valley	"Orion" Syrah "Old Vines" Syrah
Zaca Mesa Winery	Santa Barbara	Syrah Mourvèdre "Z Cuvée" (Rhône blend)

Italy in California

Italy may very well have more different wine grape varieties than any other country in the world, and quite a few of those varieties have migrated to California.

Barbera, one of the most prolific red varieties in Italy, has had some success in California over the years. (Recent Barberas from Boeger Winery in El Dorado County and Renwood Winery in Amador County are very good.) A few producers, such as Kent Rasmussen, are making a Dolcetto (a grape of Piedmontese origin). Californian vintners, however, seem unable to get good results with the noble Nebbiolo (the variety that makes Barolo and Barbaresco in Piedmont); like Pinot Noir, Nebbiolo is *very* particular about its *terroir* and has not performed well anywhere outside northwest Italy.

Sangiovese, the dominant grape of Chianti — and all of Italy — is the one Italian grape variety that seems to show the most promise of adapting to California's environment.

Seghesio Winery in Sonoma has had quite a successful history with its Chianti Station (a mainly Sangiovese wine named after an old train stop near Seghesio Winery, where many Italian immigrants lived). Another Sangiovese pioneer in California, Atlas Peak Winery in the eastern Napa hills (now owned entirely by Tuscany's Antinori Winery), has far more Sangiovese planted than any other winery in the United States.

Frankly, the quality of Sangiovese wines in California up to this point is mixed, at best. The trouble with most California Sangiovese wines is that they don't taste like Sangiovese. Try a Chianti, Brunello di Montalcino, or any Sangiovese-based wine from Italy (see Chapter 12) to see what we mean. California Sangioveses tend to be too soft and alcoholic. Perhaps they need a cooler growing climate than Napa and Sonoma.

Because winemakers have been experimenting with Sangiovese only since the mid-1980s, however, it is too early to speculate about the grape's long-term success. As two of the very best Sangioveses being made in California — those of Staglin Family Vineyard and Swanson Vineyards — both come from the Rutherford area of Napa Valley, perhaps this region will ultimately prove to have the right *terroir* for Sangiovese.

Table 7-8 includes some of the leading producers of Sangiovese in California.

Table 7-8   Leading California Sangiovese Producers

Producer	Wine	Vineyard Location
Atlas Peak Vineyards	Sangiovese	Napa Valley
Ferrari-Carano Winery	Sangiovese	Alexander Valley
Flora Springs Wine Co.	Sangiovese	Napa Valley
Long Vineyards	Sangiovese	Napa Valley
Robert Mondavi Winery	Sangiovese	California
♆ Robert Pepi Winery	"Colline di Sassi"	Napa Valley

Producer	Wine	Vineyard Location
Seghesio Winery	"Chianti Station Old Vines" (Sangiovese blend)	Alexander Valley
	"Vitigno Toscano" (100 percent Sangiovese)	Alexander Valley
Shafer Vineyards	"Firebreak" (Sangiovese blend)	Stags Leap District
Silverado Vineyards	Sangiovese	Napa Valley
♀ Staglin Family Vineyard	"Stagliano"	Napa Valley
♀ Swanson Vineyards	Sangiovese	Napa Valley
Trentadue Winery	Sangiovese	Alexander Valley

Chapter 8

Oregon, Washington, and Long Island Red Wines

• •

In This Chapter

▶ Pinot Noir's promise in Oregon

▶ Washington's success with Merlot

▶ Long Island's affinity for red

• •

*C*alifornia dominates so much of the wine scene in the United States that it's easy to forget that some really good wine is made in other states. Three states deserve special attention for their excellent wines.

Oregon is now rivaling California with some of the best Pinot Noirs in the country. And surely no one can refute that some of the finest Merlots in the world have their home in the state of Washington. Meanwhile, Long Island, New York, has found its best red wine: You guessed it — Merlot.

Pinot Noir Finds a Home in Oregon

The Oregon wine story is a recent one. If any winemaking operations existed in the state before Prohibition, they vanished during that period. In 1962, Richard Sommer, a graduate of the University of California at Davis (which boasts the most famous winemaking program in the United States), began the first modern winery in Oregon. Sommer's winery was Hillcrest Vineyards, in the Umpqua Valley, in the southwest part of the state.

In 1966, another California expatriate and U. C. Davis grad, David Lett, became the first to plant the Pinot Noir grape in the Willamette *(will AM ett)* Valley in northwest Oregon, just south of Portland. Lett's vineyard and winery, The Eyrie *(EYE ree)* Vineyards, made a serious impact on Oregon's wine future — in fact, the 1975 Eyrie Pinot Noir put Oregon on the international wine map by winning a wine competition against French red

Burgundies in Paris in 1979. Pinot Noir became the name of the game in Oregon. (Turn to Chapter 3 for information about the Pinot Noir grape.)

The Eyrie Vineyards released its first Pinot Noir wine in 1970, followed quickly by other Oregon pioneers, such as Dick Ponzi (Ponzi Vineyards), Ron Vuylsteke (Oak Knoll Winery), Dick Erath (Knudsen-Erath Winery), and Bill Fuller (Tualatin Vineyards). Word spread that the Willamette Valley was an ideal place to grow the elusive Pinot Noir grape. The region's relatively cool climate, long growing season, and mineral-laden soil (many areas, such as the Red Hills in Dundee, are rich in iron) suit the needs of Pinot Noir quite well. Figure 8-1 shows a label from a Willamette Valley Pinot Noir.

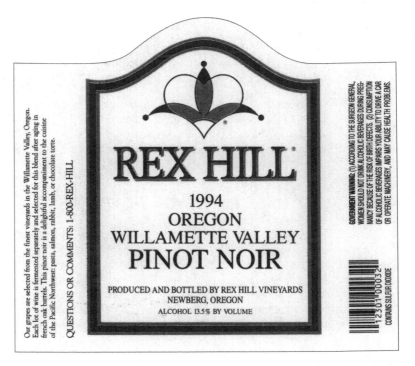

Figure 8-1: Oregon's Willamette Valley is well suited to growing the Pinot Noir grape.

Today, more than 50 wineries exist in the Willamette Valley, almost all of which feature Pinot Noir as their premium wine. Most of these wineries are small, family-run operations producing 10,000 or fewer cases of wine annually. Two notable exceptions are the huge King Estate, located just south of the Willamette Valley, and the French-owned Domaine Drouhin.

Oregon has become such an important center of Pinot Noir production that it is the site of an annual International Pinot Noir Celebration. Every year in late July, winemakers from as far away as South Africa, New Zealand, and France (and simple citizen Pinot Noir enthusiasts) visit Oregon for a three-day weekend of conferences and wine tastings at McMinnville, in the heart of Oregon's Pinot Noir region. The event usually sells out a few days after it is announced in early February. For more information, call 503-472-8964, or fax 503-472-1785.

Enjoying Oregon Pinot Noir

Legend has it that American Pinot Noir wines don't age well and should be consumed in the first eight years or so of their lives. We do believe, as a general rule, that Pinot Noir is best when it is young and vibrant, with its trademark cherry-berry aromas and delicious red-fruit flavors going strong. But certain vintages in Oregon (and certain styles of winemaking, such as those of The Eyrie Vineyards, Ponzi Vineyards, and Domaine Drouhin) make longer-lasting Pinots. For example, The Eyrie Vineyards' 1973 and 1975 Pinot Noirs are still drinking beautifully today.

The 1983 and 1985 vintages were two early successes for Oregon Pinot Noir, but most wines from these vintages are in decline today (although a few are fine). With 1988, an era of good Oregon Pinot Noir vintages began; **1990** was even better; 1991 and 1993 are really fine; and **1994** might be the best vintage yet.

Oregon Pinot Noirs are an especially fine accompaniment to the specialty of the Pacific Northwest, salmon. These wines are equally at home with chicken, duck, and beef, as well as hard cheeses such as Asiago and cheddar.

Recommended Oregon Pinot Noir wines

Oregon Pinot Noirs cost about $15 to $18 for regular bottlings and about $25 to $30 for reserve or single-vineyard wines (a few cost a bit more than $30).

We recommend the following Oregon wineries (listed in alphabetical order) for their across-the-board performance in making Pinot Noir wine; our favorite wineries are marked with a ♟ symbol.

- ✔ Adelsheim Vineyards
- ✔ ♟ Bethel Heights Vineyard
- ✔ ♟ Cameron Winery
- ✔ Chehalem Vineyards
- ✔ ♟ Domaine Drouhin
- ✔ ♟ Elk Cove Vineyards
- ✔ ♟ Domaine Serene
- ✔ ♟ Evesham Wood Vineyard
- ✔ ♟ The Eyrie Vineyards
- ✔ ♟ Oak Knoll Winery
- ✔ Panther Creek Cellars
- ✔ ♟ Ponzi Vineyards
- ✔ Redhawk Vineyard
- ✔ ♟ Rex Hill Vineyards
- ✔ ♟ Ken Wright Cellars

We particularly recommend the Oregon Pinot Noir wines listed alphabetically in Table 8-1, which are some of the best Pinot Noir wines made in America.

Table 8-1   Highly Recommended Oregon Pinot Noir Wines

Winery	Highly Recommended Wine
Adelsheim Vineyard	"Elizabeth's Reserve" Pinot Noir
Amity Vineyards	"Winemaker's Reserve" Pinot Noir
Archery Summit	Pinot Noir, Red Hills Estate
Autumn Wind Vineyard	Pinot Noir Reserve
Beaux Frères	Pinot Noir
Benton-Lane	Pinot Noir Reserve
Bethel Heights Vineyard	Pinot Noir Reserve (any of their reserve bottlings)
Brick House Wine Company	Pinot Noir

Winery	Highly Recommended Wine
Broadley Vineyards	Pinot Noir, "Claudia's Choice"
Cameron Winery	"Clos Electrique" Pinot Noir
Chehalem Vineyards	Pinot Noir, Ridgecrest Vineyards Reserve
Cooper Mountain Vineyards	Pinot Noir Reserve, Reusser Vineyard
Cristom Vineyards	Pinot Noir Reserve (any of their reserve bottlings)
Domaine Drouhin	"Lorène" Pinot Noir Reserve
Domaine Serene	Pinot Noir Reserve (any of their reserve bottlings)
Edgefield Winery	"Winemaker's Reserve" Pinot Noir
Elk Cove Vineyards	Pinot Noir, La Bohème Vineyard Pinot Noir Reserve
Erath Winery (older bottles carry the winery's former name, Knudsen-Erath)	Pinot Noir Reserve (any of their reserve bottlings)
Evesham Wood Vineyard	"Cuvée J" Pinot Noir
The Eyrie Vineyards	Pinot Noir Reserve
Foris Vineyards Winery	Pinot Noir, Maple Ranch (Rogue Valley)
King Estate	Pinot Noir
Lange Winery	Pinot Noir Reserve
McKinlay Vineyard	"Special Selection" Pinot Noir
Montinore Vineyards	"Winemaker's Reserve" Pinot Noir
Oak Knoll Winery	"Vintage Reserve" Pinot Noir
Panther Creek Cellars	Pinot Noir Reserve
Ponzi Vineyards	Pinot Noir Reserve
Redhawk Vineyard	Pinot Noir Reserve (any of their reserve bottlings)
Rex Hill Vineyards	Pinot Noir Reserve
St. Innocent	Pinot Noir (any of their single-vineyard wines)
Sokol Blosser Winery	Pinot Noir, Redland
Tualatin Vineyards	Pinot Noir Reserve

(continued)

Table 8-1 *(continued)*

Winery	Highly Recommended Wine
Willamette Valley Vineyards	"O.V.D." Pinot Noir "Founder's Reserve" Pinot Noir
Witness Tree Vineyard	"Vintage Select" Pinot Noir
Ken Wright Cellars	Pinot Noir Reserve
Yamhill Valley Vineyards	"Estate Reserve" Pinot Noir

Oregon's Other Red Wines

Although Pinot Noir dominates red wine production in Oregon, a few wineries make Cabernet Sauvignon and a little Merlot — especially those wineries in the southern (warmer) part of Oregon. That said, some of the best Cabs and Merlots are coming from Seven Hills Winery in warm, dry, northeast Oregon (at the southern end of Washington's Walla Walla Valley).

Other wineries producing good Cabernet Sauvignon are

- Girardet Wine Cellars and Henry Estate Winery (both in the Umpqua Valley)
- Foris Vineyards, Ashland Vineyards, and Valley View Vineyard (all in the extreme southwest part of Oregon, the Rogue River Valley)

Also, some surprisingly good, unctuous Merlots are coming from Foris Vineyards and Ashland Vineyards.

World-class Merlots from Washington State

Washington, the second-largest U.S. producer of wine from *vinifera* grapes (see Chapter 3), has quietly become one of the best regions in the world for Merlot in the last 15 years. Some very good Cabernet Sauvignon comes from Washington as well.

Washington had an even later start than Oregon in the American wine boom; most of the currently operating wineries weren't around before 1980. Two exceptions are the gigantic

Chateau Ste. Michelle (which, together with its brother wineries, Columbia Crest and Snoqualmie, produces more than half the wine in the state) and Columbia Winery, both founded in 1967. Today, Washington has nearly 90 wineries.

Although almost all the grapes of Washington are grown in the warm, dry, desert-like Columbia, Yakima, and Walla Walla Valleys in the southeastern part of the state, many wineries are located in the northwest, in the vicinity of Seattle, where much of the wine is actually sold.

Good-quality Washington Merlots and Cabs are quite reasonably priced; many good wines are still in the $8 to $12 range (for example, you can purchase Columbia Crest Merlot, one of the largest-selling Merlots in the United States, for under $10 retail), although reserve and small-production wines are mainly $25 to $30.

The **1983** vintage was a super one for Washington Cabernet Sauvignons, if you are lucky enough to find any. Recently, 1988, 1990, 1992, and especially **1989** and **1994** have been excellent vintages for both Merlot and Cabernet Sauvignon.

The producers named in Table 8-2 (listed alphabetically, along with their best wines) are now making some of the finest Merlots and Cabernet Sauvignons in the United States. In cases where we mention more than one wine from a particular producer, we mention what we consider to be the best wine first. The ■ symbol indicates wineries where production is so small that their wines are available by mailing list only (see Appendix C for addresses and phone numbers).

For information about buying wine directly from wineries, refer to our book, *Wine For Dummies*.

Table 8-2	Recommended Washington Merlot Wines and Cabernet Wines
Winery	**Winery's Best Red Wine(s)**
Chateau Ste. Michelle	Merlot, Indian Wells Vineyard Cabernet Sauvignon "Estate"
Chinook Wines	Merlot
Columbia Crest Winery	Merlot, Estate Cabernet Sauvignon, Estate

(continued)

Table 8-2 *(continued)*

Winery	***Winery's Best Red Wine(s)***
Columbia Winery	🍷 Merlot "Milestone," Red Willow Vineyard 🍷 Single-vineyard Cabernet Sauvignons
✉ De Lille Cellars	🍷 "Chaleur Estate" (Cabernet Sauvignon, Merlot, Cabernet Franc blend)
Barnard Griffin Winery	Cabernet Sauvignon
Hedges Cellars	"Red Mountain Reserve" (Cab/Merlot blend)
The Hogue Cellars	🍷 Cabernet Sauvignon Reserve 🍷 Merlot Reserve
Kiona Vineyards	Cabernet Sauvignon Merlot
Latah Creek Wine Cellars	Cabernet Sauvignon Reserve Merlot
L'Ecole #41	Merlot Cabernet Sauvignon Reserve
✉ Leonetti Cellar	🍷 All Cabernet Sauvignons and Merlots
Preston Wine Cellars	Cabernet Sauvignon
✉ Quilceda Creek Vintners	🍷 Cabernet Sauvignon
Seven Hills Winery	Merlot Cabernet Sauvignon
Snoqualmie Winery	Cabernet Sauvignon
Waterbrook Winery	Merlot Cabernet Sauvignon
✉ Andrew Will Cellars	🍷 All Cabernet Sauvignons and Merlots
Woodward Canyon Winery	Cabernet Sauvignon, Canoe Ridge Vineyard

Note: The Seven Hills winery is located in Oregon, but has vineyards (Walla Walla Valley) in both Washington and Oregon.

Long Island, New York: Merlot Strikes Again

The strength of New York State's principal wine region, the Finger Lakes, is white wines and sparkling wines; the Hudson Valley wine region (north of New York City) also specializes in white wines. But New York's Long Island wine region, east of New York City, is known at least as much for its red wines as for its white wines.

Back in 1973, after researching on both coasts of the United States, Alex and Louisa Hargrave decided that the North Fork of Long Island has a mild enough climate (in fact, remarkably similar to that of Bordeaux) and the proper, well-drained, sandy loam soils to support the growth of the classic French red grapes Cabernet Sauvignon, Merlot, Cabernet Franc, and Pinot Noir (as well as white grapes). The couple founded Hargrave Vineyards that year in the farming community of Cutchogue and in 1977 released their first wines.

Time has proven the Hargraves' vision correct. Today, a thriving community of about 15 wineries exists on the North Fork, centering around Cutchogue, and a few wineries exist on the island's South Fork, too.

Almost all Long Island wineries are small, family-run operations, producing between 5,000 and 15,000 cases of wine a year (half of which is sold to visitors at the wineries). Pindar Vineyards, which produces about 50,000 cases a year, is the largest winery on the island.

Merlot has emerged as the most successful red grape variety on Long Island, primarily because it has a shorter growing season than the late-ripening Cabernet Sauvignon, which needs a mild, dry autumn — not always the reality of maritime Long Island. The quick-ripening Cabernet Franc also has had some success but has not yet enjoyed recognition in the marketplace. Pinot Noir, with a few exceptions, has been a failure; the damp Long Island climate (in most years) causes too much rot for this difficult variety.

Some of the most successful wines on Long Island are blends of the so-called Bordeaux varieties: Merlot, Cabernet Sauvignon, Cabernet Franc, and sometimes even the very-late-ripening Petite Verdot. Pindar Vineyards' Mythology is a good example of this kind of wine.

Vintages on Long Island have been good lately; 1993 and **1994** (both warm and dry) produced excellent wines, equally the great **1988**. And **1995**, with its long, hot, dry summer, promises to be the best vintage yet. Most of Long Island's red wines are priced in the $12 to $15 range, with reserves and Cab/Merlot blends at around $20.

Almost every Long Island winery makes a Merlot, clearly Long Island's most successful red wine. Some wineries also make a Cabernet Franc, a Cabernet Sauvignon, and/or a blended wine from these varieties. We recommend the following wineries (listed alphabetically) for their red wines and mark our favorites with ♟:

- ✔ ♟ Bedell Cellars
- ✔ ♟ Gristina Vineyards
- ✔ ♟ Hargrave Vineyard
- ✔ Jamesport Vineyards
- ✔ Lenz Winery
- ✔ ♟ Palmer Vineyards
- ✔ ♟ Paumonok Vineyards
- ✔ Peconic Bay Vineyards
- ✔ ♟ Pelligrini Vineyards
- ✔ Pindar Vineyards ("Mythology," a Bordeaux-style blend ♟)

Chapter 9

Seeing Red Down Under: Australia, South America, and South Africa

*A*re Southern Hemisphere red wines inherently different from Northern Hemisphere reds? Do the mirror-image latitudes of Below the Equator put their unique stamp on the wines of the countries Down Under and color the quality and style of wines made there?

If the answer to either of these questions is "Yes," the rest of that answer must be "and positively so!" The red wines of Southern Hemisphere countries such as Australia, Chile, South Africa, and Argentina are making inroads — some slowly, some at breakneck speed — into the U.S. wine market. Whatever the wines from these countries have to offer, plenty of American wine drinkers want it.

Actually, what each Southern Hemisphere country has to offer in terms of red wines is slightly different. Australia offers wines with bright, vivid fruit flavors, technological superiority, and sheer taste appeal. Chile offers wines caught in a time warp, or maybe a space warp: not quite traditional European wines, smacking of centuries-old ways — and yet not quite New World wines, preoccupied with grape character to the point of near obsession. Argentina offers competent quality and value for today — and for tomorrow, promise. South Africa offers new beginnings, not only of the political sort but also of the vinous sort, the potential of an old region finding a new soul.

The wines of the Southern Hemisphere are different, yes. And original. And worth knowing. We cross the equator in 0:01 hours.

Australia: Where the Voluptuous Redheads Are

In the mid-1980s, Australia sprang into the consciousness of Americans suddenly and fully born, like Venus from the forehead of Zeus: the language of Australia, the culture of a wild yet civilized place almost too far away to visit, the exotic-yet-familiar people — and the wines of Australia.

The initial appeal of Australian wines to many wine drinkers in the United States — we must be honest — was the extremely affordable price, combined with the fact that many wines carried exactly the same names as American wines did, the names of grape varieties. Good Chardonnay for $4 a bottle: Who can resist — and why?!?

Over subsequent years, the prices of Australian wines "normalized," as wine marketers might say, and the wines of Australia today are no longer the bargain-basement attractions they once were. Instead, these wines now appeal to wine drinkers for their taste first — and their price only secondarily. Australia has managed to forge a specific style for its wines in the minds of wine drinkers worldwide, regardless of price.

What is that style? Fruity, for sure. Ask Australian winemakers what they expect of their wines, and their immediate response will probably be, "Fruit character, and plenty of it." Fresh fruit flavor is a trademark of Australian wines.

The red wines of Australia have another trademark: soft tannins. Australian winemakers lead the world in knowing how to extract just enough tannin from their red grapes, of just the right sort, to give their wines volume and weight but never bitterness or astringency.

Australian red wine with food

Because Australian red wines are generally quite ripe and full, they are perfect with barbecued and grilled meats, such as steaks, hamburgers, and sausages. They are also fine with hearty stews and casseroles and with hard cheeses, such as cheddar.

The climate of Australia certainly doesn't hinder winemakers in their efforts to make ripe, rich wines. Australia has plenty of sunshine and very little rain. As a result, grapes ripen perfectly in most of Australia's wine regions, with few rainy-weather headaches for grape growers. Really poor vintages don't exist — just average, good, and very good vintages. Australian red wines end up rich and ripe — voluptuous, easy-drinking wines. Thin, high-acid wines? No such problem, mate; not in Australia.

Australia's short and sweet winemaking past

Considering Australia's size (about the same as the United States), this country actually doesn't produce much wine — only about a third as much as the U.S. But relatively little of the Australian territory is suitable for viticulture: The northern two-thirds of Australia, hot and desert-like, is uninhabitable to wine grapes. Only in more temperate, southeastern Australia (and a small area in southwestern Australia) can wine grapes grow. Beer is the alcohol beverage of choice among Australians, but, per capita, Aussies drink three times as much wine as Americans.

Although wine has been made in Australia since the late 18th century, most of Australia's wines were the sweet or *fortified* type (wines with alcohol added) until as recently as 1960. Then, at about the same time as Americans, Australians became more aware of the pleasures of dry wine.

By the early 1980s, the wine boom was on Down Under. Australia's progress in making quality table wines, both red and white, has been remarkably rapid. Today, winemakers in the more established wine regions of Europe and the United States look to Australia to learn the latest advances in wine technology.

Australia's grapes and regions

In Australia, almost all the wines are named after grape varieties — either a single grape variety, such as Shiraz, or, quite frequently, two grape varieties that are blended together, as in Shiraz/Cabernet Sauvignon (the percentage of each is stated somewhere on the label, and the dominant variety is named first, as shown in Figure 9-1).

Figure 9-1: In Australian red wine blends, the label lists the percentage of each grape variety, with the dominant variety first.

Australia's most important red wine grape is Shiraz, the same grape as Syrah but here wearing its original Persian name. (Turn to Chapter 3 for a description of the Syrah grape.) This grape came to Australia from France's Rhône Valley in 1832. Perhaps because Australia's climate resembles that of the warm Rhône Valley in some respects, Shiraz proved capable of producing fine wines in its new home. (Recently, by the way, some Australian winemakers began to use the name Syrah for their better wines and Shiraz for their less-expensive versions. But no set rule exists.)

Cabernet Sauvignon is clearly Australia's second most important red grape. Adaptable as it is to so many different growing conditions, the Cabernet Sauvignon grape does just fine in Australia. One of the more common types of red wine in Australia is blended from the country's two major red grapes, Shiraz and Cabernet. Because Shiraz usually comprises the higher percentage in such blends, these wines are most frequently called Shiraz/Cabernet.

Pinot Noir has enjoyed little success so far in Australia, generally speaking, because most of Australia's wine regions are too warm. But a couple of exceptions exist: The Coldstream Hills Winery, for example, makes some good Pinot Noirs, thanks to its cool microclimate. Merlot has been late in getting started in Australia, but the Aussies, aware of the worldwide demand for Merlot, are catching up fast with this hot variety.

Most of Australia's wine comes from its three southeastern states: South Australia, Victoria, and New South Wales. In fact, many of Australia's large producers make inexpensive, high-volume wines by blending grapes or wine from these separate states. Those wines are labeled as wines from "South Eastern Australia" — not a specific wine region, but simply a descriptive geographic term.

South Australia

South Australia is the country's most important red wine area. Many of Australia's large wineries — such as Penfolds, Orlando, Seppelt, Peter Lehmann, Henschke, Leasingham, Petaluma, Wolf Blass, and Hill Smith — are located in South Australia, and about 58 percent of the country's wine comes from here.

The better red wines of South Australia come from wine regions around the state's capital city, Adelaide. Three regions particularly known for their red wines are

- **Barossa Valley:** This rather warm wine region north of Adelaide is famous for its Shiraz and Cabernet Sauvignon and is one of Australia's most well established fine-wine areas. Most of the large wineries are located here.

- **Coonawarra:** The coolest, and many say finest, red wine region in Australia, this area is located near the southern end of South Australia. Many of Australia's best Cabernet Sauvignons come from the famous red soil of Coonawarra.

- **McLaren Vale:** Directly south of Adelaide, this otherwise warm region is cooled by ocean breezes; some big, rich, ripe red wines come from here.

Victoria

Victoria's capital is the cosmopolitan port city of Melbourne. Although Victoria produces only 14 percent of Australia's wines, many of the country's finest small wineries are here —

along with a few larger ones, such as Brown Brothers, Mildara, Wynns, and the largest winery facility of the giant Lindemans group.

The best-known red wine regions of Victoria are

- **Glenrowan:** A warm region in northeastern Victoria, this location is known for its big, rich Shiraz wines as well as its Cabs and blends of both grapes.

- **Milawa:** Also in northeastern Victoria, this area is known for its heady, ripe red wines.

- **Murray River:** Lots of red wine comes from this northwest border region, from such wineries as Lindemans and Mildara.

- **Yarra Valley:** A cool-climate region outside Melbourne, the Yarra Valley is *the* chic new wine area in Australia. This region is cool enough to grow Pinot Noir yet warm enough to do well with Cabernet Sauvignon.

New South Wales

New South Wales is the oldest wine-growing area in Australia, and Sydney is the state capital. New South Wales makes 27 percent of Australia's wine. Many high-production, everyday wines come from the hot, interior region with the unpronounce-able name, Murrumbidgee Irrigation Area. Several of Australia's large, well-established wineries, such as Rothbury Estate, Tyrell's, Lindemans, McWilliams, Montrose, Rosemount, Wyndham Estate, Evans Family, and Hungerford Hill, are situated in New South Wales.

The state's fine wines come from the following three regions:

- **Lower Hunter Valley:** This area, about a three-hour drive north of Sydney, is Australia's single most famous wine region. The climate is less than ideal because of harvest-time rains, but most of New South Wales' wineries are located here. Among red wines, Cabernet Sauvignon does best, and Shiraz less so.

- **Upper Hunter Valley:** The climate here is drier than that of the lower valley and better for white wines than for reds — although Shiraz is grown here. This region is the home of the Rosemount Winery.

- **Mudgee:** This area west of the Hunter Valley is good for Cabernet Sauvignon and Shiraz.

Western Australia

Only a small amount of wine comes from Western Australia, with its capital city of Perth. But two cool wine regions, both in the southwestern tip of the state, hold great promise for the future:

> ✔ **Margaret River:** Some excellent Cabernet Sauvignons and Pinot Noirs come from this cool-climate region, especially from such fine estates as Cape Mentelle and Leeuwin Estate.

> ✔ **Lower Great Southern:** A large, cool region with potential that is still untapped; good, leaner-styled Cabernet Sauvignons, similar to Bordeaux, are made here.

Recommended Australian reds: Shiraz, Cabernet Sauvignon, and Shiraz/Cab blends

Because almost all of Australia's better red wines are made from Shiraz, Cabernet Sauvignon, and blends of these two varieties, we confine our recommendations mainly to wines of these types. We group our recommended wines into two categories — wines that retail under $10 and wines that retail over $10. In Tables 9-1 and 9-2, respectively, we list these wines alphabetically according to producer. We mark our favorite wines with a ♟ symbol.

Table 9-1	Recommended Australian Reds under $10
Producer	*Recommended Wines*
Black Opal	Shiraz Cabernet Sauvignon Cabernet/Merlot
Brown Brothers	Cabernet Sauvignon
Peter Lehmann	♟ Shiraz ♟ Cabernet Sauvignon
Lindemans	Cabernet Sauvignon Shiraz
McGuigan Brothers	♟ Cabernet Sauvignon "Black Shiraz"

(continued)

Table 9-1 *(continued)*

Producer	Recommended Wines
Michelton	Shiraz Cabernet/Shiraz/Malbec blend
Montrose	♟ Cabernet Sauvignon Shiraz
Orlando	Cabernet Sauvignon "Jacob's Creek"
Oxford Landing	Cabernet Sauvignon Cabernet/Shiraz
Penfolds	Cabernet/Shiraz "Koonunga Hill"
Redbank	Shiraz
Rosemount	♟ "Diamond Label" Shiraz "Diamond Label" Cabernet Shiraz/Cabernet
Rothbury Estate	♟ Shiraz
Seppelt	"Black Label" Shiraz "Reserve Bin" Shiraz ♟ Cabernet Sauvignon "Black Label" "Reserve Bin" Cabernet Sauvignon
Taltarni	♟ Shiraz Cabernet Sauvignon Merlot Merlot/Cab Franc
Tyrrell's	♟ Shiraz Cabernet Sauvignon
Wolf Blass	Shiraz "President's Selection" Cabernet Sauvignon "Yellow Label"
Wyndham Estates	Cabernet Sauvignon "Bin 444" Shiraz "Bin 555" Cabernet/Merlot "Bin 888"

Table 9-2   Recommended Australian Reds over $10

Producer	Recommended Wines
Tim Adams	Shiraz

Producer	Recommended Wines
Bowen Estate	Cabernet Sauvignon 🍷 Cabernet Sauvignon/Merlot/ Cabernet Franc blend
Cape Mentelle	Cabernet Sauvignon Shiraz
Henschke	🍷 Shiraz "Hill of Grace" 🍷 Shiraz "Mount Edelstone"
Leeuwin Estate	Cabernet Sauvignon
Peter Lehmann	"Clancy's Gold Preference" (Cabernet blend)
Lindemans	🍷 Shiraz/Cabernet "Limestone Ridge" Cabernet Sauvignon, St. George Vineyard
Michelton	🍷 Cabernet Sauvignon Victoria Reserve
Orlando	Cabernet Sauvignon "Jacaranda Ridge" Cabernet Sauvignon "St. Hugo"
Penfolds	🍷 "Grange" (formerly known as "Grange Hermitage") 🍷 Cabernet Sauvignon "Bin 707" Shiraz "Bin 128" Magill Estate Shiraz 🍷 Cabernet Sauvignon/Shiraz "Bin 389"
Petaluma	Cabernet Sauvignon (Coonawarra)
Rosemount	🍷 Cabernet Sauvignon "Show Reserve" Syrah "Balmoral Show Reserve"
Wolf Blass	Cabernet Sauvignon "President's Selection" "Black Label" (Cabernet/Shiraz blend)
Wynns	🍷 Cabernet Sauvignon "John Riddoch" (Coonawarra)

Recent good vintages for Australian red wine

Playing the vintage game for Australian reds is no trick at all. For one thing, Australian vintages don't vary as much as those of Europe and, therefore, you seldom have to worry about a poor vintage. Furthermore, most Australian red wines are made to be consumed when they are young.

With the exception of a few of the more expensive wines in Table 9-2 (such as Penfolds' Grange, Penfolds' Bin 707 Cabernet

Sauvignon, or Henschke's Shiraz wines), Australian reds do not improve much with age. Best vintages for Australian red wines are **1994** and **1986**, but 1995, 1993, 1992, 1991, 1990, 1989, 1988, and 1987 are all good. Get the picture?

One for the wish list

The Penfolds' red wine called Grange (formerly called Grange Hermitage) is Australia's greatest, most expensive red wine ($100 to $125, depending on the vintage, and difficult to find). It is made from the finest Shiraz grapes — sometimes with a little Cabernet Sauvignon added. Grange is one of the richest, most concentrated red wines in the world, with a proven record for prolonged aging. This wine is a collector's item for wine connoisseurs.

Chile: The Best Is Yet to Be

Chile is blessed with the finest conditions for grape growing that anyone could hope for — a perfect place for wine grapes to live.

The Central Valley, where most of Chile's wine grapes grow, lies between the Pacific Ocean on the west (with a range of coastal hills to block ocean moisture), and the Andes Moutains on the east. This situation gives Chilean vineyards just the right amount of moisture and offers ideal grape-growing conditions.

Also, the natural barriers of the ocean and the mountains keep Chilean vineyards free from the phylloxera louse, an insect that has ravaged most of the world's vineyards (refer to Chapter 9 of our book, *Wine For Dummies,* for more information about phylloxera). Chile's vineyards enjoy long, dry summers and cool winters.

Because of the consistent weather from year to year, every vintage in Chile is uniformly good. No wonder so many European producers (such as Bordeaux's Château Lafite-Rothschild and Spain's Torres) and so many of California's gigantic wineries are staking claims in Chile as fast as they can! Not only is Chilean wine being purchased by foreign wine companies for distribution in their home markets — because of the current shortage of fine wine grapes — but quite a few foreign wine companies also have actually built their own wineries in Chile.

Although Chile can trace its winemaking back to the 1650s, we frankly believe that the potential for making great Chilean wines has hardly been tapped. Since the 1980s, Chile's winemakers have focused on making decent, mass-produced wines in response to world demand for inexpensive varietally labeled bottlings. This development is a mixed blessing. With a focus more on price than on quality, growers have kept their vineyard yields extremely high (producing very large quantities of grapes from a vineyard negatively affects the grapes' quality), and the resulting wines — both red and white, but especially white — are thin and diluted. The word *watery* comes to mind.

Some Chilean producers, however, have made red wines, mainly Cabernet Sauvignons, that are excellent as well as being good values. We point out these wines in our "Recommended" section coming up.

Chile's red wine regions

Chile has three principal red wine regions, all in the Central Valley. From north to south, they are

- ✔ **Aconcagua:** North of the capital city of Santiago, this area is the warmest of the three regions.
- ✔ **Maipo Valley:** Directly south of Santiago; most of Chile's large wineries are here.
- ✔ **Rapel Valley:** Directly south of Maipo, this location is the coolest of the major red wine regions. (A subzone of Rapel getting some acclaim is the **Colchagua Valley**).

Cabernet Sauvignon rules in Chile

The four main red grape varieties in Chile's vineyards, in order of importance, are

- ✔ Cabernet Sauvignon
- ✔ Merlot
- ✔ Pinot Noir
- ✔ Malbec

The Pinot Noir grape has not been successful in Chile, and Malbec has not made very interesting wine.

Merlot sees a little more action. You can buy Merlot from Chile really cheaply: Concha y Toro's Merlot and the Merlot under that winery's second label, Walnut Crest (no, Walnut Crest isn't from California; that would be Walnut Creek!), are both available for less than $5, as is Concha y Toro's Cabernet Sauvignon/ Merlot blend. At the opposite end of the scale, a new winery called Casa Lapostolle, in the Colchagua district of the Rapel Valley, made perhaps Chile's finest Merlot to date with its release of the 1994 Merlot, Cuvée Alexandre.

But Chile's *best* red grape variety, hands down, is good old reliable Cabernet Sauvignon.

Recommended red wines from Chile

In Tables 9-3 and 9-4, we recommend red wines from Chile — almost all of which are Cabernet Sauvignon — in two price categories: under $10 (Chile's wines are priced as low as $4 for a 750 ml bottle) and over $10. Wines in the higher-priced category are distinctly superior to those in the lower-priced category. In both tables, we mark our favorite wines with a ▼ symbol, and we list producers alphabetically.

Table 9-3	Recommended Chilean Red Wines under $10
Producer	**Recommended Wines**
Carmen Vineyards	Cabernet Sauvignon Cabernet Sauvignon Reserve Merlot
Casa Lapostolle	▼ Cabernet Sauvignon (Colchagua district)
Concha y Toro	Cabernet Sauvignon "Casillero del Diablo"
Cousino Macul	Cabernet Sauvignon Cabernet Sauvignon "Antiguas Reservas"
De Martino	Cabernet Sauvignon
Errazuriz	▼ Cabernet Sauvignon Don Maximiano Reserva Merlot
Santa Alicia	▼ Merlot Reserve Cabernet Sauvignon Reserve
Santa Amelia	▼ Cabernet Sauvignon ▼ Merlot
Santa Monica	Cabernet Sauvignon
Los Vascos	Cabernet Sauvignon Cabernet Sauvignon Reserve

Table 9-4	Recommended Chilean Red Wines over $10
Producer	*Recommended Wines*
Casa Lapostolle	♟ Merlot, Cuvée Alexandre
Concha y Toro	♟ Cabernet Sauvignon, "Don Melchor" (single-vineyard) Cabernet Sauvignon Reserve, "Marqués de Casa"
Cousino Macul	"Finis Terrae" (Cabernet/Merlot blend)
Errazuriz	♟ Cabernet Sauvignon Special Reserve

We believe that the five wines in Table 9-4 are Chile's finest red wines at present. (Even better ones will be coming in the future). At $25, Cousino Macul's Finis Terrae is Chile's highest-priced wine. But, frankly, our very favorite Chilean red wine continues to be Concha y Toro's single-vineyard Cab, Don Melchor (at about $16), as shown in Figure 9-2. Recent vintages of Don Melchor are better than ever.

Figure 9-2: Concha y Toro's Don Melchor Cabernet Sauvignon, one of Chile's great red wines.

You can drink Chilean red wines as soon as you buy them, but you should drink most of them no later than five or six years from the vintage date. Better Chilean reds, such as those recommended in Table 9-4, hold their quality for ten years from the vintage date, however.

Argentina: Red Wine Country

Argentineans are rightly proud of their beef, and they like to drink red wine with it. Fortunately, Argentina makes plenty of red wine. The country, surprisingly enough, is the world's fourth-largest producer of wine — mainly red. (In 1995, Argentina passed the United States in wine production.) What's more, Argentineans are among the highest per capita wine drinkers in the world.

Almost all of Argentina's better wines come from the hot, dry state of Mendoza, in the northwest part of the country, across the mountains from Chile. The Andes Mountains form a natural barrier in the west, removing all moisture coming from the Pacific Ocean but providing irrigation water from melting snow. The sun shines constantly there. As in Chile, every vintage is good.

Until the 1980s, the best that could be said about most Argentine red wines was that they were inexpensive (the white wines weren't even a matter for discussion). But the same technological revolution that swept over most other New World wine countries is also beginning to influence Argentina.

Today, a number of fairly high-tech wineries exist, and some wineries employ winemaker-consultants from Europe or the United States. As a result, the best red wines of Argentina are light-years ahead in quality from those wines of ten years ago. (The wines we list in Table 9-6 are especially fine, but even the under-$10 red wines we recommend in Table 9-5 are vastly improved today.)

Malbec finds a home

In Argentina's warm climate, red grape varieties fare considerably better than white ones do. One red grape variety that's not exactly a household word in most of the wine world is particularly important in Argentina; that grape is Malbec.

Malbec is a legally permitted variety in Bordeaux, but it is shunned by most Bordelais winemakers, who prefer Cabernet Sauvignon, Merlot, and Cabernet Franc (read about Bordeaux in Chapter 10). The Malbec grape is practically unknown in California. This grape is cultivated in some places in southwest France and a little bit in Italy and Chile. But Malbec truly has found a home in Argentina, where it is the leading grape variety for fine red wines. Malbec has adapted extremely well to the country's hot, dry climate, where it makes some very dark, tannic, intensely flavored wines.

The other major red grape varieties of Argentina are more well known:

- ✔ Cabernet Sauvignon
- ✔ Merlot
- ✔ Syrah

Thanks to the many Italian immigrants who came to Argentina and brought their red grape varieties, you can find Argentine wines made from Barbera, Sangiovese, Bonarda, and even Lambrusco grapes. Spain's best red grape, Tempranillo, also puts in an appearance in Argentine vineyards.

Recommended red wines from Argentina

Of the red wines that we recommend from Argentina, most are Cabernet Sauvignons, Malbecs, Merlots, and blends of these three varieties. We believe that those are the best wines produced in Argentina today — and they are the most widely available.

Table 9-5 features wines that sell for under $10 a bottle (Argentina's wines are priced as low as $4 to $5 for a 750 ml bottle). Table 9-6 features wines that sell for over $10. Wines in the higher-priced category are clearly superior to those in the lower-priced category. Producers in both groups appear in alphabetical order. We indicate our favorite wines with a ♟ symbol.

Table 9-5   Recommended Red Argentine Wines under $10

Producer	Recommended Wines
Valentin Bianchi	Malbec Cabernet Sauvignon Cabernet Sauvignon "Reserve Particular"
Finca Flichman	♟ Cabernet Sauvignon "Caballero de la Cepa" Syrah Sangiovese Cabernet Sauvignon Reserve
Château Mendoza	Cabernet Sauvignon Malbec
Pascual Toso	Cabernet Sauvignon Malbec
Trapiche	Cabernet Sauvignon "Oak Aged" Malbec "Oak Aged"

Table 9-6   Recommended Red Argentine Wines over $10

Producer	Recommended Wines
Catena	♟ Cabernet Sauvignon, Agrelo Vineyard
Navarro Correas	♟ Cabernet Sauvignon "Coleccion Privada"
Bodega Weinart	♟ "Cavas de Weinart" (Cabernet Sauvignon, Merlot, Malbec blend) ♟ Cabernet Sauvignon ♟ Merlot "Carrascal" (Malbec, Merlot, Cabernet Sauvignon blend)

Bodega Weinart might be making Argentina's best red wines today, yet its prices range from $10 for the wine called Carrascal to $16 for its top-of-the-line Cavas de Weinart wine — extremely reasonable for wines of this quality. We think that Weinart's best-value wines are the Cabernet Sauvignon ($12 to $13) and the Merlot ($13 to $14).

The red wines of Argentina are generally ready to drink when you buy them, and you should drink most of them within five or six years of the vintage date. Better Argentine reds, such as those recommended in Table 9-6, can keep their quality for ten years from the vintage date if stored in a cool environment.

South Africa's Red Wines: A Bridge between the Old and New Worlds

If you taste a red wine from South Africa today — say a Cabernet Sauvignon, Merlot, or Shiraz (Syrah) — it is likely to remind you of a French wine. And yet it's not quite the same. Nor is it the same as a Californian or Australian red wine. South African wine has some of the leanness and subtlety of French wine, with some of the fleshy ripeness of California wine. You come to the conclusion that South African wines are somewhere in between both worlds — they're totally unique.

The abolition of apartheid and the subsequent election of Nelson Mandela as President came at a fortunate time for South Africa's wine industry. Only a few years earlier (starting with the 1986 vintage), South Africa began to show marked improvement in its dry red wines, thanks to more advanced technology. Now that sanctions directed toward South African products have been lifted in the United States, South African wines are readily available in this market. Today, as South Africa positions itself as a player in the world wine market, its wines are better than ever.

Then and now

South Africa today is the seventh largest wine producer in the world. South Africa has been a winemaking land since the 1650s, but, until recently, its wines were mainly fortified and dessert wines. In the 19th century, politics, war, and phylloxera combined to decimate the wine industry in South Africa. In response, the government approved the formation of a regulatory body, the KWV, in 1918. The KWV (initials representing a very long Afrikaans name) is, in effect, a gigantic, seminational wine cooperative that still controls South Africa's wine industry. The KWV runs 70 smaller cooperatives, which together account for 85 percent of the country's wine production.

In addition to the huge KWV, about 170 independent wineries exist in South Africa today. Many of these independent wineries focus on premium grape varieties such as Cabernet Sauvignon, Merlot, Pinot Noir, and Shiraz.

Besides wines from the classic French grape varieties, South Africa also produces a unique red wine — Pinotage *(pee noh TAHJ)*. This wine is made from a grape of the same name, born from a crossing of the Pinot Noir vine and the Cinsault vine (a

Rhône Valley variety). Pinotage combines the cherry fruit of Pinot Noir with the earthiness of a Rhône wine. In the hands of a good producer, such as Kanonkop or Simonsig, it is a delightful, delicious wine. The very best examples of Pinotage, such as Kanonkop's, cost $18 to $19, but you can also find many Pinotages in the $8 to $10 range.

South Africa's major red wine regions

Most of South Africa's best red wine regions are in Cape Province, within 90 miles of its principal city, picturesque Cape Town.

The crescent-shaped Coastal Region stretches west to the Atlantic Ocean and east to the Indian Ocean — the only wine region in the world that's situated between two oceans. Four of South Africa's best wine districts are here, where the generally hot climate is cooled by the prevailing ocean breezes:

- **Constantia:** This area is the oldest wine-producing region in South Africa, located south of Cape Town.
- **Stellenbosch:** East of Cape Town, this region is the country's most important wine region in terms of quantity and quality.
- **Paarl:** North of Stellenbosch, this warmer region is home to the KWV and some of South Africa's fine wineries, such as the Nederburg Estate.
- **Franschhoek Valley:** East of Stellenbosch, this region is the site of many innovative wineries.

Farther east and south, along the coast of the Indian Ocean, is another up-and-coming wine region worth noting:

- **Walker Bay:** This region is very cool and shows promise for Pinot Noir, especially from the excellent winery, Hamilton Russell Vineyards.

Recommended producers of red wines in South Africa

Table 9-7 names several recommended South African producers and some of their best red wines. Our recommended wines generally range in price from $8 to $18, but a few of the very best are over $18. Producers are listed alphabetically, and we indicate our favorite wines with a ▼ symbol.

Recent good vintages for South African red wine

As in other fairly warm-climate regions, vintages are consistently good in South Africa. The cooler, coastal regions can experience variable weather, however. The best recent vintages for red wine are **1995**, **1993**, **1992**, 1991, **1990**, **1987**, and **1986**. The 1992 and 1986 vintages are the very finest for red wines.

In general, South African red wines are ready to drink upon release and should be enjoyed fairly young, within five or six years of the vintage date. The better wines, for example, those we indicate as our personal favorites in Table 9-7, should hold their quality somewhat longer, up to ten years after the vintage.

Table 9-7   Recommended Red Wines from South Africa

Producer	District	Wines
Backsburg Estate	Paarl	Merlot Cabernet Sauvignon Malbec Pinotage Klein Babylonstoren (Merlot/Cabernet blend)
Boschendal Estate	Paarl	Shiraz Merlot "Grand Reserve" (Merlot/Cab)
Fleur du Cap	Stellenbosch	Merlot Shiraz
Glen Carlou	Paarl	"Grande Classique" (Cabernet Sauvignon, Merlot, Cabernet Franc blend)
Groot Constantia	Constantia	Cabernet Sauvignon
Hamilton Russell	Walker Bay	🍷 Pinot Noir
Kanonkop Estate	Stellenbosch	🍷 Pinotage Cabernet Sauvignon

(continued)

Table 9-7 *(continued)*

Producer	***District***	***Wines***
Klein Constantia	Constantia	🍷 Marlbrook (Cabernet Sauvignon, Merlot, Cabernet Franc blend) 🍷 Cabernet Sauvignon
La Motte Estate	Franschhoek	"Millennium" (Cabernet Sauvignon, Merlot, Cabernet Franc blend) Shiraz
Lievland Estate	Stellenbosch	"DVB" (Cab Sauvignon, Merlot, Cab Franc blend)
L'Ormarins Estate	Franschhoek	"Optima" (Cab Sauvignon, Merlot, Cab Franc blend) Cabernet Sauvignon Shiraz
Meerlust Estate	Stellenbosch	🍷 "Rubicon" (mainly Cabernet Sauvignon) 🍷 Merlot 🍷 Cabernet Sauvignon Pinot Noir
Middelvlei Estate	Stellenbosch	Pinotage Cabernet Sauvignon
Neil Ellis	Stellenbosch	Cabernet Sauvignon Cabernet Sauvignon/Merlot
Plaisir de Merle	Franschhoek	🍷 Cabernet Sauvignon
Rozendal Farm	Stellenbosch	"Rozendal" (mainly Merlot)
Rust En Vrede	Stellenbosch	🍷 Estate (Cabernet Sauvignon/ Shiraz) 🍷 Cabernet Sauvignon Shiraz
Simonsig Estate	Stellenbosch	Pinotage "Tiara" (Cabernet Sauvignon/ Merlot)
Thelema Mountain	Stellenbosch	Cabernet Sauvignon Cabernet Sauvignon/Merlot
Villiera Estate	Paarl	🍷 "Cru Monro" (60 % Cabernet Sauvignon/40 % Merlot) Merlot
Zonnenbloem	Stellenbosch	🍷 "Lauréat" (Cab Sauvignon/Merlot blend) 🍷 Merlot

Chapter 10
Vin Rouge Begins with Bordeaux

In This Chapter

▶ At home with the famous red wine grapes

▶ Vintages in Bordeaux — attention must be paid

▶ Left Bank versus Right Bank

▶ "Classified" wines

▶ Price levels to suit everyone's pocketbook

*F*rance is home to many of the world's most important red grape varieties, such as Cabernet Sauvignon, Merlot, Pinot Noir, Syrah, Gamay, and Cabernet Franc. What's more, many of the world's most renowned red wines — Bordeaux, Burgundy, Beaujolais, Côtes du Rhône, and Châteauneuf-du-Pape, to name a few — come from France. The French, you see, have been making wine for over 2,000 years — even before they were known as French!

France is blessed with many regions that provide excellent growing conditions for wine grapes. The French would say that they have excellent *terroir* (pronounced *terr wahr*) — a term that refers to the environment in which grapes grow, including all aspects of climate and soil.

Besides being blessed with natural resources for grape-growing, France was lucky enough to get off to an early start in the wine business. The Greeks brought grape vines to Gaul, the land now known as France, centuries before the Romans arrived to conquer the area. The wine-loving Romans subsequently encouraged cultivation of grapes among the inhabitants.

Where the Rouges Grow

Over France's centuries of experience, three regions emerged as the finest areas for growing red grapes and making red wine:

> ✔ Bordeaux
>
> ✔ Burgundy
>
> ✔ The Rhône Valley

Today, these three areas rank among the best red wine regions in the world.

Bordeaux and Burgundy are France's two most famous wine regions. Of the two, Bordeaux is by far the larger, producing about twice as much wine as Burgundy (and that's including the fairly large Beaujolais area as part of the Burgundy region, which it technically is, even though Beaujolais wines are quite different from other red Burgundy wines). The Rhône Valley offers robust red wines in all price categories.

Actually, the *vin rouge* scene extends far beyond these three regions. The Loire *(l'wahr)* Valley, for example, although more famous for its white wines, produces light-bodied to medium-bodied, undervalued red wines that are worth seeking out. And if you're looking for good red wines in the $6 to $10 range, the varietally named wines from the Languedoc-Roussillon *(lahn gweh doc roo see yon)* region in southwest France fit the bill perfectly.

We cover the red wines of Bordeaux in this chapter, and France's other major red wine regions in Chapter 11.

Table 10-1 provides a quick reference to the wines of France's principal wine regions and the grape varieties that make those wines. (Turn to Chapter 3 for a description of most of these red grapes.)

Table 10-1	Red Wine Regions of France: The Wines and Their Grape Varieties
Regions and Wines	*Grape Varieties*
Bordeaux	Cabernet Sauvignon, Merlot, Cabernet Franc, Petite Verdot, Malbec*
Burgundy	Pinot Noir
Beaujolais	Gamay
Rhône	
Hermitage	Syrah

Regions and Wines	Grape Varieties
Côte Rôtie	Syrah, Viognier*
Cornas	Syrah
Châteauneuf-du-Pape	Grenache, Mourvèdre, Syrah, and many others*
Côtes du Rhône	Grenache, Mourvèdre, Carignan, and many others*
Gigondas	Grenache, Mourvèdre, Syrah, and many others*
Loire Valley	
Chinon	Cabernet Franc, Cabernet Sauvignon*
Bourgueil	Cabernet Franc, Cabernet Sauvignon*
St.-Nicolas-de- Bourgueil	Cabernet Franc, Cabernet Sauvignon*
Languedoc-Roussillon	
Corbieres	Carignan, Syrah, Mourvèdre, Grenache, and others*
Minervois	Carignan, Grenache, Syrah, Mourvèdre, and others*
Cabernet Sauvignon	Cabernet Sauvignon
Merlot	Merlot
Syrah	Syrah

*Multiple grape varieties are blended for this wine.

Bordeaux: The Red Wine King of France

Bordeaux, the fourth-largest city in France, gives its name to France's largest fine wine region, abutting the Atlantic Ocean in southwestern France.

For many wine lovers, Bordeaux wine is *the* most prestigious red wine in the world. Although dry and sweet white wines are also made in the Bordeaux region, 83 percent of Bordeaux wine is red. In fact, when we think of Bordeaux, we automatically think *red*.

The Bordeaux region has a maritime, temperate climate: not too hot in summer, not too cold in winter. Unfortunately for the growers of Bordeaux, however, autumn rains can play havoc with the grape crop (as can an occasional devastating springtime frost). For these reasons, usually only four or five years of each decade — at best — produce truly fine wines. The 1980s were a fortunate exception; every vintage but 1980, 1984, and 1987 yielded good, very good, or great red Bordeaux wines.

Red wines from Bordeaux can cost as little as $6 per bottle or well over $100 a bottle. In a region as large as Bordeaux, quality can vary a great deal from one producer to the next and from one part of the region to the next, causing enormous variations in prices. Finer Bordeaux wines usually cost $15 and up in wine shops when they are first released, depending on the vintage, producer, and demand. As fine Bordeaux wines age, they invariably increase in price.

One of the reasons that Bordeaux wine has become so famous among wine lovers is that the best wines of the region are very good, very expensive, long-lived wines that improve for decades, taking on legendary status as they age. The region owes its reputation to the *grands vins* (great wines) made by historic *châteaux* (wine estates) such as Château Haut-Brion *(oh bree oan)*, Château Lafite-Rothschild *(lah feet roth sheeld)*, Château Latour *(lah tor)*, Château Margaux *(mahr go)*, and Château Mouton-Rothschild *(moo tahn roth sheeld)*.

Legendary wines such as these from good vintage years are nearly immortal — or at least they age better than humans do. In 1995, a few lucky wine buffs drank a bottle of 1848 Lafite (the property was not then owned by the Rothschild family) and found it extraordinary. Personally, we've been stunned by the greatness of a few examples of 1870 Bordeaux that we've been fortunate enough to drink.

Vintage Bordeaux

Great recent vintages for fine red Bordeaux are **1982, 1985, 1986, 1988, 1989,** and **1990** (the 1985 is the readiest-to-drink of this group). And the **1994** wines — available in 1997 — look promising, according to our preliminary assessment. The **1995** vintage will probably be considered better yet, but it is a vintage of rather small quantity and the wines will be expensive; at any rate, the 1995 wines won't be available until 1998.

Understanding French wine labels

All sorts of subtle communications happen between the lines of French wine labels. For example, every label specifies a geographic area where the grapes for that wine grew. But some geographic areas are considered better than others. Within any large region, such as Bordeaux or Burgundy, the *smaller* the area specified on the label, the *better* the pedigree of the wine. For example, in Bordeaux, a wine with the *appellation* (the official term for an official geographic area) of Pauillac, a commune, has a higher pedigree than a wine from the much broader appellation, Bordeaux.

For more detailed information about the subtleties of French labels, refer to *Wine For Dummies*, specifically the beginning of Chapter 10.

Petit Bacchus en verre émaillé. Nevers - XVIIIe s. Musée de Mouton

Château d'Armailhac

1991

Grand Cru Classé

PAUILLAC
APPELLATION PAUILLAC CONTROLÉE

Baronne Philippine de Rothschild g.f.a.

PRODUCE OF FRANCE   PROPRIETAIRE
75 cl   MIS EN BOUTEILLE AU CHATEAU   12.5% vol

ALC. 12.5% BY VOL. - RED BORDEAUX WINE - PRODUCE OF FRANCE - 750 ML

But the truly great, nearly immortal red Bordeaux wines make up only a tiny fraction of the region's red wines. Many very good Bordeaux wines — wines that sell in the $15 to $25 range — are made to be enjoyed within 10 to 15 years of their vintage. Inexpensive (less than $15 a bottle) red Bordeaux wines are most enjoyable when they are young, in the first 5 years of their lives. Most of the time, they don't improve with aging — in fact, they usually deteriorate.

Unfortunately for wine lovers who seek immediate gratification, age (the wine's age, that is) is very much an issue for better red Bordeaux wines. The more "serious" (over $15) red Bordeaux wines are not just capable of aging; they really taste better with 10 or more years of age.

When they are young, the finest red Bordeaux wines have a deep cranberry hue, with aromas of black currants, cassis, spice, and cedar. For the first 8 to 10 years, they can be very dry, almost austere, with tannins masking their fruit flavors. With time, their color turns slightly garnet, their tannins soften, and they develop an extraordinarily complex bouquet and taste, often reminiscent of leather, chocolate, coffee, or tobacco. Really fine Bordeaux often take 15 to 20 years to reach maturity and then remain in this optimal drinking stage for many years.

Less expensive Bordeaux, on the other hand, are lighter in color, lighter-bodied, and less complex in flavor than higher-priced Bordeaux.

Bordeaux's Two Faces

Paris has its Left Bank (of the river Seine), home of university students and *relatively* inexpensive restaurants and hotels, and its upscale Right Bank, with magisterial hotels, very expensive restaurants, and perhaps the most famous boulevard in the world, the Champs Elysées.

In the Bordeaux region, the situation is somewhat reversed. On the Left Bank of the Gironde River (the area near the Atlantic Ocean) are the famous châteaux of the Médoc *(meh doc)* and the Graves *(grahv)* districts, owned by wealthy families or corporations. The Right Bank area of Bordeaux (the eastern part) has more than its share of small properties and working farmers. Two of the wine districts on the Right Bank —

St.-Emilion *(sant ay meal yon)* and Pomerol — are well known, however. In fact, many of the most expensive and sought-after red Bordeaux wines, such as Château Petrus *(peh troos)*, Château Lafleur *(lah fler)*, and Château Trotanoy *(trot ahn wah)*, come from tiny properties in the Pomerol district.

Right Bank versus Left Bank: Vive la Difference!

Bordeaux wines from the Left Bank and the Right Bank are so markedly different from each other that many wine lovers develop distinct preferences for the wines from one side of the Gironde or the other. For one thing, the grape composition of the wines tends to be different in each area.

On the Left Bank, where gravelly soil predominates, the Cabernet Sauvignon grape does particularly well. The wines of the Médoc and the Graves/Pessac-Léognan *(grahv pay sac lay oh nyahn)* districts are therefore predominantly (typically, two-thirds) Cabernet Sauvignon. (Pessac-Léognan is the northern-most subdistrict of Graves and a notable red wine area.)

The balance of the grape blend in Left Bank wines is Merlot and Cabernet Franc, often with a small amount of two lesser grapes. (See "Red Bordeaux at a glance" in Chapter 4.)

On the Right Bank, clay soil, user-friendly to the Merlot grape, prevails. Therefore, Bordeaux wines from St.-Emilion, Pomerol, and all other red wine districts east of the Gironde are predominantly (usually about 70 percent or more) Merlot; Cabernet Sauvignon and Cabernet Franc make up the rest of the blend.

The Cabernet Sauvignon-dominated wines of the Left Bank are normally austere and tannic with a pronounced black currant flavor. They usually need many years to develop and can age for a long time, sometimes for decades — typical of a Cabernet Sauvignon-based wine.

The Merlot-based wines of the Right Bank are usually softer and more approachable than Left Bank wines. They are less tannic, richer, and more plummy in flavor, and you usually can enjoy them sooner, often within eight years of the vintage.

If you are new to red Bordeaux wines, we suggest that you begin with the wines from the Right Bank, especially those wines from the St.-Emilion or Pomerol districts.

More on the Médoc

Although the Right Bank wines are easier to enjoy young, the wines of the Left Bank — especially those of the Médoc — are more famous. Many of the names you're likely to hear when wine lovers discuss Bordeaux are names of villages and châteaux of the Médoc.

Four of Bordeaux's most important wine villages are located in the southern part of the Médoc district, which is known as the Haut-Médoc *(oh may doc)*. From north to south, these villages are

- ✔ St.-Estèphe *(sant eh steff)*
- ✔ Pauillac *(poy yac)*
- ✔ St.-Julien *(sant jewl yen)*
- ✔ Margaux *(mahr go)*

Table 10-2 describes the typical wines of each of the four villages.

The names of these districts or communes are officially part of the wine's name and always appear on the label.

Table 10-2 The Four Principal Communes in the Haut-Médoc

Commune	Wine Characteristics	Typical Wine
St.-Estèphe	Tannic, full-bodied, earthy, acidic, chunky, slow to mature	Château Montrose
Pauillac	Powerful, firm, tannic, full-bodied, and long-lived; aromas of black currants and cedar; home of three First Growths (Latour, Lafite-Rothschild, and Mouton-Rothschild)	Château Lynch-Bages
St.-Julien	Medium- to full-bodied, well-balanced; cedary bouquet; wines show elegance and finesse	Château Beychevelle *(baysch vel)*
Margaux	Fragrant, perfumed bouquet; medium-bodied; supple, complex	Château Palmer

Classified growths

 The most renowned red Bordeaux wines are those of the lucky 61 châteaux that were named in the legendary 1855 Classification. (For an explanation of this classification, refer to Chapter 10, "Classified Information," of *Wine For Dummies*.) Each of the 61 properties is ranked as either a First Growth (the highest level) or a Second, Third, Fourth, or Fifth Growth. The appendix of *Wine For Dummies* lists all 61 properties.

The 61 classified wines are often referred to as great growths or *grands crus classés* (pronounced *grahn crew clas say*). If you consider that over 8,000 wine estates exist in all of Bordeaux, you can appreciate what a privilege it is to be part of the 1855 Classification.

These 61 wines all hail from the Left Bank, which was the most important production area in the middle of the last century. Today, the St.-Emilion district has its own classification of properties, although Pomerol estates remain unclassified.

Two other less-well-known villages in the Haut-Médoc are Listrac *(lee strahk)* and Moulis *(moo lees)*. Wines from these two villages are usually very good values.

Any château located in the Haut-Médoc but not within these six areas cannot by law specify a village name on its labels; those properties must instead use the district name, Haut-Médoc, along with the name of the property. Those châteaux with vineyards situated in the northern part of the Médoc may specify only the location Médoc on their labels, along with the château name.

Bordeaux Wines to Buy

To appreciate the difference between Right Bank wines and Left Bank wines, or between a classified-growth wine (see the sidebar, "Classified growths") and a lesser Bordeaux red, you have to taste for yourself. In the following section, we recommend numerous red Bordeaux wines that you can try, according to your interest and your budget. We begin with the most prestigious, most expensive wines and then move to more affordable options.

Recommendations: Some of the best Bordeaux wines

We hope that you have an opportunity to try some of the very fine Bordeaux wines listed in this section. The Haut-Médoc wines we recommend in Table 10-3 are all *classified growths,* and many of them are expensive, special-occasion wines (although you're allowed to drink them once a week after winning the lottery).

We list these wines alphabetically by commune. Prices for all these wines vary from about $20 to $55 a bottle (with a few more expensive exceptions, as noted — wines marked with double dollar signs may cost as much as $75 or more).

Table 10-3	Recommended Haut-Médoc Wines
Village	*Wine*
St.-Estèphe	Château Cos d'Estournel
	Château Montrose
Pauillac	Château Clerc-Milon
	Château Duhart-Milon-Rothschild
	Château Grand-Puy-Lacoste
	$ $ Château Lafite-Rothschild
	$ $ Château Latour
	Château Lynch-Bages
	$ $ Château Mouton-Rothschild
	Château Pichon-Baron
	Château Pichon-Lalande
St.-Julien	Château Beychevelle
	Château Branaire-Ducru
	Château Ducru-Beaucaillou
	Château Gruaud-Larose
	Château Lagrange
	Château Léoville-Barton
	Château Léoville-Las Cases
	Château Léoville-Poyferré

Producer	Wine
Margaux	Château Lascombes
	$ $ Château Margaux
	Château Palmer
	Château Rausan-Sègla
Haut-Médoc	Château La Lagune

Our recommendations in the following alphabetical bulleted lists include wines from three other important districts in Bordeaux. Prices for these wines also range from about $20 to $55 a bottle (with a few more expensive exceptions, as noted — wines marked with double dollar signs may cost as much as $75 or more).

We recommend these **Graves/Pessac-Léognan** wines:

- ✔ Domaine de Chevalier
- ✔ Château de Fieuzal
- ✔ Château Haut-Bailly
- ✔ $ $ Château Haut-Brion
- ✔ Château La Louvière
- ✔ $ $ Château La Mission Haut-Brion
- ✔ Château Pape Clément

Recommended **Pomerol** wines are

- ✔ Château Certan de May
- ✔ Château Clinet
- ✔ Château La Conseillante
- ✔ Château L'Evangile
- ✔ Château La Fleur de Gay
- ✔ Château Latour à Pomerol
- ✔ $ $ Château Trotanoy
- ✔ Vieux-Château-Certan

(We are not recommending two excellent Pomerols — Château Petrus and Château Lafleur — because of their very high retail price, $300 and $250 per bottle, respectively.)

Recommended **St.-Emilion** wines include the following:

- ✔ Château L'Arrosée
- ✔ Château Canon
- ✔ $ $ Château Cheval Blanc
- ✔ Château La Dominique
- ✔ Château Figeac
- ✔ Château Pavie
- ✔ Château Pavie-Macquin
- ✔ Château Troplong Mondot

Some good, affordable Bordeaux wines

For great value among Bordeaux wines, look for Médoc wines that were *not* included in the 1855 Classification (see the sidebar, "Classified growths"). About 400 such red Bordeaux are grouped in the category, *cru bourgeois*. These wines generally sell in the $12 to $22 price range. Some of them are quite age-worthy and are even as good as the lesser-quality classified growths. We recommend these *cru bourgeois* wines:

- ✔ Château d'Angludet
- ✔ Château Chasse-Spleen
- ✔ Château Haut-Marbuzet
- ✔ Château Les Ormes-de-Pez
- ✔ Château Meyney
- ✔ Château Monbrison
- ✔ Château de Pez
- ✔ Château Phélan-Segur
- ✔ Château Poujeaux
- ✔ Château Sociando Mallet

Even less expensive is the huge group of Bordeaux wines that never received a classification; they are known as *petits châteaux*. These wines can retail for $6 to $10. They are usually light bodied and ready to drink when they are released. The *petits chateaux* are the Bordeaux wines of choice in restaurants when you are looking for a young, inexpensive, approachable Bordeaux with dinner. Unfortunately, these wines are not labeled *petits châteaux;* you can recognize them only by their affordable price.

When (and where) to drink red Bordeaux

We generally don't order fine Bordeaux in restaurants; the young wines are too tannic and austere, and the older wines are too expensive. We prefer to age fine Bordeaux ourselves (in a cool place!) and enjoy them at home, after the wines have time to develop and mature.

If you really want a red Bordeaux with your dinner in a restaurant, order an inexpensive one. Although it may be less important and prestigious than the more expensive wines, chances are good that it will be less tannic than the finer wines and more enjoyable.

Red Bordeaux goes well with lamb, venison, simple grilled meats, and hard cheeses, such as cheddar or aged Gouda. If you plan to serve a fine red Bordeaux that's less than ten years old, you should pour the wine into a decanter (see Chapter 6 of our book *Wine For Dummies* or the sidebar "To decant or not to decant" in Chapter 5 of this book) and let it breathe for about an hour before you drink it. This procedure softens the tannins in the wine somewhat. Older Bordeaux (more than ten years old) also need decanting, in order to separate the sediment at the bottom of the bottle from the wine. Serve the wine at about 63° to 65° F (18° to 19° C).

Chapter 11

The Other Great French Reds: Burgundy, Rhône, and Company

- ▶ The scarcity factor in Burgundy
- ▶ The golden slope
- ▶ Burgundy — classified information
- ▶ The Burgundy called Beaujolais
- ▶ Affordable Rhône reds
- ▶ Lighter reds from the Loire Valley

*W*hen wine lovers name the greatest red wines of France — if not the world — the red wines of France's Bordeaux region share the spotlight with their perennial rivals, the red wines of Burgundy.

Burgundy might actually have more of a claim to the status of *greatness* because of the incomparable characteristics of its wines. Bordeaux's red wines, after all, are born of the Cabernet Sauvignon and Merlot grape varieties, and you can find good examples of wines made from these grapes throughout the world's wine regions. But nowhere else in the world (including the United States) has the difficult Pinot Noir grape risen to such heights as it has in the Burgundy region of France.

A certain part of the Burgundy region is the world champion in growing another red grape variety, one called Gamay. That district is Beaujolais. Not only are the wines of Beaujolais made from a different grape variety (and sold in a much lower price range) than other red Burgundy wines, but they also represent a completely different style of wine. Wine lovers treat Burgundy with reverence, respect, and even awe; Beaujolais is a fun wine, one to quaff at parties and picnics.

South of the Burgundy region, the warm Rhône Valley wine region boasts red wines of two quality levels:

- ✓ Inexpensive, lighter-bodied Côtes du Rhône wines — perfect, versatile everyday reds
- ✓ The more serious, Sunday dinner wines: Châteauneuf-du-Pape, Côte Rôtie, and Hermitage

The latter two, from the Northern Rhône wine district, are two of the world's finest examples of wines based on the Syrah grape variety.

On occasions that call for a good, dry, light-bodied red wine without too much tannin — such as summertime, or meals with relatively light foods — the little-known red wines of another French wine region, the Loire Valley, are delightful.

We end this chapter on French red wines with a brief trip to the Languedoc-Roussillon region of southern France. The wines of this area defy the image of French wines as expensive beverages. Here you can find good-quality $6 French red wine — even many with familiar names, such as Cabernet Sauvignon, Merlot, and Syrah.

Status, prestige, fun, flavor, and value await you among France's red wines.

The Magic of Burgundy

France's Burgundy region — known locally as Bourgogne *(bor guh nyeh)* — is one of the most famous wine regions in the world.

Burgundy's fame derives from the unique aspects of the region's wines:

- ✓ No place else in the world has ever been able to duplicate the velvety, delicious red wines — made from that most fickle of all grape varieties, the Pinot Noir — that we call red Burgundy.
- ✓ No place else in the world has ever been able to create the delicious, quaffable, fruity red wines, made from the Gamay grape, that are known as Beaujolais.
- ✓ No place else in the world does the Chardonnay grape rise to such heights as it does in Burgundy. Burgundy's wine excellence even extends to white wines (see "White Burgundies" in our book, *White Wine For Dummies*).

Yes, there is magic in this land known as Burgundy — a magical combination of soil, climate and grape variety.

Situated in eastern France, Burgundy is just a few hours' drive southeast from Paris.

Burgundy's climate is continental — rather hot summers and cold winters. Localized hailstorms are not unusual in the summer. The combination of fairly harsh climate and a very sensitive red grape variety, Pinot Noir, results in the reality that Burgundy is fortunate to average about three good-to-better vintages each decade.

The soils in the areas of Burgundy known for the region's best red wines, mainly limestone and red clay soil, seem particularly suited for the Pinot Noir grape. Farther south in the region, where the soil becomes granitic and sandy, the Gamay grape thrives. That area is the home of Beaujolais.

Although the Beaujolais district is part of the Burgundy region, wine lovers never refer to Beaujolais wines as Burgundy, and they never mean Beaujolais when they say Burgundy. They reserve the term "red Burgundy" for those wines of the Burgundy region that are made from the Pinot Noir grape.

The real thing

Some inexpensive red wines from California go by the name Burgundy. You usually see these wines in large, jug-type bottles. These wines have absolutely no relationship to true Burgundies from Bourgogne, France (as if!). The grape varieties used to make these imposter-Burgundies are common, ordinary types. The wines emanate from large, industrial vineyards in the hot Central Valley, far away from the best wine regions of the cool California coastline — let alone the hills of Burgundy. If someone offers you a California imposter and calls it Burgundy, just say, "Hello? This is not Burgundy!"

Getting Down to Detail in Burgundy

Unfortunately for wine drinkers who are eager to experience the magic of Burgundy in their wine glasses, Burgundy happens to be one of the most complex wine regions in the world. Many details complicate the process of understanding the red wines of Burgundy, such as:

- ✔ Subdivisions of the region
- ✔ Rankings and classifications of vineyards
- ✔ Tiny vineyard plots with multiple owners
- ✔ Producers who might or might not actually make their own wine

In order to purchase red Burgundy wine wisely and to understand exactly what you're drinking, you really do need to know about these issues. We discuss them one by one in the sections that follow.

Two red coats, one trimmed in gold

The grapes for red Burgundies grow along two rather narrow strips of land running from north to south.

The northerly strip, directly south of the city of Dijon, is known as the Côte d'Or *(coat door)*, or Golden Slope. The Côte d'Or itself is made up of two areas:

- ✔ The Côte de Nuits *(coat deh nwee)*, its northern half, named for the village of Nuits-St.-Georges *(nwee san jorj)*
- ✔ The Côte de Beaune *(coat deh bone)* in the south, named after the town of Beaune.

All the famous and most highly sought-after red Burgundies come from the Côte d'Or.

The southerly strip of red Burgundy vineyards is called the Côte Chalonnaise *(shal oan naize)*. This area produces lower-priced ($12 to $25) red Burgundies.

Classified information

Up and down the Côte d'Or and the Côte Chalonnaise, the soils differ slightly. In the Côte d'Or, for example, soils vary not only from hillside to hillside but also from the top of each hill to the middle of the hill to the bottom. As a result of these soil differences, certain vineyards are able to produce finer red grapes, and finer wine, than other sites.

French wine law recognizes these very best vineyard sites in Burgundy and ranks them higher than the other vineyard sites of the region. Wines from the favored vineyards are entitled to be named for the vineyard itself, rather than just for the region at large (Burgundy), the district (such as Côte de Beaune), or the village in which the vineyard is situated.

Red Burgundies, like most of France's best wines, are named for the place where the grapes grow. The smaller and more specific the place indicated by the wine name, the finer that wine is considered to be — and the more expensive. From least to most specific, the names of red Burgundy wines are

- ✔ Regional names (the least specific)
- ✔ District names
- ✔ Village (or *commune*) names
- ✔ Vineyard names (at the top of the ladder)

The premier cru and grand cru category

Although the top vineyard sites of Burgundy hold higher status than other vineyards of the region, these top vineyards do not all have the same status. Some of them are ranked as premier cru *(preem yay crew)*, and others are ranked higher, as grand cru. (*Premier cru* translates as "First Growth" — but wine lovers always use the French phrase rather than the English translation to avoid confusion with the Bordeaux wines designated First Growths in the 1855 Classification, which we discuss in Chapter 10.)

In Burgundy, 561 vineyards hold premier cru status; about 75 percent of these vineyards grow red grapes, and the rest make white Burgundy. Premier cru wines account for only about 11 percent of Burgundy wines, red and white (not counting Beaujolais). Red premier cru Burgundies range in retail price from $30 to $75 a bottle.

Thirty-two vineyards in Burgundy hold grand cru status — 25 of them for red wine and 7 for white wine. These 32 grand cru vineyards are so special that their wines represent only 1 percent of all Burgundy! Prices for grand cru red Burgundies start at about $65 to $70 per bottle and can go well over $100; Romanée-Conti, a grand cru wine that is typically Burgundy's — if not the world's — most expensive red wine, usually costs about $800 (per bottle, that is!) in a good vintage.

The village category

Luckily for regular wine drinkers, the great majority of red Burgundies come from neither premier cru nor grand cru vineyards. Occupying the middle ground of quality (and price) are wines that are named after specially-ranked villages. (Wines named after districts of Burgundy are one notch lower in price and quality. At the bottom of the pyramid are wines named after the region itself, Bourgogne.)

So-called *village Burgundies* — those with the name of a specific village — are made from grapes growing in nonranked vineyards within the specific village. (If the grapes come from a premier cru or grand cru vineyard in that village, the producer names the wine after the vineyard so that the wine can command a higher price.) Fifty-three villages in Burgundy are entitled to use their name as an official wine name. Village wines make up 23 percent of all Burgundies; they are mainly in the $20 to $30 per bottle price range, retail.

For a listing of the leading ranked communes or villages in Burgundy and a brief description of their wines, see "The Côte d'Or" section of *Wine For Dummies,* Chapter 10.

The district and regional category

The two broadest categories of Burgundies — regional wines (such as Bourgogne Rouge) and district wines (such as Côte de Nuits-Villages, pronounced *coat deh nwee vey lahj*) — comprise about 65 percent of all Burgundies.

At these last two levels — regional Burgundy and district-level Burgundy — red Burgundy wines are affordable; regional and district Burgundies are in the $10 to $18 retail price range.

Table 11-1 illustrates Burgundy's classification system with real-life examples of wine names.

Table 11-1   The Burgundy Classification System

Category	Examples
Regional wine	Bourgogne Rouge
District wine	Côte de Beaune-Villages
Commune or village wine	Nuits-St.-Georges Pommard Volnay

Category	Examples
Premier cru wine	Vosne-Romanée Clos des Réas Volnay Champans
Grand cru wine	Corton Chambertin Richebourg

Reading the rank from the label

You can tell the difference between a village Burgundy, a premier cru, and a grand cru by looking carefully at the label.

✔ A commune or village Burgundy's name is the same as the village name (usually a hyphenated name, such as Morey-St. Denis or Vosne-Romanée, pronounced *vone roh mah nay*), as in Figure 11-1.

✔ A premier cru Burgundy carries the name of the village *plus* the vineyard name in same-sized letters (such as CHAMBOLLE-MUSIGNY LES CHARMES). If the label shows what seems to be a vineyard name, but that name is in smaller print, that vineyard is not a premier cru but is merely the name of a single vineyard from which the wine originated.

✔ Grand cru Burgundies carry only the name of the vineyard, such as CHAMBERTIN or MUSIGNY, on the label.

Growers versus négociants

The names of Burgundy wines are not the only things about Burgundy that are fragmented and complicated. The vineyards themselves are fragmented. Any one vineyard — even if it is small — may have dozens of owners; some of these owners might own as little as two or three rows of grapevines.

As a result of this fragmentation, many grape growers traditionally have not been in a position to sell wine under their own names. (Selling 12 or 16 different wines, each available in miniscule quantities, is a marketer's nightmare!) Instead, growers have usually sold their wines to *négociant houses,* large firms that buy grapes and/or wine from growers and blend the

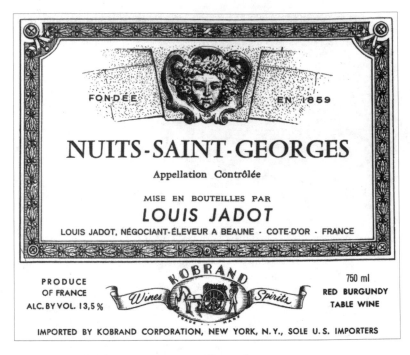

FONDÉE   EN 1859

NUITS-SAINT-GEORGES

Appellation Contrôlée

MISE EN BOUTEILLES PAR

LOUIS JADOT

LOUIS JADOT, NÉGOCIANT-ÉLEVEUR A BEAUNE · COTE-D'OR · FRANCE

PRODUCE
OF FRANCE
ALC. BY VOL. 13,5 %

KOBRAND
Wines Spirits

750 ml
RED BURGUNDY
TABLE WINE

IMPORTED BY KOBRAND CORPORATION, NEW YORK, N. Y., SOLE U. S. IMPORTERS

Figure 11-1: Label from a commune or village wine.

wines or grapes of many growers to produce their own Burgundy wines in their own house style. Some of the well-known
négociant houses in the Burgundy region are Louis Jadot,
Joseph Drouhin, Louis Latour, and Georges Duboeuf.

During the early part of this century, a few Burgundian growers
started bottling and selling their own wine. After World War II,
more and more growers followed suit, usually for both eco-
nomic and status motives. Today, about half of all Burgundy
wine is made and sold by growers themselves.

Direct-selling by growers has its advantages and disadvantages.
Some truly outstanding, unique Burgundies come from the
individual plots of many growers. Unfortunately, most of these
growers are very small producers (some make as little as 50 to
100 cases of each of their wines for the entire world). Consequently, many grower Burgundies are very difficult to obtain
and very expensive.

Buying and drinking red Burgundy

Burgundy is not a large area to begin with — it produces only about 25 percent as much wine as Bordeaux (not counting Beaujolais wines in Burgundy's statistics). The fragmentation of the region into hundreds of vineyards, and the fragmentation of each vineyard into dozens of individual producers, guarantees that the available quantity of any single red Burgundy wine will be small. Small production makes it a certainty that the wines will be expensive and difficult to find.

Consider this: The typical Burgundian winemaker's production varies from 500 cases to 1,000 cases a year (for the whole world!). In Bordeaux, the average château owner makes 15,000 to 20,000 cases of wine annually. Add to these considerations the fact that red Burgundy wines are truly unique in the world, and the inescapable conclusion is that good red Burgundy will always be scarce.

Because red Burgundy wines (that is, excluding Beaujolais wines and one minor exception) are always 100 percent Pinot Noir, their color is invariably lighter than Cabernet Sauvignon or Merlot-based wines — such as Bordeaux reds. Burgundy's hues range from light cherry to ruby red, depending on the vintage and producer. As red Burgundy wines age, they turn to garnet, especially around the rim.

Red Burgundy wine is typically medium bodied (compared to other red wines), dry, and relatively low in tannin. Because of these characteristics, red Burgundy is usually an excellent choice in restaurants. It is enjoyable young and goes well with fish and seafood as well as meat. The typical aroma of red Burgundies is that of small red fruits, such as cherries and/or berries; often the wine has damp-earth or woodsy aromas as well. As it ages, red Burgundy takes on a natural softness and sweetness of fruit flavors.

Red Burgundy wines are usually best if consumed within ten years of the vintage (with the exception of powerful vintages — years when the wine is more intense, such as 1978 or 1990). In lighter vintages, such as 1992, Burgundy should be consumed within six to eight years or even sooner. (See Appendix D for further information about Burgundy vintages.)

Our most important advice on red Burgundy

The very fine level of detail of Burgundy's classification system makes it seem reliable and trustworthy. You can easily assume that grand cru red Burgundies are the best wines, for example, followed by premier cru Burgundies, and so on down the line to regional wines — as if Burgundians would make things that easy for you!

Actually, the classification rank of a particular red Burgundy wine is the *least important* criterion to consider when you are buying red Burgundy in a store or restaurant. In order of importance, you should rely on the following criteria:

- ✔ The producer's reputation, based on other wines that producer has made in recent years. (In the next section, we recommend some of the best red Burgundy producers.) A lower-ranking wine from a good producer is usually better quality than a higher-ranking wine from a less talented producer.

- ✔ The vintage — almost as important a consideration as the producer — because fluctuations in quality are quite significant from year to year.

- ✔ The *appellation* (the formal name of the wine, that is, the regional, district, village, or vineyard name that indicates the wine's classification ranking). Normally, a good producer's greatest Burgundy is his grand cru (if he makes one), followed by his premier cru, his village Burgundy, and so on. The wines are priced accordingly.

Vintage variations

Recent good vintages for red Burgundy are 1985 (although some wines from this vintage are showing signs of growing tired), 1988, 1989, **1990** especially, 1991 (for those Burgundies in the northern part of the Côte d'Or, the Côte de Nuits), and 1993. The 1995 vintage looks promising, but it's really too early to make a final judgment at this point.

Recommended Producers of Red Burgundy

We happen to believe that drinking a really good red Burgundy is one of the greatest gastronomic experiences on this planet. If you want to experience some of the best examples of red Burgundy (a reasonable request!), this section — in which we mention some of our favorite red Burgundy producers and their most renowned wines — should prove invaluable to you. Bear in mind, however, that you don't necessarily have to spring for the best wines from these excellent producers; even their least expensive wines, such as Leroy's Bourgogne Rouge ($15 to $18) are still fine examples of red Burgundy.

Two in a class by themselves

For red Burgundy, two producers truly stand out (and, as you might expect, their best wines are extremely expensive):

- ✔ Domaine Leroy (and the négociant house, Maison Leroy)
- ✔ Domaine de la Romanée-Conti

Domaine Leroy *(lay wah)*, run by Lalou Bize-Leroy, makes top-quality Burgundy wines from its own vineyards. The company's grand cru wines such as Richebourg, Musigny, and Chambertin sell for $300 to $500 per bottle in good vintages! Even most of Domaine Leroy's village-level Burgundies, such as Nuits-St.-Georges or Gevrey-Chambertin, are $65 and up, depending on the vintage.

Bize-Leroy — a great Burgundy palate

Madame Bize-Leroy *(beeze lay wah)*, the redoubtable owner of Domaine Leroy and Maison Leroy, is reputed to have one of the finest palates for wine in the world. When she buys wines for her négociant house, she tells growers to bring her only their best wines, regardless of the cost. And then she picks the best of their best. No one in Burgundy has higher standards, and no one makes better Burgundy than Leroy.

For a more affordable sampling of the winery's quality, look for Domaine Leroy's lesser-known wines from Savigny-les-Beaune — both premier cru and village-level — which are often in the $45 to $55 price range, and Maison Leroy's Bourgogne Rouge d'Auvenay, which costs about $15. With the exception of the Bourgogne Rouge, Leroy's Burgundies are clearly the longest-lasting red Burgundies made today. These wines truly improve with age, and most are at their best between 20 and 30 years of age.

The Domaine de la Romanée-Conti (nicknamed DRC by those in the know) makes the most famous and sought-after red Burgundy wines of all. DRC is the only real rival of Domaine Leroy in terms of both the quality and longevity of its wines. The six red Burgundies of Domaine de la Romanée-Conti — all grand cru wines — are (in descending order of quality) Romanée-Conti, La Tache, Richebourg, Romanée St.-Vivant, Grands Echézeaux, and Echézeaux. In an average vintage, these wines range in price from about $90 to $100 for the lowest-priced (Echézeaux) to $600 to $800 for Romanée-Conti, depending on the vintage. Romanée-Conti is, in fact, the world's most expensive wine when it is first released.

If you would prefer not to part with $800 for a bottle of Romanée-Conti, Aubert de Villaine, the coproprietor of Domaine de la Romanée-Conti, makes some fine, inexpensive Burgundies at his private estate, Domaine A. P. de Villaine, in Bouzeron, a village to the south of the Côte d'Or (in the Côte Chalonnaise district). Try his Bourgogne Rouge La Digoine *(lah dee gwahn),* at around $15, for a great example of regional red Burgundy at its best.

Other great red Burgundy producers

In this section, we recommend producers whom we believe are making some of the best red Burgundies available today, and give examples of some of their best wines — all of which are from the Côte d'Or. Table 11-2 lists these producers in our rough order of preference. Please forgive us if we have left out one of your favorite producers. We have omitted those wineries where production is so tiny that the wines are almost impossible to obtain.

For affordable and good red Burgundy wines, look for these producers' less expensive wines, such as their Bourgogne Rouge, Côte de Nuits-Villages, or Côte de Beaune-Villages, in the $10 to $18 price range — especially in better vintages.

Table 11-2   Producers of the Best Red Burgundies

Producer	Producer's Best Wines
Henri Jayer	Echézeaux Any of his Vosne-Romanée premier crus
Ponsot	Clos de la Roche (Vieilles Vignes) Chambertin
Hubert Lignier	Clos de la Roche Charmes-Chambertin
Méo-Camuzet	Corton Richebourg Vosne-Romanée Les Brûlées
Domaine des Chézeaux	Griotte-Chambertin Clos St.-Denis (Vieilles Vignes)
Jean Gros	Richebourg Vosne-Romanée Clos des Réas
Georges Roumier	Musigny Chambolle-Musigny Les Amoureuses
Armand Rousseau	Chambertin-Clos de Beze Gevrey-Chambertin Clos St.-Jacques
Domaine Maume	Mazis-Chambertin Charmes-Chambertin
Louis Jadot	Romanée St.-Vivant Musigny Beaune Clos des Ursules
Chopin-Groffier	Clos de Vougeot
Jean-Jacques Confuron	Romanée St.-Vivant Nuits-St.-Georges Aux Boudots
Christian Serafin	Charmes-Chambertin Gevrey Chambertin Les Cazétiers
Marquis d'Angerville	Volnay Clos des Ducs Volnay Champans
Robert Chevillon	Nuits-St.-Georges Les St.-Georges Nuits-St.-Georges Les Vaucrains
Domaine des Varoilles	Gevrey-Chambertin Clos des Varoilles
Domaine Comte Armand	Pommard Clos des Epeneaux

Recommended producers in the Côte Chalonnaise

Another way to save money when buying red Burgundy wines — in addition to sticking to regional- and district-level Burgundies from our recommended Côte d'Or producers — is to seek out the lesser-known red Burgundy wines of the Côte Chalonnaise.

Burgundies from the villages of Mercurey *(mer cure ay)*, Rully *(rue yee)*, and Givry *(gee vree)* — both at the commune level and at the premier cru level — sell for $15 to $25 per bottle. They are 100 percent Pinot Noir, but a bit earthier and more rustic in style than the Côte d'Or Burgundies. The red Burgundies of Mercurey are particularly good.

In Table 11-3, we list our recommended producers in rough order of preference, according to commune.

Table 11-3	Recommended Côte Chalonnaise Red Burgundy Producers
Village	*Producer*
Mercurey	Château de Chamirey
	Domaine Meix Foulot
	Domaine Bordeaux-Montrieux
	Domaine Michel Juillot
	Domaine J. Naltet Père et Fils
	Antonin Rodet
Givry	Domaine Joblot
	Domaine Thierry Lespinasse
	Domaine du Gardin-Clos Salomon
	Paul et Henri Jacqueson
	Domaine Thenard
Rully	Domaine Jean-Claude Breliére
	Domaine de la Folie
	Château de Rully
	Antonin Rodet
	Domaine Michel Briday
	Domaine de la Rénarde

A Nouveau kind of Beaujolais

Some people call Zinfandel "America's wine" (see "Zinfandel" in Chapter 7), but Beaujolais Nouveau can also qualify for that title, because most of it is sold and consumed in the U.S.

Each year, Beaujolais producers earmark a certain portion of their wine to make Beaujolais Nouveau — a light, grapey style of wine that is the first wine to be released from each new vintage. Beaujolais Nouveau wine is released amid great fanfare each year on the third Thursday in November (just in time for Thanksgiving and Christmas, by the way), when the wine is a mere six weeks old, very fruity, and very easy to drink. The wine sells (very successfully) for about $6 a bottle and is often sold out by Christmas. Beaujolais Nouveau drinks best within six months of its release.

Beaujolais: Easy-Drinking and Affordable

Although Beaujolais is officially a part of the Burgundy region (the southernmost part), it is such a famous wine that it stands on its own. Beaujolais uses an entirely different grape variety from other red Burgundies — all Beaujolais wine is 100 percent Gamay (see Chapter 3 for a description of the Gamay grape).

Beaujolais is a light-bodied, fairly simple, fruity red wine (a tiny bit of Beaujolais Blanc is made, but the quantity is really insignificant) that's meant to be quaffed with gusto — ideally with summer lunches or barbecues — rather than sipped in quiet contemplation. Beaujolais is a fun wine, a party wine, a wine for young (or young-at-heart) wine drinkers.

If you are just getting into red wine, Beaujolais is the wine of choice. Beaujolais makes a great crossover wine from white, rosé, or blush wines because it is low in tannin, fruity, easy to drink, and inexpensive: Most Beaujolais are in the $6 to $10 per bottle price range.

Just as real Burgundy is made only in Burgundy, France, real Beaujolais comes only from the Beaujolais district of France. But some wines made in California and elsewhere do carry the word Beaujolais on their labels. The American wines are often called Gamay Beaujolais, a local name for a grape related to Pinot Noir (not the Gamay grape at all), but they really don't taste very much like true Beaujolais.

True to its Burgundian roots, the Beaujolais area is subdivided into sections and ranked vineyards — although the categories are not nearly so confusing as they are in the rest of Burgundy. The sandy, southern part of Beaujolais makes the simplest, most inexpensive ($6 to $7) wines, simply called Beaujolais, and the northern part, with granite soil, makes the better Beaujolais wines.

These better Beaujolais wines fall into two distinct categories:

Beaujolais-Villages: Wines blended from Gamay grapes grown in 39 specific villages and considered to be of higher quality than simple Beaujolais; Beaujolais-Villages wines usually cost only about a dollar more than Beaujolais. They are more substantial wines, and they are well worth the dollar more.

Cru Beaujolais: Wines from ten specific villages and vineyard sites that make the highest-quality (more full-bodied and more distinctive) Beaujolais wines. Cru Beaujolais wines carry only the cru's name, in large letters, on their labels (rather than Beaujolais or Beaujolais-Villages). Following are the ten cru Beaujolais, from south to north:

- Brouilly *(broo yee)*
- Côte de Brouilly
- Regnie *(ray nyay)*
- Morgon *(mor gohn)*
- Chiroubles *(sheh roob leh)*
- Fleurie *(flehr ee)*
- Moulin-á-Vent *(moo lahn ah vahn)*
- Chénas *(shay nahs)*
- Juliénas *(jhool ee ay nahs)*
- Saint-Amour *(sant ah more)*

For a description of stylistic differences among the ten cru Beaujolais wines, see Table 10-8 in *Wine For Dummies*.

Cru Beaujolais wines range in price from $8 to $14. One of our favorite crus is Chiroubles because it is usually one of the most perfumed Beaujolais wines; it is delicate and delicious — the quintessential Beaujolais. For a more full-bodied, consistently reliable Beaujolais, choose a Moulin-á-Vent, Juliénas, or Fleurie. These three cru Beaujolais wines can hold their quality for a few years — but most Beaujolais wines should be enjoyed within two or three years of the vintage.

Almost all Beaujolais wine is sold by large négociants (see "Growers versus négociants" earlier in the Burgundy section). Two of the largest and most reliable négociants to look for when buying Beaujolais are Louis Jadot and Georges Duboeuf.

Beaujolais at its best

Visiting the Beaujolais district is quite a treat. Located just north of the city of Lyon, the Beaujolais area is in the heart of one of the great gastronomic regions in the world, with many of the superb restaurants of France nearby. At a bistro in Lyon (or Paris, for that matter), a carafe of young Beaujolais is perfect with pâté or charcuterie.

We drink our Beaujolais slightly chilled (about 55° F or 13° C) to enjoy its lively, fruity exuberance. The more serious cru Beaujolais wines, however, should be served at about the same temperature as other red Burgundies — 60° to 62° F, or 17° C.

The Warm Rhône Valley Reds

The Rhône Valley, a wine region of southeastern France directly south of Lyon and north of Provence, traditionally has been a fine source of hearty, generous red wines. The wines vary from simple, inexpensive Côtes du Rhône wines to long-lived, aristocratic Hermitage *(er mee tahj)* wines. The better Rhône reds have warm, robust flavors, firm tannin, and are fairly high in alcohol. They are ideal winter wines.

In fact, the Rhône Valley wine region encompasses two distinct subregions — the Northern Rhône and the Southern Rhône. Each grows different red grapes and makes distinct wines within the Rhône's hearty, generous red wine prototype.

The southern Rhône: Land of values

The southern Rhône Valley is a large area with a warm, dry, Mediterranean climate, where red grapes thrive. In fact, 95 percent of all Rhône wines (red and white) come from here; most of them are called Côtes du Rhône.

Côtes du Rhône and Côtes du Rhône-Villages

The major grape variety in most Côtes du Rhône red wines is Grenache (a variety that is high in alcohol, with flavors often suggestive of raspberries; see Chapter 3), but winemakers can legally blend many different varieties in making southern Rhône red wines. In practice, although Grenache dominates, Cinsault, Syrah, Carignan, and Mourvèdre are other major grape varieties of southern Rhône reds.

For everyday drinking, if great Bordeaux or Burgundy is too expensive, a Côtes du Rhône red wine for $6 to $8 is ideal. For a few dollars more ($9 to $12), you can experience the next step up in quality: Côtes du Rhône-Villages wines. These wines come from 16 villages where the vineyards are judged superior to those making simple Côtes du Rhône.

Most Côtes du Rhône-Villages wines are blended from grapes that come from two or more villages, and their labels read Côtes du Rhône-Villages. If a wine's grapes come entirely from a specific village, however, the village name can appear on the label along with the name Côtes du Rhône-Villages. Two of the better-known villages, for example, are Cairanne and Rasteau.

Whereas many Côtes du Rhône wines are relatively simple and fruity and are meant to be consumed in their first two years, Côtes du Rhône-Villages wines are usually more concentrated and complex, and they can age for up to eight years.

Certain villages that were formerly part of the Côtes du Rhône-Villages group have "graduated," and their own village name now appears on the label without the designation Côtes du Rhône-Villages. One such wine is Gigondas *(jhee gohn dahs)*, which sells in the $15 to $18 range, a particularly robust and long-lived red (ten years or more in good vintages). Another is Vacqueyras *(vah keh rahs)*, a wine that's a bit lighter but also less expensive (about $10).

Côtes du Ventoux

Another area of the southern Rhône that is a reliable source of inexpensive red wines is Côtes du Ventoux *(vahn too)*. Wines from this area are very similar to Côtes du Rhône but perhaps are a bit lighter bodied; they sell for $6 to $7 per bottle. Paul Jaboulet Aîné is one Côtes du Ventoux producer to seek out.

Châteauneuf-du-Pape

The most important, and probably the most renowned, red wine in the southern Rhône is Châteauneuf-du-Pape *(shah toe nuf dew pahp)*. (A little white Châteauneuf-du-Pape is also made; see *White Wine For Dummies.*) Red Châteauneuf-du-Pape wine can derive from as many as 13 grape varieties, but in practice Grenache, Mourvèdre, and Syrah predominate. One of the amazing features of the sunny vineyards of Châteauneuf-du-Pape is the very large stones that form their "soil." The hardy grapes manage to not only survive, but also thrive, in this terrain.

Châteauneuf-du-Pape at its best is a rich, full-bodied wine that is fairly high in alcohol (12.5 to 14 percent) and that, in good vintages, ages and improves for 15 to 20 years. Most Châteauneuf-du-Pape wines are in the $18 to $25 price range, not bad for wines of such quality.

Table 11-4 lists five outstanding Châteauneuf-du-Pape producers.

Table 11-4   Five Outstanding Châteauneuf-du-Pape Producers

Producer	Comments
Château Rayas	Very old vines, 100 percent Grenache
Château de Beaucastel	Perhaps the longest-lived
Chapoutier	Especially since 1989
Domaine de la Janasse	An up-and-coming producer
Vieux Telegraphe	Highly reliable

Recent good vintages in the southern Rhône

The southern Rhône and the northern Rhône have distinctly different microclimates; therefore, vintages differ. Both **1989** and **1990** were outstanding vintages in the southern Rhône, and 1988 and 1994 were good, as was the 1993. The **1995** vintage shows the potential to rival the '89 and '90 vintages in quality.

The majestic northern Rhône reds

Although the northern part of the Rhône Valley produces far less wine than the southern part, the two best red wines of the entire Rhône Valley wine region, Côte Rôtie *(coat roe tee)* and Hermitage *(er mee tajh)*, come from the north. Both are made from the noble Syrah grape variety (although a little white Viognier, pronounced *vee ohn yay,* is sometimes added to Côte Rôtie). Hermitage and Côte Rôtie are two of the best examples in the world of Syrah — only Australia's best Syrah-based wines (called Shiraz) can rival these two northern Rhône wines in quality. (See Chapter 9 for more information about Australian Shiraz.)

Côte Rôtie

Both Côte Rôtie and Hermitage are rich, full-bodied wines, but the former emphasizes finesse and elegance a bit more. Côte Rôtie wines have marvelously fragrant aromas, often reminiscent of green olives, and soft, lush, ripe, black raspberry fruit flavors. In good vintages, they can age for 20 years or more.

Guigal is the most renowned Côte Rôtie producer; his single-vineyard wines — La Mouline, La Landonne, and La Turque — are truly outstanding, if prohibitively expensive ($125 per bottle). Most Côte Rôtie wines sell in the $25 to $45 price range. Besides Guigal, other outstanding producers of Côte Rôtie (in alphabetical order) are

- Gilles Barge
- Pierre Barge
- Alain Burgaud
- Chapoutier
- Clusel-Roch
- Henri Gallet
- Gentaz-Dervieux
- Jamet
- Michel Ogier
- René Rostaing
- Vidal-Fleury

Hermitage

Red Hermitage wines (a lesser-known white Hermitage also exists; see *White Wine For Dummies*) are the sturdiest, most long-lived wines of the Rhône Valley. Hermitage is more tannic, more full bodied, and more black peppery than Côte Rôtie, but in other respects the wines are similar. In good vintages, Hermitage wines need about 15 years to mature, and these wines can age for 30 years or more.

Most red Hermitages sell in the $25 to $55 price range. Some of the best Hermitage producers include

- ✔ Jean Louis Chave
- ✔ Chapoutier
- ✔ Ferraton Père et Fils
- ✔ Paul Jaboulet Aîné (for his best Hermitage, "La Chapelle")
- ✔ Henri Sorrel

Cornas, Crozes-Hermitage, and St. Joseph

Côte Rôtie and Hermitage are not the only wines of the northern Rhône, however. Three other important wines are Cornas, Crozes-Hermitage, and St. Joseph, all made entirely from the Syrah grape. Cornas is the sturdiest, most tannic, and long-lived (20 years or more) of the three. In many ways, Cornas resembles the more expensive Hermitage, but Cornas is more rustic and never quite develops the extraordinary bouquet or complex flavors of Hermitage.

The wines of Cornas are in the $20 to $30 price range. Some of the best Cornas producers include

- ✔ August Clape
- ✔ Alain Voge
- ✔ Noel Verset
- ✔ Marcel Juge
- ✔ Robert Michel

Both Crozes-Hermitage and St. Joseph are medium-bodied wines that can be enjoyed within five to eight years of the vintage (although Jaboulet's excellent Crozes-Hermitage, Domaine de Thalabert, can be more long-lived). Most Crozes-Hermitage and St. Joseph wines are in the $15 to $20 price range.

Recent good vintages in the northern Rhône

The northern Rhône has experienced a string of excellent vintages for its red wines: **1988**, **1989**, **1990**, and **1991**, with 1989 particularly fine for Hermitage and 1991 outstanding for Côte Rôtie. 1994 is also quite good, as were the 1983 and 1985 vintages. And at this point, **1995** looks as if it will be a fine vintage for northern Rhône wines as well.

Rhône wines with food

 Most Rhône red wines are hearty, warming, and generous and are best suited for sturdy foods, such as steaks, roasts, stews, and cassoulet. The (relatively) lighter-bodied Rhônes, such as Côtes du Rhône and Côtes du Ventoux wines, are fine with hamburgers, chicken, or pizza.

The Lighter Red Wines of the Loire Valley

Although the cool Loire Valley is better known for its white wines, some very interesting, light- to medium-bodied red wines exist here.

The best Loire reds come from the Touraine region (named after the city of Tours) in the central Loire Valley and are made mainly from the Cabernet Franc grape, with up to 10 percent Cabernet Sauvignon allowed. These wines include

- Chinon *(she nohn)*
- Bourgueil *(bor goye)*
- Saint-Nicolas-de-Borgueil *(san nih coh lahs deh bor goye)*

These wines have fragrant aromas, frequently suggestive of raspberries and/or violets, and fairly high acidity, combined with the characteristic vegetal flavors of Cabernet Franc — often reminiscent of green bell peppers.

 Loire red wines are generally meant to be consumed when they are young, although the more rustic wines of Bourgueil often improve with a few years of aging. Look especially for the Chinon of Charles Joguet (up to the 1993 vintage), the region's best producer. Prices range from $6 for the simplest Loire reds to $18.

Three excellent vintages for the Loire red wines are 1988, **1989**, and **1990** (the 1990 is especially great), and **1995** looks to be of the same high quality. 1993 is also quite good. Roast chicken, duck, pork, and rabbit, plus chèvres and sheep-milk cheeses, are the traditional foods to enjoy with these wines.

France's Wine Lake: Languedoc-Roussillon

The sunny, dry Languedoc-Roussillon *(lahn gweh doc roo see yon)* region of southern France, also known as the Midi *(mee dee)*, produces more than half of France's red wines. If quantity were the sole consideration, this region would be the most famous wine region in all of France. In reality, however, the wines from this area are not well known because for most of the region's history, Languedoc-Roussillon wines were of mediocre quality and were seldom exported.

But a revolution has been taking place in Languedoc-Roussillon during the past ten years. Modern winemaking technology, a new quality consciousness on the part of some producers, and a large-scale replanting of vineyards with higher quality grapes has changed the face of Languedoc-Roussillon reds. As a result, these inexpensive wines (most are under $10) are now readily available outside France.

The traditional red grape varieties in Languedoc-Roussillon are

- ✔ Carignan
- ✔ Cinsault
- ✔ Grenache

Nowadays, more and more Syrah, Mourvèdre, Cabernet Sauvignon, and Merlot vines are being used.

Some of the more popular red wines from the region include Corbières and Minervois, both from the traditional local grape varieties. Many small wine estates make good examples of these and other traditional wines, which are usually full bodied and intensely flavored. Other small producers, such as the excellent Mas-de-Daumas Gassac property, base their wines on Cabernet Sauvignon or other grapes not traditional to the area.

Increasingly important in terms of export are the many clean, well-made red wines varietally labelled with the names of famous newcomer grapes such as Cabernet Sauvignon, Merlot, and Syrah. These wines, usually made by very large wineries, sell in the $6 to $10 price range and carry on their labels the *table wine* appellation of Vin de Pays d'Oc. (Refer to Chapter 8 of *Wine For Dummies* to find out the precise meaning that the French and other Europeans give to the term "table wine.") Two well-known brands of inexpensive red varietal wines from Languedoc-Roussillon are Fortant de France and Réserve St. Martin.

Chapter 12

Vino Rosso, Vino Tinto, Vinho Tinto

● ●

In This Chapter

▶ Some of our favorite wines are Italian

▶ The home of Chianti and his big brother

▶ Bullish on Spanish reds

▶ Portuguese red wines: Still great values

● ●

*E*urope produces 75 percent of the world's wine. Logically, the two countries that lead the world in red wine production — France and Italy — are situated there. Other countries might be catching up, but these two have had a big head start: Italy, like France, has been making wine for over 2,000 years.

In Chapters 10 and 11, we discuss the famous red wines of France — wines made from grape varieties that are familiar to many wine drinkers, such as Cabernet Sauvignon, Merlot, Pinot Noir, and Syrah. Italy has her own unique grape varieties; as a result, most Italian red wines are completely different from French wines and from other wines of the world made with "French" grapes.

Perhaps the greatest thing about Italian red wines is how well they go with Italian food. (Do you know anybody who doesn't like Italian cuisine? We would never associate with such a person!)

Talking about wonderful food, when was the last time you had that delicious Spanish specialty, paella — or perhaps a plate of Spanish seafood or chicken with rice and beans? You may have enjoyed a pitcher of Sangria (red wine with fruits) with it, a real treat in warm weather. But Spain does make more serious red wines, too, such as Rioja — which also happen to be terrific red wines with food.

On Portugal's wine scene, the times they are a-changin'. Although Portugal has always been acclaimed for great-value red wines, her winemaking methods were somewhat old-fashioned until recently. You can now find dramatically improved Portuguese red wines, and they still are fine values.

We end this chapter with a reference to some really inexpensive red wines from Eastern European countries.

The Wonder of Italy

Italy is a truly amazing country. It's smaller than the state of California, and about two-thirds of the country is mountainous, yet it leads the world in wine production (and is second to France in per capita wine consumption).

As you travel throughout Italy, you see grapevines — along with olive trees — almost everywhere you see soil. We can't remember a lunch or dinner in Italy at which wine was not served. Wine is as much a part of an Italian's life as those other essentials: air, water, bread, cheese, and family.

Because Italy's terrain is so varied — from coastlines to plains and hills to mountains — each tiny section of the country has its own particular combination of soil and climate, and therefore its own unique wines. The number of different types of red wine in Italy is mind-boggling.

Like French wines, Italian wines are named after the place where the grapes grow, such as Chianti (see Figure 12-1) or Valpolicella. Some wines have names that combine the grape variety name and the place, such as Barbera (the grape) d'Alba (of Alba, the place).

Because many of the grapes used to make Italian wines are varieties of purely local importance, we suggest that you not become fixated on grape varieties when exploring Italy's wines — unless you plan to become an Italian wine specialist or are a dedicated collector of wine trivia.

Italy's 20 regions all make red wine, but two regions are famous for their red wines: Piedmont and Tuscany. We discuss the wines of those two regions in some depth in the sections that follow.

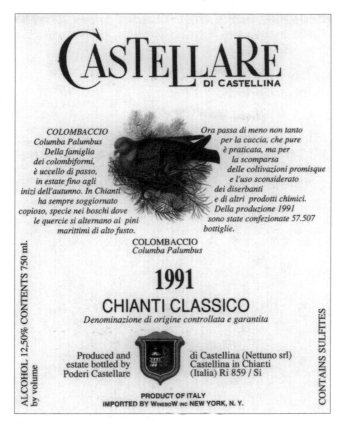

Figure 12-1: Italian wines are named after the place where the grapes grow — in this case, the Chianti Classico district.

Piedmont Reds: From Simple to Monumental

The Piedmont region in northwestern Italy, bordering France and Switzerland, is home to some of the greatest and most unique red wines — not just in Italy but in the world. Much of the Piedmont region is actually the foothills of the mighty Alps — and it is in these foothills that Piedmont's best red grapes grow. A district in southeast Piedmont called the Langhe *(LAHN gay)* hills, around the town of Alba, is particularly important for red wine.

The majestic Barolo *(bah RO lo)* and Barbaresco *(bar bah RES co)* wines come from the Langhe hills, as do three important, "everyday" red wines:

- ✔ Barbera *(bar BEAR ah)*
- ✔ Dolcetto *(dohl CHET oh)*
- ✔ Nebbiolo *(neb bee OH lo)*

(These three names are the names of the grape varieties from which each wine is made; on their actual labels, each wine has a proper name that includes the place where the grapes for that wine grow, such as Barbera d'Alba, as shown in Figure 12-2.)

Figure 12-2: This label gives the name of the grape variety as well as the name of the place where the grapes grow.

Dolcetto, Barbera, and Nebbiolo grow in other parts of the Piedmont region besides the Alba zone. Six other distinct wine zones exist for Dolcetto, and two others for Barbera. In addition, the Novara-Vercelli hills of northeastern Piedmont make an important Nebbiolo-based wine called Gattinara *(gah tee NAH rah)*.

The Piedmontese people drink their finest red wines, Barolo and Barbaresco, on special occasions or for Sunday dinners. Their *everyday* red wines are Dolcetto, Barbera, and Nebbiolo. These three wines retail mainly in the $10 to $15 range in the United States. You can find some for under $10, and a few Barberas do cost over $20.

Dolcetto: Young, fun, and dry

Dolcetto is a medium-bodied, dry wine with somewhat grapey flavors, low acidity, and quite a bit of tannin. The Piedmontese usually serve Dolcetto as their first red wine in a dinner, often with pasta or risotto but sometimes as an aperitivo, before dinner, accompanied by prosciutto.

Some of the best Dolcetto wines come from the Alba district and are called Dolcetto d'Alba. Although weather in that area can be variable from year to year, vintage variation is less of a problem for Dolcetto than for wines such as Barolo and Barbaresco, because Dolcetto grapes are harvested quite early and usually escape potentially damaging late-season weather.

We recommend that you drink Dolcetto while it is young — within three or four years of the vintage. Our recommended Barolo or Barbaresco producers, listed later in this chapter, are reliable for Dolcetto as well.

Barbera: The perfect everyday red

Barbera wine is very popular in Italy; in fact, the Barbera grape, along with Tuscany's Sangiovese grape, is the most widely planted grape variety — red or white — in the country.

If we had to nominate just one wine as our favorite, everyday red, it would be Barbera. We love its rich, tart-cherry, fruity flavors and cleansing acidity. We find Barberas especially appealing with pastas, pizza, or any tomato-based dish, but they're versatile wines that you can enjoy with all sorts of foods.

We particularly like Barbera wines from the Alba and Asti zones (the wines are called Barbera d'Alba and Barbera d'Asti, respectively). Most of these wines are unoaked wines; they are either made entirely in stainless steel tanks or are made in old oak casks that give practically no oak character to the wine. Besides having no oaky character, Barbera wines have crisp acidity and hardly any tannin. (Barbera is unusual among red grapes because it has very little tannin.)

Some producers age their Barbera in small barrels of French oak, which impart oaky flavors and complexity to the wine and increase the wine's tannin; oak-aged Barberas can be expensive ($20 to $35).

These Barbera vintages are especially good: 1988, **1989**, **1990**, and 1993, with **1995** promising to be excellent. Barbera is enjoyable in its youth, when it is first released two years after the vintage, but it is capable of aging for ten or more years in good vintages. Table 12-1 shows six of our very favorite Barbera producers and their wines.

Table 12-1   Recommended Barbera Producers and Their Wines

Producer	Wine(s)
Vietti	Barbera d'Alba, Scarrone or Bussia (single-vineyards)
Giacomo Conterno	Barbera d'Alba
Giuseppe Mascarello	Barbera d'Alba (any of his Barberas)
Giuseppe Rinaldi	Barbera d'Alba
Angelo Gaja	Barbera d'Alba "Vignarey" (oak-aged)
Giacomo Bologna	Barbera di Rocchetta Tanaro "Bricco dell'Uccellone" or "Bricco della Bigotta" (both are from the Asti area; they are oak-aged)

Nebbiolo: Baby Barolo

If you want to experience Piedmont's Nebbiolo grape without paying the hefty price of Barolo wine or Barbaresco wine — the two loftiest examples of this grape variety — buy a simple Nebbiolo wine. (These wines are named Nebbiolo d'Alba or sometimes Nebbiolo Langhe.)

The grapes for the more simple Nebbiolo wines are grown outside the official Barolo and Barbaresco districts, and the wines are, therefore, less intense and not so complex. But they can be excellent buys ($10 to $15), especially in the better vintages (look for them in 1988, **1989**, **1990**, and 1993 — and **1995** when it's released). Drink Nebbiolo wines within five or six years of the vintage (in good vintage years, they are capable of aging a few more years).

Nebbiolo wines, which are light to medium bodied, are fine with pastas and meat sauce, with chicken, or with veal. Our recommended Barolo or Barbaresco producers, listed later in this chapter, are reliable for Nebbiolo as well.

Nebbiolo: Tar and roses

The Nebbiolo grape is named after the Italian word *nebbia*, which means "fog" — a climatic condition that's common in the hills of Piedmont in the mornings and evenings of the long, rather warm, moist autumns. Growing conditions in Piedmont apparently suit the Nebbiolo grape ideally, because Piedmont is the only place on Earth that is truly successful in growing this grape variety.

Nebbiolo produces sturdy, very dry, full-bodied wines, with typically high alcohol (13 to 14 percent), high tannin, and high acidity levels. Tar and roses are just two of the many aromas that wines made from Nebbiolo can develop. Although Nebbiolo-based wines are a deep ruby color when young, they normally develop a garnet or brick-red rim as they age.

The two big B's of Piedmont

Barolo and Barbaresco are the twin stars of Piedmont, and these wines are two of the greatest red wines in all of Italy. Each wine is named after a village situated within that wine's production zone, and each is made entirely from the Nebbiolo grape. The Barolo and Barbaresco wine zones are close to each other; Barbaresco is slightly northeast of the town of Alba, and Barolo lies southwest of Alba.

Barolo and Barbaresco are two of the most robust, driest red wines in the world. They are also probably the two least appreciated great red wines in the world because they are normally not easy to drink when they are young; their tannins need the softening that age brings. After you taste a mature Barolo or Barbaresco from a good producer, however, you can recognize the greatness of these wines.

In addition to inaccessibility in their youth, Barolo and Barbaresco present another handicap to wine drinkers — one that these wines share with France's Burgundies: You simply must know who the good producers are to buy a great wine (especially true for Barolo).

Barolo and Barbaresco producers, in fact, resemble Burgundy producers more so than Bordeaux producers with regard to the size of their production. The typical Barolo/Barbaresco producer makes only about 2,000 to 3,000 cases of either wine each year. As a result, good Barolo and Barbaresco wines will always be scarce.

Your best bet is to buy these wines soon after they are released for sale (about three years after the vintage for Barbaresco and four years after the vintage for Barolo) and age them yourself.

Enjoying Barolo and Barbaresco

Because Barolo and Barbaresco come from the same grape variety, grown in areas that are relatively close to each other, they are quite similar in style. Both are complex, richly textured wines with aromas suggesting tar, violets, roses, camphor, licorice, ripe strawberries, and sometimes even white truffles.

Both wines are at their best after many years of aging — often ten or more years in good vintages. (Some producers age their wine in barrels of French oak, however, resulting in somewhat atypical wines that mature more quickly.) Barolo is somewhat fuller bodied than Barbaresco and usually requires a little more aging.

To learn whether a particular producer of Barolo and Barbaresco is a traditionalist, whose wines mature slowly, or a modernist, whose wines are approachable sooner, see Chapter 11 of our book *Wine For Dummies*.

Like most Italian red wines, Barolo and Barbaresco really are at their best when accompanied by food. Both Barolo and Barbaresco are excellent with roasted meats, such as beef, especially when the meat is cooked in the same wine. (To cut costs, we often use Barbera to cook the meat.) Also try them with game, such as venison, boar, or rabbit; with flavorful game birds, such as pheasant or duck; or with hard cheeses, such as fontina, Gouda, or cheddar.

Because they are such sturdy, tannic wines, Barolo and Barbaresco benefit from a few hours of aeration before drinking, especially if they are younger than six years old. (See Chapter 6 of *Wine For Dummies,* or the sidebar "To decant or not to decant" in Chapter 5 of this book, for information about why and how to aerate wine.)

Most good Barolos and Barbarescos sell in the $25 to $45 price range; a few of the very best are more expensive.

Both Barolo and Barbaresco experienced three great vintages in a row recently: 1988 and especially **1989** and **1990**. You can still find a few wines from these vintages in some retail stores. **1985** was also excellent; 1993 was good; **1995** will be very fine, but will not be in the stores until 1998 (in the case of Barbaresco) and 1999 (in the case of Barolo).

Piedmont: Our second home

Those who know us know how much we love Piedmont. We visit there more than any other wine region in the world because we love the wine, the food, the people, and the beautiful landscape. Tucked away in a remote corner of Italy, Piedmont is off the beaten tourist track — which we like. It has no Rome, Florence, or Venice to attract hoards of tourists from all over the world. The hard-working, humble, friendly Piedmontese people are proud of their wine and food (with good reason). Go there in the autumn for a plate of pasta covered with white truffles and a bottle of Barbera in one of the region's outstanding restaurants. You will say to yourself (or anyone else who is listening), "This is what life is all about."

Recommended Barolo wines

Many producers make more than one Barolo wine each year. Some wines are made from the grapes of a specific vineyard, and the vineyard name is indicated on the label; other wines are made from the grapes of several vineyards, and no vineyard name appears on the label. Wines labeled *riserva* are aged longer before release (and, presumably, are better wines worthy of that longer aging).

In Table 12-2, we list our recommended Barolo wines in rough order of preference. (Because many producers make multiple wines, their names can appear at multiple points on our list of preferred wines.) The vineyard name of each wine, if any, follows the wine name.

Check our recommended vintages — either from our suggestions earlier in this chapter or in Appendix D — when selecting these wines. When we believe that a producer has made a very good Barolo in a less than stellar vintage, we indicate that information in the table.

As an introductory wine to some of the superb Barolos listed in Table 12-2, we recommend that you try 1990 Le Terre del Barolo (about $15). This Barolo is a lighter-bodied version of the preceding wines and is drinkable now; otherwise, its characteristics are similar to the more expensive Barolos in Table 12-2. It's a particularly good buy in a great vintage, such as 1990.

Table 12-2	Recommended Barolo Wines
Producer	*Recommended Wine(s)*
Giuseppe Mascarello	Barolo Monprivato (good in 1991, also)
Giacomo Conterno	Barolo Riserva "Monfortino" (good in 1987, also)
Vietti	Barolo Riserva Villero (especially the 1990) Barolo Rocche Barolo Lazzarito
Giacomo Conterno	Barolo "Cascina Francia"
Giuseppe Rinaldi	Barolo Brunate (good 1983 and 1986, also)
Bartolo Mascarello	Barolo (good 1986, also)

Producer	Recommended Wine(s)
Bruno Giacosa	Barolo Rionda di Serralunga Barolo Falletto di Serralunga
Ceretto	Barolo Bricco Rocche (especially the 1990)
Aldo Conterno	Barolo Bussia Soprana Barolo, Vigna Colonnello (small-production wine) Barolo, Vigna Cicala (small-production wine) Barolo, Granbussia (small-production wine)
Angelo Gaja	Barolo Sperss (good 1991, also)
Pio Cesare	Barolo Ornato (especially 1990)
Giuseppe Mascarello	Barolo Villero
Ceretto	Barolo Brunate Barolo Prapó
Carretta	Barolo Cannubi
Renato Ratti	Barolo Marcenasco
Prunotto	Barolo Bussia Barolo Cannubi
Luciano Sandrone	Barolo Cannubi Boschis (difficult to find)
Paolo Scavino	Barolo Bric' del Fiasc'
Manzone	Barolo Gramolere
Pio Cesare	Barolo
Marcarini	Barolo Brunate Barolo La Serra
Roberto Voerzio	Barolo Cerequio Barolo Brunate Barolo La Serra
Fontanafredda	Barolo Vigna La Rosa
Marchesi di Barolo	Barolo Cannubi Barolo Sarmassa
Conterno-Fantino	Barolo Sori' Ginestra Barolo Vigna de Gris

Recommended Barbaresco wines

As with Barolo, many producers of Barbaresco make more than one Barbaresco wine each year. Some wines are made from the grapes of a specific vineyard, and the vineyard name is indicated on the label; other wines are made from the grapes of several vineyards, and no vineyard name appears on the label. Wines labeled *riserva* are aged longer before release (and, presumably, are better wines worthy of that longer aging).

In Table 12-3, we list our recommended Barbaresco wines in rough order of preference. The vineyard name of each wine (if any) follows the wine name. Check our recommended vintages when selecting these wines.

Table 12-3	Recommended Barbaresco Wines
Producer	*Recommended Wine(s)*
Bruno Giacosa	Barbaresco Riserva Santo Stefano
Angelo Gaja	Barbaresco Sori' San Lorenzo Barbaresco Sori' Tildin
Ceretto	Barbaresco Bricco Asili
Marchesi di Gresy	Barbaresco Cru Gaiun Barbaresco Camp Gros
Cigliuti	Barbaresco Serraboella
Angelo Gaja	Barbaresco
Moccagatta	Barbaresco Basarin Barbaresco Cole
Produttori del Barbaresco	Barbaresco Asili Barbaresco Rabajá
Bruno Giacosa	Barbaresco Gallina di Neive
Ceretto	Barbaresco Faset
Marchesi di Gresy	Barbaresco Martinenga
Castello di Neive	Barbaresco Santo Stefano

Another good (and less expensive) Piedmontese red

 Barolo and Barbaresco get most of the attention from wine critics, but Gattinara, which always derives at least 90 percent from the Nebbiolo grape, is the best buy of the "serious" red Piedmontese wines. Gattinara offers most of the wonderful aromas and flavors of its more famous brothers, but in a more reasonable price range ($15 to $20). Gattinara wines are somewhat lighter bodied than Barolo and Barbaresco wines, however. On the other hand, they are more approachable.

 Two Gattinara producers to look for are Antoniolo and Travaglini, in the same vintages that we recommend for Barolo and Barbaresco (listed earlier in this chapter).

In northeastern Piedmont, in the vicinity of the town of Gattinara, the Nebbiolo grape goes by the local name of Spanna *(SPAH nah)*. Some wines from that general area that are not made specifically in the Gattinara zone carry the grape name, Spanna.

Tuscany: The Home of Chianti

Wine producers in California and Washington have discovered the Sangiovese grape, and several of them now make Sangiovese wines (we discuss them in Chapter 7). To experience Sangiovese at its best, however, you must try the red wines from the region of Tuscany, in north-central Italy.

Sangiovese has always been the main grape in Chianti wine. The permissible blend has changed gradually over the years, and now Italian wine regulations allow some Chianti wines (specifically those from the district known as Chianti Classico) to be made entirely from the Sangiovese grape. Sangiovese clearly is a grape whose star is on the rise, not only in the United States but also on its home turf.

The Chianti production zone, in central Tuscany, has the great city of Florence at its northern border and Florence's traditional rival, the colorful old city of Siena, at its southern end. This large wine zone has seven districts:

✔ The greatest district is *Chianti Classico*, in the heart of the Chianti zone; most of the renowned Chianti wines are made from grapes grown on the hillsides of the Classico district. (Such wines are labeled "Chianti Classico.")

✔ The only Chianti district that rivals Chianti Classico in quality is *Chianti Rufina* (pronounced *ROO fee nah*).

✔ Five additional districts are entitled to append their name to the word Chianti, for example *Chianti Colli Senesi*; these wines are rarely seen outside Italy, and so we don't bother to list them here.

✔ The lightest, most inexpensive Chianti wines carry the simple designation Chianti (without reference to a specific district).

Chianti is a very dry red wine with aromas of cherries and violets, flavors of tart cherries, and very high acidity. Many different versions of Chianti exist, from very light-bodied wines to rather intense, fuller-bodied wines. Some of the better Chianti wines age about a year longer than other Chiantis before release, to earn the designation *riserva*. (Some *riserva* Chiantis age in French oak barrels — barrels made from oak grown in French forests, considered the finest oak for wine barrels — resulting in a particularly intense style.)

The finest Chianti wines usually are at their best from five to eight years after the vintage, but they can age for ten years or more in good vintages. Riserva wines are capable of aging a bit longer, beyond ten years. The lightest wines (those simply labeled "Chianti") are ready to drink when they are released, usually just a year after the vintage. (For a further description of Chianti, see "Chianti, Il Magnifico" in Chapter 4.)

Chianti wines are still wonderful values. Simple Chianti wines sell for as low as $6, while Chianti Classico and Chianti Rufina wines cost $10 to $15. Riservas can range in price from $11 or $12 to about $18.

Recent great vintages for Chianti are the **1985**, **1988**, and **1990**. **1995** also will be very fine, while 1991 and 1993 are fairly good.

Recommended Chianti producers

Most Chianti producers make several different Chianti wines. Depending on how large a producer is, he or she might make a simple Chianti, one or two Chianti Classicos (with different vineyard or estate designations; some producers own several different properties), and one or two Chianti Classico Riservas (each from grapes of a different vineyard or estate).

In the following two lists, we do not indicate individual wines (too many exist), but we list producers whom we recommend. In our experience, every Chianti from the better producers is good, for its style. All but three of the producers we list make Chianti Classico (the three Chianti Rufina producers are identified).

We divided our favorite Chianti producers into two groups, and we list them alphabetically in each group. Although we slightly prefer the producers in the first group, do not hesitate to buy a Chianti from a producer in either group; we think that they all are good. Please forgive us if we have left out one of your favorite producers.

- ✔ Antinori
- ✔ Badia a Coltibuono
- ✔ Brolio (since 1993)
- ✔ Castell'in Villa
- ✔ Castellare
- ✔ Castello dei Rampolla
- ✔ Castello di Fonterutoli
- ✔ Castello di Volpaia
- ✔ Fattoria di Felsina
- ✔ Fontodi
- ✔ Monte Vertine
- ✔ Podere Il Palazzino
- ✔ Ruffino
- ✔ San Giusto a Rentennano

More good Chianti producers include the following:

- ✔ Castello di Ama
- ✔ Castello di Cacchiano
- ✔ Castello di Gabbiano
- ✔ Dievole
- ✔ Frescobaldi (Chianti Rufina)
- ✔ Isole e Olena
- ✔ Melini

- Monsanto
- Renzo Masi (Chianti Rufina)
- San Felice
- Selvapiana (Chianti Rufina)
- Villa Cafaggio
- Villa Cerna
- Viticcio

The "super-Tuscan" red wines

When the Chianti region was suffering economically in the 1970s, innovative producers such as Piero Antinori, Marchesi Incisa della Rocchetta (Antinori's cousin), and the Castello dei Rampolla winery stimulated sales by creating new wines that, for lack of a better name, are referred to as super-Tuscan wines. (Later, Lodovico Antinori, Piero's younger brother, began his own winery, where he makes his own super-Tuscan wine.)

Most of these wines are blends of internationally known grape varieties, chiefly Cabernet Sauvignon (but in some cases Cabernet Franc, Merlot, and even Syrah), with the traditional grape of the region, Sangiovese. Some of these wines are made entirely from Sangiovese (thus departing from the legal Chianti grape blend at that time).

The pioneering super-Tuscan wines, still perhaps the most famous of what is now a large number of wines, are the following:

- **Antinori:** "Tignanello" and "Solaia"
- **Incisa della Rocchetta:** "Sassicaia"
- **Castello dei Rampolla:** "Sammarco"
- **Lodovico Antinori:** "Ornellaia"

What all the super-Tuscan wines have in common, besides high quality, is that they are expensive and often difficult to obtain because they're made in small quantities. These wines range in price from $30 to $40 per bottle retail — and up to $75 to $125 for the most sought-after wines, such as Sassicaia and Solaia. In prized vintages such as 1985, the latter two wines can cost as much as $200 a bottle. (1988 and 1990 are two other fine vintages for these wines.)

Now that the Chianti region and its namesake wine have recovered economically, the expensive super-Tuscan wines are less important. But most major Chianti producers still make at least one of these wines. We have two particular favorite super-Tuscan wines, both made from 100 percent Sangiovese grapes and aged in French oak barrels:

- ✓ **Monte Vertine:** "Le Pergole Torte"
- ✓ **San Giusto a Rentennano:** "Percarlo"

At $35 to $40, these two wines are not so expensive as some of the other super-Tuscans, and we believe that they are among Tuscany's finest wines. Look for them in the 1990, 1993, and 1995 vintages (the latter available around 1999).

Just as you would do with young Barolos or Barbarescos, we recommend that you decant young super-Tuscan wines several hours before serving. They improve with aeration.

Chianti's big brother: Brunello di Montalcino

South of the Chianti region is the majestic old fortress town of Montalcino, which gives its name to two wines based on the Sangiovese grape:

- ✓ Brunello di Montalcino
- ✓ Rosso di Montalcino

In the Montalcino area, a subvariety of the Sangiovese grape called Sangiovese Grosso (and formerly called Brunello) makes fuller-bodied, more intense, more complex, longer-lived wine than Chianti. The wine known as Brunello di Montalcino *(brew NEL lo dee mon tahl CHEE no)*, in fact, is not only Italy's but also one of the world's longest-lived red wines. Together with Piedmont's big two "B" wines (Barolo and Barbaresco), Brunello completes the triumvirate of Italy's truly classic red wines.

Brunello di Montalcino resembles a Chianti on steroids. It's a muscular, concentrated, tannic wine that demands aging (at least 20 years or more in good vintages). The 1975 vintage of Brunello, for example, is finally drinking well now. Brunello di Montalcino normally needs several hours of aeration before serving, especially when it is young.

Most good Brunellos sell in the $30 to $50 price range, although you can find a few for around $25. The riserva versions are more expensive. The two most expensive Brunello di Montalcino wines — that of Biondi-Santi and Soldera's Case

Basse — usually cost over $100 per bottle! (The Biondi-Santi family "created" Brunello di Montalcino in the 19th century; their 1891 Brunello is legendary.)

If you don't have the patience — or don't want to invest the money — for Brunello di Montalcino, we heartily recommend that you try the "junior" version of Brunello, called Rosso di Montalcino. This wine is made entirely from Sangiovese Grosso grapes from the same vineyards that produce Brunello, but usually from younger vines whose fruit is not yet of the very finest quality.

Rosso di Montalcino is a lighter-bodied, less complex, less expensive ($10 to $15), readier-to-drink edition of its more well-known sibling. We believe that Rosso di Montalcino wines are among the world's best red wine values. And you don't have to age them; drink them within eight years of the vintage. Try a Rosso di Montalcino from any of the recommended Brunello producers listed in the next section.

Recommended Brunello di Montalcino producers

In the following list, alphabetically within two groups, are our favorite producers of Brunello di Montalcino. We have a slight preference for the producers in the first group, but their wines do tend to be more expensive than those in the second group. Like Chianti wines, Brunellos were great in **1985**, **1988**, and especially **1990**. 1991 was fairly good, 1993 was good (not available until 1997 or 1998), and **1995** will be excellent (available in 1999 or 2000).

Our very favorite Brunello di Montalcino producers include

- ✔ Altesino, for the Montosoli vineyard bottling
- ✔ Biondi-Santi
- ✔ Caparzo, for the wine called "La Casa"
- ✔ Case Basse (producer, Soldera)
- ✔ Ciacci Piccolomini, for the Pianrosso vineyard and regular Brunello wines
- ✔ Costanti
- ✔ Pertimali (producer, Sassetti)

- Poggio Antico
- Il Poggione
- La Torre

More of our favorite Brunello di Montalcino producers include

- Altesino, for his regular and riserva Brunello wines
- Argiano
- Castello Banfi
- Fattoria dei Barbi
- Campogiovanni (producer, San Felice of Chianti Classico)
- Caparzo, for his regular and riserva Brunello wines
- Castelgiocondo (producer, Frescobaldi of Chianti Rufina)
- Col d'Orcia
- Il Greppone Mazzi
- Lisini
- Pieve Santa Restituta (producer, Angelo Gaja)
- Val di Suga

Two other noteworthy Tuscan reds

Vino Nobile di Montepulciano *(NO be lay dee mon tay pul chee AH no)* and Carmignano *(car mee NYAH no)* are two other Tuscan reds worth trying.

The vineyards around Montepulciano, a town southeast of the Chianti zone, make a wine similar to Chianti from a Sangiovese subvariety locally called Prugnolo Gentile. The best producers of Vino Nobile, such as Avignonesi, Boscarelli, Dei, and Poliziano, make wines that can rival the better Chianti Classicos at about the same price. Good vintage years are the same as in the Chianti and Brunello zones. Vino Nobile producers also make a Rosso di Montepulciano: a less expensive, lighter, readier-to-drink version of Vino Nobile di Montepulciano.

The Carmignano wine zone lies in the northern part of Tuscany, west of Florence. Carmignano wine is predominantly from the Sangiovese grape, but Cabernet Sauvignon can legally be blended (up to 10 percent) into this finesseful wine. The two fine producers of Carmignano are Villa di Capezzana and Ambra. Good vintage years are the same as in the Chianti region, and prices for Carmignano are similar to those of Chianti Classico.

Red Tuscan wines with food

Light-bodied, inexpensive Chianti wines and Rosso (di Montalcino or di Montepulciano) wines are fine with hamburgers or pasta with meat sauce. Younger Chianti Classico wines, Vino Nobile, and Carmignano are excellent with roast chicken and other poultry dishes. With Chianti Classico Riservas and mature Chianti wines, steak or prime ribs go very well, as does that wonderful Italian cheese, Parmigiano Reggiano. Tuscans also enjoy their fuller Chianti Riservas with game, such as wild boar. Brunello di Montalcino calls for steak, game birds (such as pheasant), game (such as venison), or aged cheeses, such as Gouda or Parmigiano.

Elsewhere in Italy . . .

Italy makes so much wine, especially red, that it's impossible to highlight all of this country's wonderful wines. In this section, we mention some of the other important or interesting red wines from Italy's various regions, starting in the north and working our way down to Sicily.

The Veneto region

The Veneto wine region of northeast Italy, centered around the picturesque old city of Verona and beautiful Lake Garda, is one of Italy's largest wine-producing areas. Chianti might be Italy's most famous red wine, but two red wines from the Veneto, Valpolicella *(val po lee CHEL lah)* and Bardolino *(bar doe LEE noh)*, certainly vie with Chianti in worldwide popularity.

Valpolicella is a dry, light- to medium-bodied wine that is best when consumed within four or five years. Bardolino wine is very light bodied and just a bit deeper in color than a rosé; it's a dry, crisp, warm-weather red that is delightful when served slightly cool. Drink Bardolino within three years of the vintage.

Bolla and Masi are two large, reliable producers of both wines with worldwide distribution; these producers' wines are in the $6 to $8 range. For a bit more serious, and a bit more expensive, version of Valpolicella, try these producers (listed alphabetically):

- Alighieri
- Allegrini
- Guerrieri-Rizzardi (also recommended for Bardolino)
- Le Ragose
- Tommasi

Amarone della Valpolicella, which has long been one of Italy's most popular full-bodied red wines, is made from the same grapes as Valpolicella and Bardolino (Corvina, Rondinella, and Molinara).

In Amarone production, the ripe grapes are dried on straw mats for several months, thus dramatically concentrating their grape sugars and flavors.

The resulting wine is a rich, velvety, powerful (14 to 16 percent alcohol), long-lasting wine that is at its best when it has at least 10 years of bottle age. We find Amarone wines to be even better when they're about 20 years old. Try Amarone with steak or with mature, hard cheeses, such as Parmigiano, cheddar, or aged Gouda, on a cold winter's night.

We recommend these producers of Amarone, listed alphabetically:

- Allegrini
- Bertani
- Bolla
- Masi
- Quintarelli
- Le Ragose
- Tommasi

Lombardy

One of the few places outside Piedmont to successfully grow the Nebbiolo grape is the Valtellina wine zone in northern Lombardy, near the Swiss border. Here, four Nebbiolo-based wines are produced: Grumello, Inferno, Sassella, and Valgella.

All four wines are light bodied, inexpensive (under $10), and — unlike the tannic, full-bodied Barolo and Barbaresco wines of Piedmont — should be enjoyed when they are young (within six years), because they do not age well.

Emilia-Romagna

Some food critics maintain that Italy's best food comes from the Emilia-Romagna region. (Considering how good the food is throughout Italy, that endorsement is impressive!) Two of Italy's gastronomic capitals, Bologna and Parma, are in Emilia-Romagna.

Lambrusco, the red wine consumed in Emilia-Romagna with the fine local food, is well known throughout the world. This slightly effervescent, grapey wine has a particular style in its home region: drier than most export versions and more bubbly. The Bolognese maintain that Lambrusco is the perfect wine with their rich cuisine; it's especially fine with the local sausages.

Umbria

Beautiful, mountainous Umbria boasts the towns of Assisi, Perugia, and Orvieto. Two fine red wines are made here.

Torgiano *(tor gee AH no)*, a Sangiovese-based wine similar to Chianti, is produced around the walled town of Torgiano. One excellent, well-known producer, Lungarotti, makes an acclaimed, age-worthy Torgiano called Rubesco Riserva. (His Rubesco sells for about $12; the Rubesco Riserva costs $18 to $25, depending on the vintage.)

Around the town of Montefalco, an elegant, medium-bodied red wine called Sagratino di Montefalco (made from the local Sagratino grape variety) is produced. We believe that Sagratino di Montefalco is Italy's best unknown red wine; it's not even well known outside Umbria — let alone on the other side of the Atlantic Ocean.

Abruzzo

Montepulciano d'Abruzzo *(mon tay pul chee AH noh dah BRUTE so)*, a typically inexpensive (under $5), easy-drinking, low-tannin, low-acid red wine, comes from the Adriatic coast region called Abruzzo. The Montepulciano grape variety is similar to, and undoubtedly related to, Sangiovese. Most of the wines from the Abruzzo region are simple quaffing wines, and the wines from this region are very good values.

Two more serious producers of Montepulciano d'Abruzzo are Edoardo Valentini and Emidio Pepe. (Pepe's grapes are still crushed the old-fashioned way: by foot.) If you ever come across Valentini's Montepulciano, in particular, we suggest that you buy it (about $25 to $30); one of Italy's great red wines, it can age for 20 years or more in good vintages.

Campania

Taurasi, the most serious red wine of southern Italy, is made from the Aglianico *(ah lee AHN ee coh)* grape variety in the region of Campania, near Naples. Full-bodied and tannic, Taurasi is one of Italy's longest-lived red wines. The 1968 Taurasi from Mastroberardino, the region's outstanding producer, is still drinking well. We especially recommend Mastroberardino's single-vineyard Taurasi, Radici (about $18 to $20).

Basilicata

One important red wine is made in the southern region of Basilicata, which forms the instep of the Italian boot: Aglianico del Vulture *(ah lee AHN ee coh del VUL toor ay)*. The Aglianico grape variety is regarded by some critics as one of the three great red grapes of Italy, along with Nebbiolo and Sangiovese. Aglianico del Vulture's leading producer is D'Angelo; the wine sells for about $12 (the riserva, $15). Drink it within six to eight years of the vintage.

Apulia

The region of Apulia (also known as Puglia, pronounced *POO lyah*), on the Adriatic coast, makes more wine than any other region in Italy. Its most well-known red wine, Salice Salentino *(SAH lee chay sah len TEE noh)*, is a warm, full-bodied, low-acid wine. Dr. Cosimo Taurino is a leading producer; his Salice Salentino sells for about $8, and his more elegant (but still very hearty) Notarpanaro costs about $10 to $11.

Sicily

Like Apulia, the island of Sicily also produces a great deal of wine, much of it red. Two leading Sicilian wine producers are Corvo and Regaleali.

Corvo is the brand name of the wines made by the gigantic Duca di Salaparuta winery. The everyday red wine known as Corvo Red retails for under $10; it is especially popular in southern Italian restaurants. Duca di Salaparuta's top red wine,

Duca Enrico, is a rich, full-bodied, concentrated red wine with an intense bouquet; it sells for about $32 to $34. Introduced only in 1989, Duca Enrico has already established itself as one of Italy's great red wines.

Regaleali *(ray gah lay AH lee)* is a smaller, quality-conscious producer whose grapes grow at high altitudes to counteract Sicily's warm climate. Regaleali Rosso sells for about $9; Regaleali's fine red wine, Rosso del Conte — a medium-bodied, elegant wine that resembles a red Bordeaux — retails for about $17 to $18.

The Red Wines of Spain

Although Spain ranks third in the world in wine production after Italy and France, it actually has more land under vines than any other country. Dry, hot, mountainous Spain is also one of the world's leaders in wine consumption, much of which is red.

Not long ago, Spanish red wines were generally of mediocre quality. Many of them aged too long in wood, losing their freshness; the taste of oak predominated over the flavors coming from the grapes. That tradition has been changing during the past 10 to 15 years. Quality is definitely on the upswing throughout Spain, to the point that Spanish wines, especially red wines, now compete successfully with other fine wines of the world.

We discuss Spain's three most important red wine regions in this section: Rioja *(ree OH ha)*, Ribera del Duero *(ree BEAR ah del doo AIR oh)*, and Penedés *(pen eh DAIS)*, with a nod to Navarra, an upcoming region formerly known mainly for its rosé wines.

Rioja: Tradition makes way for modernity

Rioja wine, a type of red (and white) wine named for the region in which it is made, is not only Spain's most famous type of red wine but also one of the classic red wines of the world. (See the section "Rioja" in Chapter 4.)

The Rioja wine region in north-central Spain has been the country's most important red wine region for more than 100 years. Naturally, tradition plays a strong role in winemaking practices there, but modern influences have arrived.

Fewer and fewer Rioja wines are tired and overoaked today, as they typically were in the past. Now, most producers of red Rioja strive to preserve their wine's fruit character by aging the wine less in wood (where it loses its freshness) and more in bottle. In the more progressive Rioja cellars, casks of American oak, which traditionally gave Rioja wines their distinctive vanillan aromas, now share their work with French oak casks, which impart subtler aromas. (In some cases, French oak has replaced the traditional American oak completely.)

Also, an amazing increase in the number of wineries in Rioja during the past 15 years — from 42 to around 150 — indicates remarkable progress for a "traditional" wine region!

By law, Rioja wine producers may use four red grape varieties:

- ✔ Tempranillo, Spain's greatest red grape variety (see Chapter 3), is the major grape in all Rioja's better wines.

- ✔ Garnacha (known as Grenache in France and the United States), once the leading red grape, today plays a lesser role because its wines are too high in alcohol and oxidize too quickly.

- ✔ The Graciano grape variety is highly regarded but difficult to grow; nevertheless, quite a few Rioja producers use a small percentage of it in their wines.

- ✔ The equally difficult-to-grow Mazuelo is seldom used nowadays.

The Rioja wine region has three districts: the cooler Rioja Alavesa and Rioja Alta, home mainly to the Tempranillo grape, and the warmer Rioja Baja, where Garnacha thrives. Although many Rioja wines are blends of grapes from all three districts, most of the best Riojas come from the Rioja Alta and Alavesa districts.

The world sees three different types of red Rioja, each wine aged differently:

- ✔ *Crianza* wines (about $8 to $10) are the lightest-bodied and readiest-to-drink wines. Aged a combined two years in oak cask and bottle at the winery, they require no further aging; drink them within five or six years of the vintage.

- ✔ *Reserva* wines, medium bodied and elegant, represent a big step up in quality. Aged a combined three years in oak and bottle, they nevertheless require a few years' keeping, especially in the better vintages. Rioja reservas can age for ten years or more; they retail in the $10 to $15 price range.

✔ *Gran Reservas* (sometimes also called *Reserva Especial*) wines are the finest, most complex Riojas and are usually made only in good vintages. Aged 5 years or more in oak and bottle, they are at their best with at least 10 years of aging, but these wines can further age and improve for 20 years or more. At $18 to $25, they are great values.

The best recent vintages for Riojas are the **1994**, **1989**, **1982**, and **1981**. 1995 will be good, as are the 1993, 1990, and 1988 vintages. Try buying some 1989 Gran Reservas while they are still available and age them for a few years.

Recommended Rioja producers

Tables 12-4 and 12-5 list our recommended Rioja producers in two groups, alphabetically within each group. We recommend all the red Rioja wines of each producer, but for some producers, we list specific wines that we particularly like. The wines of the producers in the first group tend to be more expensive than those of the producers in the second group.

Table 12-4	Recommended Producers of Better Rioja Wines
Recommended Producer	**Specially Recommended Wine(s)**
CVNE	"Imperial" Gran Reserva
R. Lopez de Heredia	"Viña Tondonia" Reserva
Bodegas Muga	"Prado Enea" Gran Reserva
Bodegas Remelluri	Gran Reserva
La Rioja Alta	"Reserva 890" "Reserva 904"

Table 12-5	Additional Recommended Producers of Rioja Wines
Recommended Producer	**Specially Recommended Wine(s)**
Marqués de Arienzo	
Marqués de Cáceres	
Campo Viejo	
Marqués de Griñon	

Recommended Producer	Specially Recommended Wine(s)
Martinez Bujanda/Conde de Valdemar	
Bodegas Montecillo	"Viña Monty" Reserva/Gran Reserva
Marqués de Murrieta Ygay	Reserva Especial
Marqués de Riscal	
Bodegas Sierra Cantabria	

Newly serious in Ribera del Duero

Ribera del Duero, between Rioja and Madrid, is the up-and-coming red wine region of Spain. Recognized by the Spanish government as an official wine region only in 1982, the area boasts several fine producers, whose wines are either highly regarded or destined to be.

One producer, Vega Sicilia *(VAY gah see SEAL yah)*, dominated the Ribera del Duero area for many years, long before the region was recognized as an official wine region. Vega Sicilia's "Unico Reserva" wine (and its Reserva Especial) are legendary wines that command extremely high prices ($90 and up). The Unico *(OON ee coh)* and Reserva Especial are rich, intensely concentrated, tannic, complex wines that can age 40 or 50 years without a problem and, in fact, improve with age, becoming less massive and more velvety. Valbuena *(val boo AIN ah)*, a junior version of these wines, can age for 15 to 20 years. The wines are a blend of 60 percent Tempranillo (called Tinto Fino in this region), 20 percent Cabernet Sauvignon, and 10 percent each of Merlot and Malbec.

Vega Sicilia now has real competition from other wineries in the region, especially from producer Alejandro Fernandez and his Pesquera wine. The Pesquera, primarily from the Tempranillo grape, is a rich, oaky, velvety, intensely fruity red wine that benefits from some aging. It sells for $16 to $20 (the reserva is around $25). Four other fine producers in Ribera del Duero are

- ✔ Bodegas Ismael Arroyo
- ✔ Bodegas Mauro
- ✔ Viña Mayor (Antonio Barcelo)
- ✔ Viña Pedrosa (Bodega Pérez Pascuas)

Navarra: More than just a rosé

In the region of Navarra, long a source of pleasant, inexpensive rosé wines, a wine revolution has been taking place. You can now find some excellent Navarra red wines (mainly Tempranillo-based, but also some Cabernet Sauvignon, Merlot, and various blends of all three). And the prices are right, often less expensive than Rioja wines. Look for the red Navarra wines of the following producers:

- Bodegas Julian Chivite *(HOO lee ahn chi VEE tay)*, especially his 1985 or 1988 "125 Aniversario" Gran Reserva (100 percent Tempranillo)

- Bodegas Guelbenzu (his wines are 50 percent Cabernet Sauvignion, 40 percent Tempranillo, 10 percent Merlot)

- Bodegas Magana's 1990 or 1991 "Eventum" (70 percent Merlot, 30 percent Tempranillo)

The Torres family of Penedès

Undoubtedly, the most well-known name on Spanish wine labels — both red and white — is that of Torres. The company started in Penedès, a region in northeast Spain near Barcelona, and the Penedès area is still its base. But you can now find Torres' wines being made in California (under the label Marimar Torres Estate), Mexico, and Chile. The Torres firm is run by Miguel Torres, Jr., a brilliant, French-trained winemaker who introduced Cabernet Sauvignon, Pinot Noir, and many other French grape varieties to Penedès; he has made the Torres firm one of the most modern wine estates in Spain.

All Torres' wines are clean, well-made wines and good values. The red wines include

- Sangre de Toro (about $6) and Gran Sangre de Toro (about $10), both Garnacha-based
- Coronas (about $7), mainly Tempranillo
- Gran Coronas (about $14), mainly Cabernet Sauvignon
- The famous Gran Coronas Black Label ($28 to $32), Torres' top red wine, entirely Cabernet Sauvignon (see Figure 12-3)

Figure 12-3: Torres is perhaps the most well-known producer of Spanish wine.

The Black Label, an elegant, long-lived wine comparable to a good Bordeaux, has, in fact, competed successfully with Bordeaux wines in international competitions. Look for the 1987 or 1990 Gran Coronas Black Label; 1994, not yet released, will be especially fine.

Jean León is another producer who has made fine Cabernet Sauvignon for 25 years in Penedès; his winery was recently purchased by the Torres firm, who will continue making wines under the Jean León label.

The Old and New Reds of Portugal

In a wine world full of Cabernet Sauvignon, Merlot, and Chardonnay, Portugal stands out as a fiercely independent nonconformist. You have to look very hard to find any of these "international" grape varieties in Portugal. She has enough of her own grapes, thank you — varieties unknown outside Portugal, such as Touriga Nacional and Castelão Frances.

Portugal has never had to worry about exporting its red wines; almost all of them are consumed at home! Although only tenth in the world in wine production, Portugal has always been third or fourth in per capita consumption. While selling the world the slightly sweet, effervescent rosés such as Mateus and Lancer's and the famous dessert wines Port and Madeira, the Portuguese kept their dry red wines for themselves, for the most part.

Portuguese wine language

The following wine terms appear on some Portuguese wine labels:

- **Colheita** *(col YAIT ah):* Vintage year

- **Garrafeira** *(gar ah FAIR ah):* A *reserve* wine of higher quality that has been aged for a minimum of three years

- **Quinta** *(KEEN ta):* Wine estate or vineyard

- **Tinto** *(TEEN to):* Red

- **Vinho** *(VEEN yo):* Wine

The picture is starting to change a bit since Portugal joined the European Union in 1986. Modern winemaking practices — along with an influx of foreign winemakers, mainly Australian — have put Portugal in a position to build a strong export market for red wine. With its rich variety of climates (maritime near the coast, hot and dry in the mountainous inland), Portugal certainly has the potential to join Italy, France, and Spain as a world leader in producing quality red wines.

Recommended Portuguese Red Wines

Spain has its Vega Sicilia Unico; Portugal also has its great red wine, but not nearly so famous — in fact, known outside Portugal by only a few wine connoisseurs. The wine called Barca Velha comes from the Douro region in northern Portugal, where Port wine is made. A dry, full-bodied, tannic, concentrated wine made by the Ferreira Port House, Barca Velha needs many years to develop fully. (The 1964 Barca Velha is drinking beautifully now.)

Barca Velha is produced from the same local grapes that are used to make sweet Port and is made only in good vintage years. Even though Barca Velha is probably Portugal's greatest dry red wine, it doesn't cost two arms and a leg (such as Vega Sicilia's Unico); 1985, the last available vintage released (as of this writing), retails for about $35. It is made in small quantities, unfortunately.

The Douro Valley has the potential to be Portugal's greatest dry red wine region. Another Port house, Ramos Pinto (now owned by the great Roederer Champagne firm), makes an excellent, inexpensive, dry red wine called Duas Quintas. We are very impressed with this rich, velvety, supple wine, with its plummy fruit flavors. The 1992 Duas Quintas sells for about $8 to $10; the 1991 Duas Quintas Reserva, a more full-bodied, intense wine, is a bargain at $18 to $20.

Some of our other favorite Portuguese red wines include

- **Quinta do Carmo:** This estate is in the up-and-coming Alentejo region of southern Portugal. Bordeaux's Château Lafite-Rothschild apparently believes in the region's potential, because it recently purchased the property. Look for it to only get better. The 1988 sells for $16 to $17.

- **J. M. da Fonseca Successores' red wines:** The firm of J. M. da Fonseca (no relation to the Fonseca Port House) makes some of Portugal's best red wines, including Quinta da Camarate, Morgado do Reguengos, Rosado Fernandes, and all of the winery's Garrafeiras.

- **Quinta de Pancas:** This wine, made from 50 percent Cabernet Sauvignon and 50 percent of the local Castelão Frances grape variety (which the winery calls Periquita), comes from the Alenquer region north of Lisbon; the 1992 is a best buy at about $8 to $9.

- **Quinta de Parrotes:** The same firm that produces the Quinta de Pancas makes this wine entirely from Castelão Frances; the 1992 sells for about $7.

- **Quinta da Bacalhôa:** This Cabernet Sauvignon-Merlot blend made by J. P. Vinhos resembles a French Bordeaux; the 1992 sells for about $12.

- **Tapada do Chaves:** This rich and full-bodied red wine hails from the Portalegre region in eastern Portugal. The 1985 is one of the most impressive Portuguese red wines we've ever had.

✔ **Quinta do Cotto** and **Quinta de la Rosa:** Two other Douro red wines to look for, made in the style of Barca Velha (but less expensive).

Recent good vintages for Portuguese red wines are the **1994**, **1992** (excellent), **1991**, 1990, 1988, 1986, and 1985.

The red wine bargains of eastern Europe

If you're looking for decent, everyday red wines in the $3 to $6 range, by all means try the red wines from Eastern Europe. They are generally light bodied, and you must drink them while they're young (within five or six years of the vintage), but they are easy-drinking wines that are perfect for quick, weekday dinners after work.

We suggest that you try some of the following wines, currently available in the United States (additional wines from these countries surely will be available in the future):

✔ **Bulgaria:** Balkan Crest Cabernet Sauvignon (less than $4); Trakia Cabernet Sauvignon or Merlot ($5 to $5.49); Domaine of 60 Ships Cabernet Sauvignon ($4; Reserve, $4.49)

✔ **Romania:** Premiat Cabernet Sauvignon, Merlot, or Pinot Noir ($5 to $5.49)

✔ **Slovenia:** Avia Cabernet, Merlot, or Pinot Noir ($3.50 to $4); Cabernet Sauvignon Reserve ($4 to $4.49)

✔ **Hungary:** Egri Bikaver ("Bull's Blood"), $6; Duna Cabernet Sauvignon or Merlot ($5)

Part III
The Part of Tens

In this part . . .

*H*ow long has it been since you had a homework assignment — especially one that you actually *enjoyed?* The next time you want to feel virtuous and have a good time while you're at it, march right into the dining room and do your homework, young man or young lady! Taste that wine, refine your palate, and don't come out until you understand the difference between Cabernet and Pinot Noir once and for all!

Besides wine-tasting exercises that make homework fun, the chapters in this part of the book answer your FAQs (Frequently Asked Questions) regarding red wine and describe several red wines that you may want to make the acquaintance of.

Chapter 13

Ten Little-Known Red Wines Worth Knowing

. . . .

In This Chapter

▶ A dry red wine from Port country

▶ Our favorite everyday red

▶ A Bordeaux wine on the fast track

▶ Affordable Burgundy and Pinot Noir

▶ Green & Red red

▶ A lusty South African blend

. . . .

*W*e are firm believers in experimentation. Trying wines that differ from those you normally drink can be a real adventure. Sometimes you discover a type of wine that you enjoy even more than your "usual" — and sometimes you discover how much you really do like your "usual" in comparison. Either way, you win.

In this chapter, we describe ten red wines that we hope you'll try. Some of them are easy to find, and some of them are more difficult to track down. Those we indicate as generally available should be relatively easy to get; the others are available mainly in large cities and specialty wine shops or fine restaurants (after all, they're "little-known" reds!). We don't indicate specific vintages because we don't know which vintages will be available when you go shopping; instead, we offer some specific vintage information in the description of many of the wines.

We list each wine like this: name, producer, region of production, and country. (Remember, though, that for many European wines, the wine name *is* the region.)

Duas Quintas, Ramos Pinto, Douro, Portugal

From the Douro Valley, home of the great red dessert wine, Port, comes this exceptional dry red wine, made by the Port house of Ramos Pinto from various local grape varieties that are also used in producing Port wine. (See Chapter 14 of our book *Wine For Dummies* for more information about Port.)

The wine called Duas Quintas (pronounced *DOO ahs KEEN tahs* and translated as "two estates") may not have the intensity of Portugal's greatest dry red wine, Barca Velha, but for less than one-third the price (under $10), we believe that the plummy, velvety Duas Quintas is a steal. It stands above other wines of the area for the freshness of its fruit flavor; typically, wines from this hot region have flavors of stewed fruit or cooked fruit rather than fresh fruit. You can probably find the 1992 or 1993 vintage now.

Barbera d'Alba, Vietti, Piedmont, Italy

If we had to name our favorite everyday red wine, Barbera wine from the Alba zone in Piedmont would get our vote. This dry, fruity, high-acid red goes so well with the Italian foods we love — pasta with tomato sauce, pizza, and so on — and it's one of the most versatile food wines around (refer to "The tanninless wonder" in Chapter 5).

The Vietti winery is one of the best Barbera producers in Piedmont (Giacomo Conterno and Giuseppe Mascarello are two others). Vietti makes three single-vineyard Barberas — Bussia *(boo SEE ah)*, Scarrone *(skahr ROH nay)*, and Pian Romualdo *(pee an roh m'woo AHL doh)*. The Scarrone vineyard bottling is our favorite (about $13 to $14), but they're all good — particularly for the intensely ripe fruit flavors they have. Look for the 1993, 1994, or 1995 vintages (the 1995 becomes available in 1997).

125 Aniversario Gran Reserva, Bodegas Julian Chivite, Navarra, Spain

The Navarra region in northern Spain has always been known for its pleasant, dry rosé wines. But producers in Navarra have been really working lately to catch up with the region's next-door neighbor, Rioja, which makes some of Spain's best *red* wines. Julian Chivite's *(HOO lee ahn chi VEE tay)* 125 Aniversario Gran Reserva (especially his 1985 or 1988) is an outstanding example of a wine made entirely from Spain's finest red grape variety, Tempranillo. The 125 Aniversario is one of Chivite's most expensive wines (about $25 to $27), but it's worth the price. We also like Chivite's other red wines, which are very similar to young, well-made Riojas (his Chivite Reserva is about $11 to $12).

Like a good Rioja wine, the 125 Aniversario ages well (for ten years or more in good vintages). Enjoy it with steak, lamb, or roast chicken.

Pinot Noir Reserve, Domaine Serene, Willamette Valley (Oregon), U.S.

So many good Pinot Noirs have been coming out of Oregon's Willamette Valley in the last few years that it's difficult to keep up with them! One small producer, Domaine Serene, with the talented Ken Wright as its winemaker, has been making exceptional Pinot Noirs.

Domaine Serene's 1990 Pinot Noir Reserve bowled us over with its intense, lush fruit flavors. Look also for the 1994 (a great vintage in Oregon). The Reserve costs over $30, but the winery's basic Pinot Noir, also very good, is half the price.

Other up-and-coming, small Oregon Pinot Noir producers to look for are Chehalem, Cameron, and Evesham Wood (plus a couple of always reliable, sometimes overlooked producers, Bethel Heights Vineyard and Elk Cove Vineyards). Although Domaine Serene may be a little hard to find, some of these other wines are more generally available.

Château Troplong-Mondot, St.-Emilion, France

Of all the great red Bordeaux wines being made, Château Troplong-Mondot *(troh long mon doh),* a premium wine from the St.-Emilion region, stands out as one of the most improved wines of the entire area. Troplong-Mondot has gone from being a merely good Bordeaux to being a great one in the last six or seven years.

The 1990 Château Troplong-Mondot is one of the best Bordeaux wines of a great vintage, but it now costs over $30 — if you can find it. Look for this property's more recent vintages, such as the 1993 or 1994 (the latter available in 1997), at a more reasonable price than the 1990.

Bourgogne Rouge d'Auvenay, Leroy, France

Madame Bize-Leroy is one of the great winemakers not only in Burgundy but in the entire world as well. Unfortunately, her superb Burgundies are very expensive. But her basic red Burgundy wine, the Bourgogne Rouge d'Auvenay, is always well made, and it's a good buy at $15 to $16.

Look for the 1991 or 1993 or later vintages. Leroy's name on the label is as good a guarantee as you can get in Burgundy. This wine is generally available.

At around the same price, another fine, basic red Burgundy wine is the Bourgogne Rouge La Digoine of A.& P. DeVillaine.

Rubicon, Meerlust, Stellenbosch, South Africa

South Africa's wines have improved tremendously in the last decade. One of the country's finest producers is Meerlust, who is making a superb Cabernet Sauvignon and Merlot as well as a wine called Rubicon, which is a blend mainly of Cabernet Sauvignon, with a little Merlot and Cabernet Franc. Rubicon is a richly textured wine that tastes more expensive than its price (about $16). This wine is worth seeking out.

Pinot Noir, Napa Ridge, North Coast (California), U.S.

California's Napa Ridge Winery, part of Beringer Estate Wines, is performing a miraculous feat by producing a really high-quality Pinot Noir for less than $10 (actually, about $6 to $7). The Napa Ridge Pinot Noir displays good, clean Pinot Noir berry-like fruit flavors and has been consistently fine from vintage to vintage. Truly a best buy, and generally available.

Zinfandel, Green & Red Vineyard, Napa Valley (California), U.S.

Red Zinfandels are California's most versatile wines: They go well with so many different foods. One of our favorites is the lean, claret-style Zinfandel (refer to the Zinfandel section in Chapter 7 for a discussion of Zinfandel styles) that Green & Red Vineyard makes from its Chiles Mill Vineyard. Green & Red doesn't get as much attention as some other red Zin producers, but its Zinfandels have been consistently fine for over ten years and are great food wines. About $15 and generally available.

Chianti Classico Riserva, San Giusto a Rentennano, Tuscany, Italy

Chianti Classicos, particularly the Riservas, are among Italy's greatest red wines, especially when made by an outstanding producer such as San Giusto a Rentennano *(san JEWS toh ah ren ten NAH noh)*. This little-known producer has been making particularly exceptional Chianti wines since 1985. The Riserva, which goes well with lamb or steak, sells in the $16 to $18 range.

Chapter 14

Answers to Ten Frequently Asked Questions about Red Wine

In This Chapter

▶ Red wines for white wine drinkers

▶ Dry and less dry

▶ When vintages matter

▶ Wines that age and wines that don't

▶ The right temperature

▶ The best wine for pizza

▶ Red wine, headaches, and health

I've been a white wine (or rosé, or beer) drinker. What red wines should I try first?

We recommend that you begin with lighter-bodied, low-tannin red wines, which are more user-friendly to people not accustomed to drinking red wines. A Beaujolais (from France) would be an ideal first red wine. It's a medium-bodied, fruity, low-tannin, inexpensive (under $10) wine, and you can drink it slightly chilled to appreciate its fresh fruitiness. Beaujolais Nouveau wines (very young Beaujolais) are especially grapey in flavor and very likable; the Nouveau version of Beajoulais is available only from late November until about the end of the year.

Other red wines that we recommend to new red wine drinkers are inexpensive Merlots, Pinot Noirs, and red Zinfandels. From Italy, we recommend two light-bodied red wines: Bardolino and inexpensive (under $10) wines from the Barbera grape.

How do I know whether a red wine is dry (or how dry it is)?

First of all, most red wines nowadays are dry (that is, not sweet). But even wines that are technically dry can give an *impression* of sweetness or taste slightly sweet to some people; the perception of dryness or sweetness depends on the individual wine and the person tasting it.

To find out how dry a wine really is, ask a knowledgeable salesperson in your wine shop. Two clues that can help you decide on your own are the following:

- ✔ Very dark-colored red wines are normally dry and tannic (see Chapter 1 for information about tannin), as well as full bodied; tannin enhances the impression of dryness in the wine. (Hold the bottle up to a light to see how dark the wine looks.)
- ✔ Check the alcohol percentage of the wine; high-alcohol wines (over 13 percent), such as some red Zinfandels and Cabernet Sauvignons, give an impression of sweetness because of the ripeness of their grapes and their alcohol itself, which can seem sweet.

In general, red wines from Europe, especially those of Italy, France, and Spain, tend to be *very* dry. Red wines from Australia tend to be less dry. American red wines — particularly Cabernet Sauvignons — range from fairly dry (at lower price levels) to quite dry.

Why do I get headaches when I drink red wines?

If you get headaches only when you drink red wines and have no problems with white wines, you may be reacting to the histamines that are present in the skins of red wine grapes. Some people we know have found relief from this allergic reaction by taking an antihistamine before drinking red wine (but check with your doctor first).

Other possible causes of headaches are any of the other natural compounds found in red wine but not in white wine, or the alcohol itself. But sulfites (sulfur compounds that exist naturally in wine and other fermented beverages but are also added to wine) are probably *not* the cause; white wines generally contain higher sulfite levels than red wines do.

What's the difference between a Cabernet Sauvignon and a Merlot?

Cabernet Sauvignon and Merlot are two different grapes that are used to make red wine (see Chapter 3 for more information about these grapes).

Most Cabernet Sauvignon wines generally are dry, austere, and tannic in style. Merlot wines, although equally dark, if not darker, in color, are usually softer, lower in tannin, and more approachable than Cabernet Sauvignons. Because Merlots are typically less austere and tannic than Cabs, they do not need as much aging before they are ready to drink. A young Merlot is more pleasurable than a young Cabernet Sauvignon.

If you are just starting to drink red wine, you'll probably find Merlots more palatable than Cabernet Sauvignons. (Cabernet Franc wines — made from yet another grape — fall somewhere in between, but they are closer in style to Cabernet Sauvignon than to Merlot.) Very inexpensive ($6 or less) Cabernet Sauvignons (as well as Merlots) are lower in tannin and drinkable sooner than more expensive versions and can be very pleasing to novice red wine drinkers.

I've seen the word "Meritage" on the label of some red wines. Does it mean that the wine is of high quality?

Some American wine producers use the term *Meritage,* usually for their best red wine. The Meritage Association, headquartered in California, regulates use of the term.

Red Meritage wines must be a blend of two or more of the five grape varieties that are used for red Bordeaux: Cabernet Sauvignon, Merlot, Cabernet Franc, Petite Verdot, and/or Malbec. The quality of a Meritage wine ultimately depends on the quality of the individual producer. Generally speaking, however, most Meritage wines are of high quality.

How long should a bottle of red wine age before it is ready to drink?

The answer to this question varies according to the type of red wine. But we can offer you a few simple guidelines:

✔ Many red wines that are very dark colored need several years of aging to reach their prime drinking stage. Some examples include Bordeaux wines that sell for over $12 a bottle, Rhône wines (other than inexpensive Côtes du Rhône wines; see Chapter 11), California Cabernet Sauvignon wines, Petite Sirah wines, Barolo, and Brunello di Montalcino (the last two are from Italy). Australian Shiraz or Shiraz-Cabernets are exceptions in that, although quite dark in color, most are ready to drink when they are young.

✔ Inexpensive (under $10) red wines are usually made in a way that makes them drinkable as soon as they are released.

✔ Lighter-colored red wines, such as Bardolinos from Italy, Beaujolais wines from France, and inexpensive Pinot Noirs, Merlots, and Zinfandels, are usually ready to drink immediately after you buy them.

If you want to buy young red wines and let them age properly, your storage conditions must be good. Refer to Chapter 15 of our book, *Wine For Dummies,* for details about good storage.

Which foods go with red wine?

In Chapter 5, we discuss the hows and whys of matching red wine with food. To give a quick answer to this common question, though, we mention some good food/red wine combinations here:

✔ Lighter-bodied red wines — such as Beaujolais; Côtes du Rhône; inexpensive Cabernet Sauvignon, Merlot, Pinot Noir, and Zinfandel; and Valpolicella and Bardolino — are excellent with roast chicken, hamburgers, or veal cutlets.

✔ Medium-bodied red wines, such as Chianti Classico, moderately priced ($10 to $20) California Cabernet Sauvignon or Merlot, or Rioja from Spain, go well with steaks, pork chops, or roasts.

✔ Full-bodied red wines, such as expensive (over $20) Cabernet Sauvignon or Bordeaux, Barolo, or Brunello di Montalcino, can accompany beef, lamb, or game. Lamb and Chianti Classico Riserva are particularly good together.

✔ Italian Barbera is especially fine with pasta in tomato sauce or with pizza.

✔ Red Burgundies from France go well with roast beef — but don't stop there! Wines made from the Pinot Noir grape (as red Burgundy wines are) go great with salmon, many other fish or chicken dishes, and all sorts of medium-weight dishes.

✔ Hard cheeses, such as cheddar, aged Gouda, and Asiago, are usually excellent with all red wines.

We offer these combinations just as suggestions; in the business of wine and food pairing, no hard-and-fast rules exist. Some people love California Cabernet Sauvignon with chocolate!

At what temperature should red wine be served?

Most red wines taste best at cool-room temperature — between 62° and 65° F. Lighter-bodied red wines, such as Beaujolais or Bardolino, are best when served slightly chilled (between 56° and 60° F). Red wines served too cold often taste bitter, metallic, or tannic. If they're served too warm (over 70° F) — a frequent occurrence in many restaurants, by the way — red wines taste flabby, dull, and lifeless, or overly alcoholic.

A bottle of red wine should feel cool to the touch. If a restaurant serves you a bottle of red wine that feels warm to your hand, we suggest that you have it placed in an ice bucket for five to ten minutes to "revive" the wine.

Is red wine good for my health?

Many recent studies have found that all wines, when consumed in moderation, seem to promote longevity. Wine appears to be especially beneficial to the cardiovascular system. Some studies indicate that red wine in particular might be most beneficial of all.

Red wine contains many vitamins and minerals, including the B vitamins, iodine, iron, magnesium, zinc, copper, calcium, and phosphorus. A four-ounce serving of dry red wine contains about 110 calories.

Do I have to know about good vintage years to buy red wine?

No, you don't — and yes, you do, depending on the wine you're buying.

The quality of the *vintage year* (the growing season of the grapes) on a bottle of red wine is an important consideration only for better (over $10) red wines, especially from certain wine regions where the weather varies from year to year, such as in most of the wine regions of France and Italy. In general, year-to-year weather variation is much less significant in non-European wine countries, such as the United States, Australia, Chile, Argentina, and South Africa — and the quality of the vintage year is therefore less important.

California, for example, had a string of six fine vintages from 1990 to 1995. France and Italy shared four excellent vintage years in the past 15 years: 1982, 1985, 1988, and 1990. In particular, 1990 seems to have been an excellent vintage throughout the world's wine regions.

Chapter 15
Ten Hands-On Wine-Tasting Exercises

*A*n unfortunate downside to learning about wine is that, inevitably, words fall short in describing how wines taste. To fully understand the difference between Cabernet Sauvignon and Pinot Noir — or to grasp any other concept regarding the taste of wine — you simply have to taste for yourself. (Hey, maybe that's not a downside after all!)

The following exercises provide structure for your hands-on learning about red wines. You can do the exercises in any order you like, but we do believe that you'll get more out of the experience if you try the first four exercises first.

We recommend that you invite a friend or two to try each exercise with you, because you learn faster when you can discuss your tasting impressions with someone else. (And plenty of wine will be left over to drink with dinner.) Be sure to fill your glasses no more than halfway so that you can swirl the wines and notice their aromas. Sip water if you like between tastes, or nibble on plain bread, but don't eat cheese or anything else while you perform an exercise or you'll diminish your ability to taste the differences between the wines. (If you don't want to taste wine on an empty stomach, eat something before tasting, but not while you're tasting.)

In most cases, we don't recommend specific brands of wine for you to use in your tasting experiments. You can buy whichever brand of the suggested type of wine is available where you live. (Ask a knowledgeable person in your wine shop to advise you on which wines to buy if you feel that you need help.) The character of the specific wines you taste may vary slightly from our examples, but the general gist of the exercise should come through nevertheless.

Exercise #1: High Tannin versus Low Tannin

Recognizing tannin in a red wine is fundamental to tasting red wine because tannin is one of the main structural components of red wine — meaning that it is one of the main substances that make up red wine. (Turn to Chapters 1 and 2 for a quick review of tannin and the other structural elements of red wine.) When wine experts break red wines of the world into stylistic camps, tannin is one of the criteria they use most frequently. A wine's tannin level is also fundamental to how that wine pairs with food (see Chapter 5).

To experience tannin for yourself, buy two wines: one a Beaujolais *(bo jhoe lay)* and the other a Bordeaux *(bor DOE)* wine, both from France. If you are doing this exercise between late November and the end of the year, look for a bottle of Beaujolais Nouveau, the young Beaujolais of the latest vintage; otherwise, buy an inexpensive bottle of simple Beaujolais wine or, as a third choice, a bottle of Beaujolais-Villages (the least ideal of the three because it is likely to have slightly more tannin, and this wine is meant to represent the low-tannin end of the spectrum). For your Bordeaux selection, look for a wine that has the words *Haut Médoc* on the label, because those wines are likely to be more tannic than other Bordeaux wines.

After pouring a glass of each wine, note the differences in color and aroma if you wish, although those attributes are not crucial to this exercise. Then taste the two wines, starting with the Beaujolais and going back and forth between the two. Here's what you're likely to discover:

- ✔ The Beaujolais is soft in your mouth and smooth.
- ✔ The Bordeaux seems firmer in your mouth and less smooth.
- ✔ The Bordeaux might make your mouth pucker a little or make your cheeks seem to stick to your gums.
- ✔ After you swallow the Beaujolais, your mouth doesn't feel particularly dried out.
- ✔ After you swallow the Bordeaux, your mouth does feel dried out.

You might decide that the Bordeaux tastes more "serious" than the Beaujolais, even if you like it less. Try to notice whether the tannin in the Bordeaux wine — which is responsible for most of the impressions that we just described — makes the wine taste heavier, thicker, and more substantial than the wine with less tannin. That impression of substance is one of the positive results of the wine's tannin.

If you decide to drink the two wines later with food, notice how each one works differently with the dish. With simple meats or cheese, the tannic Bordeaux wine should taste much better than it did without food. Chapter 5 features advice for pairing tannic or low-tannin wines with food.

Exercise #2: Light Body versus Full Body

Like many beginning wine drinkers, you may instinctively understand the difference between light-bodied, medium-bodied, and full-bodied wines. But how light is light? And how full is full?

For this exercise, buy a bottle of Bardolino *(bar doh LEE noh)* and a bottle of Amarone *(ah mah ROH nay)*. The Amarone should set you back about $20 because it is a special, unusual type of wine. Because both wines come from the same region of northern Italy and are made from the same grapes (native Italian grapes; turn to Chapter 12 to find out their names), they have much in common — but definitely not their body.

As soon as you pour yourself a glass of each wine, you can see a big difference in appearance between the two wines; the Bardolino is much paler, which is rather typical of lighter-bodied reds. The Bardolino also smells lighter and fresher, while the deep-colored Amarone smells intense.

When you taste each wine, consider how heavy it feels when you hold it in your mouth. The lighter-bodied Bardolino probably doesn't strike you as heavy at all, whereas the full-bodied Amarone seems to fill your mouth because it is so heavy. Go back to the Bardolino, and you immediately see in comparison just how light the Bardolino is.

Consider which you prefer and for which occasions. If you're on our wavelength, you'll probably decide that the light-bodied wine would be better in the summer, at lunchtime, or when you're having just a light, simple meal. The fuller-bodied wine would be better in the winter with a big chunk of strong cheese and a good, crusty loaf of bread.

To further refine this exercise on body, you can add a third wine: Valpolicella *(val poh lee CHELL lah)*, from the same region and grapes as the Bardolino and Amarone (in fact, related to the Amarone, which is a sort of super-Valpolicella). It falls in the middle ground of body; it's somewhat richer than the Bardolino but way lighter than the Amarone.

Exercise #3: Lower Alcohol versus Higher Alcohol

Some (but not all) of the contrast in body that you notice between the two wines in Exercise #2 is due to the big difference in alcohol content. (Bardolino typically has about 12 percent alcohol, while Amarone can have 14 percent or even more.) The higher a wine's alcohol content, the fuller-bodied that wine is, generally speaking.

But high alcohol has other effects on a red wine as well. To explore the role of alcohol in the taste of a red wine, buy two Cabernet Sauvignon wines: one from Chile and one from California. For the California wine, choose a wine that sells for at least $12 a bottle in order to have an example that works well in contrast to the inexpensive ($4 to $8) Chilean Cabernet. Depending on which brands you choose, the Chilean wine might have about 12 or 12.5 percent alcohol, while the California Cabernet might have about 13.5 percent. (The alcohol content of each wine appears somewhere on the label; unfortunately, you can't trust the number completely on wine sold in the U.S., because U.S. labeling law allows wine producers a 1.5 percent margin of error in stating the alcohol content on their labels.)

When you smell the two wines, you might find that the higher-alcohol California wine has a more obvious aroma because the wine's alcohol carries the aromas to your nose as it evaporates; you might also detect a headiness to the aroma. The Chilean Cabernet, in comparison, has a more reticent aroma.

In your mouth, the California wine tastes richer, fuller, and probably sweeter, although it is technically a dry wine; it has more weight and more presence. The Chilean Cabernet is lighter bodied, dryer, and *thinner,* or less rich.

Now pay attention particularly to the tannin of each wine (refer to Exercise #1 for a brush-up on tannin). The Chilean wine probably tastes slightly more tannic than the California wine;

that is, it feels firmer and less soft in your mouth. One reason for this impression is that the Chilean wine has less (softening) alcohol to counterbalance its (hardening) tannin; the higher-alcohol California wine feels softer because its alcohol does counterbalance its tannin.

Consider which wine you prefer and in which circumstances you might prefer it. Although higher-alcohol wines are usually more appealing and delicious when you first taste them, you can tire of them more quickly; lower-alcohol wines are easier to drink over the course of a meal. Lower-alcohol red wines are easier to drink in hot weather, too.

Exercise #4: Acid versus Tannin

You can enjoy red wine happily for the rest of your life without ever learning the fine distinction between acid and tannin in the taste of a wine. But if you do want to learn the difference, try the following exercise.

Distinguishing between acid and tannin in red wine is quite a challenge for wine drinkers (us included!) because both components of red wine do somewhat the same thing: They make the wine feel firmer and less soft in your mouth. In fact, tannin and acid in red wines work hand in hand and reinforce each other's impact. But the tannin in a red wine changes as the wine ages (it softens) and even physically falls out of the wine as sediment in the bottom of the bottle, while acidity hangs in there. Age can soften tough, young red wines to the extent that their tannin is responsible for their hardness and toughness — but age only exaggerates a wine's acidity. When you need to decide whether to age a red wine, distinguishing between the wine's acidity and tannin can help you make the right decision.

For this exercise, we recommend two entirely different red wines. One is a Barbera d'Alba wine from the Piedmont region of Italy. Choose a Barbera that costs less than $18, or it might have some oak tannin that confuses the issue of the wine's acidity. For the second wine, choose a Cornas wine from the northern Rhône Valley wine region of France.

Don't expect to find differences in the wines' appearance and aroma that are attributable to tannin or acid, except perhaps for a certain freshness of aroma in the higher-acid Barbera wine. In your mouth is where the differences due to tannin and acidity are likely to show themselves.

As you taste each wine, notice that neither is totally soft. Both wines have a good backbone of firmness, although the firmness has a different cause in each case; acidity firms the Barbera, whereas tannin firms the Cornas. Taste the Barbera and focus your thoughts on the sides of your tongue, where acidity tends to show itself. Then taste the Cornas, focusing on the rear of your tongue for tannic roughness.

Here are some of the observations you are likely to make regarding the two wines:

- The acidic Barbera has a juicy quality and a pronounced, fresh fruity flavor.
- Although the Barbera tastes firm, it is also smooth.
- The tannic Cornas is rough in texture, and you might be inclined to call it "chewy."
- The Barbera seems to have more depth than the Cornas — that is, it seems to have layers on your tongue.
- The Cornas has more breadth in your mouth — that is, its flavors seem to push across the width of your tongue.
- After you swallow the Barbera, its acidity makes your mouth water.
- After you taste the tannic Cornas, your mouth feels rough and completely dried out.

Taste the Cornas with some Gruyère or Swiss cheese and notice how the tannin seems less harsh. The Barbera tastes fine with the cheese, but the cheese doesn't transform the wine the way it does the more tannic Cornas.

Exercise #5: Pinot Noir versus Cabernet Sauvignon

Cabernet Sauvignon and Pinot Noir are two of the most important red grape varieties in the world, but they are very different from each other — and their wines are vastly different, too.

Buy a bottle of U.S. Pinot Noir (either from California or Oregon) and a bottle of U.S. Cabernet Sauvignon (from California, Washington, or Long Island). Don't skimp too much on the Cabernet, or you won't get an appropriate example; plan to spend at least $12 on that wine.

In appearance alone, you can tell that the two wines are different. The Cabernet wine is very dark, while the Pinot Noir wine is much paler; this difference is due to less pigmentation in Pinot Noir grapes and more in Cabernet grapes.

The aroma of the Pinot Noir wine suggests berries — strawberries, raspberries, or blackberries — or maybe plums, and you might detect some woodsy aromas, such as underbrush. The aroma of the Cabernet wine might suggest black currants or cassis, and it might be slightly vegetal or herbal.

When you taste the two wines, you'll probably notice some of these differences:

- The flavors of each wine vary, just as the aromas do.
- The Pinot Noir is less tannic than the Cabernet and might feel smoother.
- The Pinot Noir is likely to seem fruitier than the Cabernet.
- The Cabernet is thicker in texture, fuller bodied, and "chewier" than the Pinot Noir.
- Although the Pinot Noir has plenty of flavor, the taste of the Cabernet is more intense.

Exercise #6: Varietal Character

This exercise builds on the preceding exercise comparing Cabernet Sauvignon and Pinot Noir.

Open a bottle of Merlot wine and a bottle of Zinfandel wine (the red kind, of course!), both from U.S. wineries; spend about the same on each bottle as you did on the Cabernet and Pinot Noir in Exercise #5. Taste the Merlot and Zin alongside the Cabernet Sauvignon and the Pinot Noir and compare the color, aroma, and taste of each wine.

You are likely to discover some of the following:

- The Pinot Noir is the palest of the four wines; the others are very saturated in color.
- The Merlot slightly resembles the Cabernet in aroma and flavors (each wine probably has some of the other grape blended in it), but the Merlot smells plummy and maybe slightly chocolatey. Both the Merlot and the Cabernet wines smell smoky, toasty, spicy (especially cinnamon or cloves), or vaguely perfumey from the oak barrels in which they aged.

- The Zinfandel has a fresh, exuberant aroma of berries, but its fruit smells much richer and riper than the berries of the Pinot Noir.

- Both the Zinfandel and the Merlot are softer and less tannic than the Cabernet (see Exercise #1 regarding tannin).

- Both the Zinfandel and the Merlot seem at least slightly higher in alcohol than the Cabernet (refer to Exercise #3 on alcohol).

- The Pinot Noir is the most fresh-tasting and the lightest of the four wines.

If you taste with friends and discuss the four wines, you'll probably make many more comparisons among the wines, depending on which brands you choose. Be sure to discuss which wine you would prefer with which type of food. Zinfandel and Tex-Mex, anyone?

Exercise #7: Ordinary Wine versus Fine Wine

Most wines today are decent-quality wines. But some wines are obviously considered finer quality than others. (Why else would such a wide range of prices exist, even for the same type of wine?) What characteristics do fine wines have that other wines don't?

The criteria relating to quality in wine are elusive concepts such as *complexity, balance, length, depth, concentration,* and *trueness to type.* (You can read more about these criteria in Chapter 2 of *Wine For Dummies.*) What makes these concepts elusive is that you cannot measure them objectively; the only way to determine whether a wine has high-quality characteristics, and to what extent, is to taste the wine — and because everyone tastes somewhat differently, everyone has a different opinion about the wine's quality.

Although the following exercise won't be enough to qualify you as a professional wine judge, it can give you some firsthand experience in distinguishing average-quality wine from fine-quality wine. It also enables you to experience personally the principal quality criteria of wine.

Buy an inexpensive red Bordeaux wine whose *appellation of origin* (official place-name) on the label is simply Bordeaux (such a wine costs about $10). Then buy a bottle of fine red Bordeaux, preferably from the same vintage, whose appellation of origin on the label is a specific district of Bordeaux, such as St. Julien or Pauillac. Depending on how far you want to stretch the comparison, you can spend $20 to $40 for that bottle. Do consult a specialist in your wine shop, and read about Bordeaux wine in Chapter 10, in order to make a good choice on the second wine.

Pop the corks and compare the two wines. The less expensive wine is probably easier to see through and less deep in color. The aroma of the less expensive wine is fresh, moderately intense, and rather direct: aromas of black currants and plums, with perhaps some vegetal character or some slight charriness of oak. That wine is quite pleasant when you taste it; it's probably light to medium bodied, fairly smooth, not too tannic, and easy to drink.

You might be surprised to discover that the more expensive wine actually tastes less pleasant (at the moment) than the less expensive wine. At first, you smell just toasty, spicy oak in the wine, and you have to swirl your glass a lot in order to bring out other aromas (black currants, lead pencil, tobacco, and earthy smells, for example) because they are reticent. In your mouth, the wine is too hard, too tough, and too tannic to be enjoyable now.

But wine quality does not necessarily correlate to immediate pleasure. Some wines — such as most of the finest Bordeaux red wines — need several years to harmonize and become truly pleasurable. In this exercise, instead of judging the wine for its pleasure quotient, look for the following characteristics of quality in the more expensive wine:

- Although the wine is tannic, when you concentrate you can notice that it has quite a lot of fruit, too — enough to match the tannin.
- A lot is happening in your mouth when you taste the wine. The longer you hold it on your tongue, the more you taste; it is *complex*.
- The wine seems to get better and better as it sits in the glass.
- Unlike the less expensive wine, which simply "is what it is," the better wine has layers of flavor and interest (*depth*).

   ✔ The wine seems more saturated with flavor *(concentrated)* than the inexpensive wine.

   ✔ The flavors of the better wine stretch back farther on your tongue and hang in longer after you swallow (the wine has *length*).

   ✔ The better wine is more interesting.

If you taste a fully mature fine Bordeaux, you discover an extraordinary complexity and harmony in the wine that far exceeds the simple, pleasant balance of the inexpensive wine.

Exercise #8: Bordeaux versus California Cabernet

This exercise represents a fascinating study of regional *terroir* (the growing conditions that make a wine what it is) as well as psychological terroir — the traditions and attitudes of the people of an area that affect the style of a wine.

Buy a good red Bordeaux wine from the Left Bank (see Chapter 10, or ask your wine merchant for advice) that costs about $20 to $25 a bottle, and buy a comparably priced bottle of Cabernet Sauvignon from California.

Both wines are based on the Cabernet Sauvignon grape. The California wine probably has some Merlot blended in (up to 25 percent is legal), even if the label mentions nothing but Cabernet; the Cabernet Sauvignon in the Bordeaux wine is probably blended with Cabernet Franc as well as Merlot, and perhaps another minor grape. To the extent that the wines derive mainly from the same grape variety, they should be similar — but are they?

When you compare the two wines, you'll probably decide that they are more different than they are similar. Their similarities include

   ✔ Deep, dark color — although the California wine might be deeper in color

   ✔ Aromas of cassis and toasty, spicy oak

   ✔ Firm tannin

Their differences are likely to include the following:

- ✔ The aroma of the California wine is much more open and pronounced, as well as being more overtly fruity.
- ✔ The California Cab has a thick, relatively soft texture and seems slightly sweet compared to the Bordeaux.
- ✔ The California wine has an exuberantly fruity character in your mouth.
- ✔ The Bordeaux wine is austere and reticent; you have to concentrate more to appreciate it.
- ✔ The aromas and flavors of the Bordeaux wine are less fruity and more earthy than those of the California Cab.
- ✔ The texture of the Bordeaux wine is drier and maybe tougher.

The California Cabernet (if it tastes as we think it will) reflects the fruit-first priorities of a winemaker working with very ripe grapes; the Bordeaux wine reflects less ripe grapes and a winemaking direction governed more by the traditional styles of the area than by the need to express fruitiness.

Exercise #9: Shiraz versus Syrah

Shiraz and Syrah are different names for the same grape, so what's to compare? Just about everything!

Shiraz is the name of the Syrah grape, and the wines made from it, in Australia and South Africa. Syrah is the name of the grape elsewhere in the world, including the Rhône Valley of France, where the grape has staked its claim to fame in the fine wines of Hermitage and Côte Rôtie (see Chapters 4 and 11 for more information about these two wines).

Because of different climates, soils, and approaches to winemaking, the wines of the Syrah grape in Australia are very different from the Syrah-based wines of the Rhône Valley in France. Try this exercise to see, smell, and taste for yourself.

Buy a bottle of inexpensive Australian Shiraz and a bottle of Crozes-Hermitage, Cornas, or other red wine from France's Northern Rhône Valley wine region. Here's what you'll probably find when you compare the color, aroma, and flavor:

- ✔ The Shiraz might be paler in color.
- ✔ The Shiraz has an exuberant fresh fruity nose, like ripe strawberries, compared to the earthy, rustic, vegetal, and spicy aroma of the Rhône wine.

✔ The Rhône wine is fuller in body and much more tannic than the Shiraz.

✔ The flavors of the Rhône wine are earthier and less fruity than those of the Shiraz.

✔ The Shiraz is soft and easy to drink.

✔ The Rhône wine is intense and serious and less easy to enjoy.

Australian winemakers are the world leaders in making attractive, fruity, low-tannin red wines from grape varieties that elsewhere make tough, dense wines that require long aging. This Shiraz/Syrah comparison is a perfect example of the Australians' success.

Exercise #10: Cool Climate versus Warm Climate

Chapter 2 describes the effect of climate on wine style: The cooler the climate, the less ripe the grapes and the lighter bodied the wine, and the warmer the climate, the riper the grapes and the fuller the wine. (Naturally, all sorts of variables apply, but as generalizations go, this one is fairly solid.)

To test the climate effect for yourself, buy a bottle of Merlot from northeastern Italy (the regions of Veneto, Friuli-Venezia Giulia, or Trentino-Alto Adige; see Chapter 12) and a bottle of Merlot from California in the $10 to $12 range.

The Italian wine is probably paler and has a slightly vegetal aroma, which suggests low ripeness of Merlot grapes. It is light bodied or medium bodied, not very high in alcohol, and quite dry, with crisp acidity and not much tannin.

In contrast, the California Merlot is deeply colored and has a full, fruity nose suggesting plums. (It probably smells oaky, too, which has more to do with winemaking style than climate.) Typical of a warm-climate wine, the California Merlot is full bodied and soft, with fairly high alcohol, ripe fruit flavors, and rich, soft tannins. The wine's combined ripeness of fruit and its high alcohol might even give a slight impression of sweetness.

Consider which of the two wines you would prefer to drink by itself and which would go better with food. Then light the grill and test that theory for yourself!

Part IV
Appendixes

In this part . . .

*T*his is the part of the book you should turn to for a quick definition of a technical wine term or to settle your bet on how to pronounce *Vosne Romanée*. If you win the bet, the Vintage Chart might come in handy to help you select a wine to celebrate with.

Appendix A

Pronunciation Guide to Red Wine Terms

• •

Accented syllables, if any, are indicated with capital letters.

Aglianico	*ah lee AHN ee coh*
Aglianico del Vulture	*ah lee AHN ee coh del VUL toor ay*
Araujo	*ah RAU ho*
Barbaresco	*bar bah RES co*
Barbera	*bar BEAR ah*
Bardolino	*bar doe LEE noh*
Barolo	*bah RO lo*
Beaujolais	*boh jhoe lay*
Beaulieu	*bo l'yuh*
Bourgogne	*bor guh nyeh*
Bourgueil	*bor goye*
Brouilly	*broo yee*
Brunello di Montalcino	*brew NEL lo dee mon tahl CHEE no*
Canaiolo	*can eye OH loh*
Carmenet	*car meh nay*
Carmignano	*car mee NYAH no*
Château Beychevelle	*shah tow baysch vel*
Château Haut-Brion	*oh bree oan*
Château Lafite-Rothschild	*lah feet roth sheeld*
Château Lafleur	*lah fler*
Château Latour	*lah tor*
Château Margaux	*mahr go*

Château Mouton-Rothschild	*moo tahn roth sheeld*
Château Petrus	*peh troos*
Château Trotanoy	*trot ahn wah*
Châteauneuf-du-Pape	*shah tow nuf dew pahp*
Chénas	*shay nahs*
Chianti	*key AHN tee*
Chianti Rufina	*key AHN tee ROO fee nah*
Chinon	*she nohn*
Chiroubles	*sheh roob leh*
Clos du Val	*clo dew val*
Colheita	*col YAIT ah*
Côte de Beaune	*coat deh bone*
Côte Chalonnaise	*coat shal oan naize*
Côte d'Or	*coat door*
Côte de Nuits	*coat deh nwee*
Côte de Nuits-Villages	*coat deh nwee vee lahj*
Côte Rôtie	*coat roe tee*
Côtes du Ventoux	*coat due vahn too*
Dolcetto	*dohl CHET oh*
Domaine Leroy	*doh men lay wah*
Eisele	*EYE seh lee*
Estancia	*eh STAHN see ah*
Etude	*ae tood*
The Eyrie Vineyards	*EYE ree*
Fleurie	*fluh ree*
Garrafeira	*gar ah FAIR ah*
Gattinara	*gah tee NAH rah*
Gigondas	*jhee gohn dahs*
Givry	*gee vree*
grands crus classés	*grahn crew clas say*

Graves	*grahv*
Haut-Médoc	*oh may doc*
Hermitage	*er mee tahj*
Julian Chivite	*HOO lee ahn chi VEE tay*
Juliénas	*jool yay nahs*
La Jota	*lah HO tah*
Languedoc-Roussillon	*lahn gweh doc roo see yon*
Listrac	*lee strahk*
Loire	*l'wahr*
Margaux	*mahr go*
Médoc	*may doc*
Mercurey	*mer cure ay*
Meritage	*MER eh tej*
Montepulciano d'Abruzzo	*mon tay pul chee AH noh dah BRUTE so*
Morgon	*mor gohn*
Moulin-á-Vent	*moo lahn ah vahn*
Moulis	*moo lees*
Nebbiolo	*neb bee OH lo*
Niebaum-Coppola	*NEE baum COPE poh lah*
Nuits-St.-Georges	*nwee san jorg*
Pauillac	*poy yac*
Penedès	*pen eh DAIS*
Pessac-Léognan	*pay sac lay oh nyahn*
Pinotage	*pee noh TAHJ*
premier cru	*prem yay crew*
Quinta	*KEEN ta*
Regaleali	*ray gah lay AH lee*
Regnie	*ray nyay*
Ribera del Duero	*ree BEAR ah del doo AIR oh*

Rioja	ree OH hah
Rully	*rue yee*
Saint-Amour	*sant ah more*
Saint-Nicolas-de-Bourgueil	*san nih coh lahs deh bor goye*
Sangiovese	*san joe VAY say*
Seghesio	*seh GAY see oh*
Spanna	*SPAH nah*
St.-Estèphe	*sant eh steff*
St.-Julien	*san jewl yen*
St.-Emilion	*sant ay meal yon*
Tempranillo	*tem prah NEE yoh*
Tinto	*TEEN toe*
Torgiano	*tor gee AH no*
Vacqueyras	*vah keh rahs*
Valpolicella	*val po lee CHEL lah*
Vega Sicilia	*VAY gah see SEAL yah*
Vieilles Vignes	*vee ay vee nyeh*
Vinho	*VEEN yo*
Vino Nobile di Montepulciano	*NO be lay dee mon tay pul chee AH no*
Vosne-Romanée	*vone roh mah nay*
Willamette Valley	*will AM ett*

Appendix B
Glossary of Red Wine Terms

• •

acidity: A component of wine, generally consisting of tartaric acid (a natural acid in grapes) and comprising approximately 0.5 to 0.7 percent of a wine by volume.

aerate: To expose wine to air in preparation for drinking it, usually with the intention of allowing off-odors to escape from an older wine or of softening the harshness of a younger wine.

alcohol level: The percentage of alcohol by volume that a wine has; most red wines have an alcohol level between 11 and 14 percent.

amplitude: A quality of fullness and expansiveness in the mouth.

AOC: Abbreviation for *Appellation d'Origine Contrôllée,* sometimes shortened to *Appellation Contrôllée* and abbreviated as AC; translates as "protected place name." France's official category for its highest-ranking types of wine, whose name, origin, grape varieties, and other defining factors are regulated by law.

appellation: Name; often used to mean the official geographic origin of a wine, which is part of a wine's official name.

American oak: Oak wood from U.S. forests, and the barrels made from such wood. Some winemakers in certain wine regions (such as Spain and Australia) favor American oak for aging their wines.

aroma: General term for the smell of a wine. More precisely, *aroma* refers to the youthful scents of a wine, whereas *bouquet* refers to a wine's developed scents.

aromatic compounds: Organic substances in grapes that are responsible for many of the aromas and flavors of wines.

astringent: A descriptor for the mouth-drying, mouth-roughening effect of some wines caused by tannin, acid, or a combination of both.

balance: The interrelationship of a red wine's alcohol, residual sugar, acid, and tannin. When no one component stands out obtrusively on the palate, a wine is said to be well balanced; balance is prized in wines.

barrel: A relatively small wooden container for aging red wine, generally 60 gallons in size and made of oak.

black grapes: Wine grapes that have a reddish or blue pigmentation in their skins and are used to make red wine.

blend: To mix together two or more individual lots of wine, usually wines from different grape varieties; a wine derived from the juice of different grape varieties.

bodega: A winery in Spain.

body: The perceived weight of a wine in the mouth, partially attributable to a wine's alcohol content.

bottle age: Maturation of a wine after it has been bottled. Most red wines undergo a short period of bottle age at the winery before release; fine red wines require additional bottle age from the consumer.

bouquet: Evolved, mature aromas of a wine.

cask: A relatively large wooden container for making or storing wine.

castello: Italian for "castle;" refers to a winery estate.

château: A French name for a grand winery estate, commonly used in the Bordeaux region as well as in other regions.

classico: An Italian term applicable to certain DOC wines whose vineyards are situated in the original, classic part of the territory from which that particular type of DOC wine can be made. See also *DOC.*

clone: A subvariety of a grape variety, exhibiting characteristics that are specific to itself as compared to other manifestations of that grape variety.

colheita: Vintage year, in Portuguese.

commune: A village.

complex: Not simple. A complex wine has many different flavors.

cosecha: Vintage year, in Spanish.

crisp: A textural term for wines that are high in acidity.

decant: To transfer wine from a bottle to another container, either for the purpose of aerating the wine or to pour a red wine off its sediment.

depth: A characteristic of fine wines that gives the impression of having underground layers of taste rather than seeming flat and one-dimensional.

district: A geographic entity more specific than a region and less specific than a commune.

DO: Abbreviation for *Denominación de Origen,* which translates as "place name." Spain's official category for wines whose name, origin, grape varieties, and other defining factors are regulated by law.

DOC: Abbreviation for *Denominazione di Origine Controllata,* which translates as "controlled place name." Italy's official category for wines whose name, origin, grape varieties, and other defining factors are regulated by law. Also an abbreviation for Portugal's highest official wine category, *Denominação de Origen Controlada,* translated similarly and having the same meaning.

DOCG: Abbreviation for *Denominazione di Origine Controllata e Garantita,* which translates as "controlled and guaranteed place name;" Italy's official category for its highest-ranking wines.

domaine: A French term for wine estate, commonly used in the Burgundy region.

dry: The opposite of sweet.

estate: A property that grows grapes and produces wines from the grapes of its own vineyards. Wines labeled *estate* are made from vineyards owned by (or in some cases, under the direct control of) the same entity that owns the winery and makes the wine. Use of the term *estate* is regulated by law in most areas.

fermentation: The natural process by which the sugar in grape juice is transformed into alcohol (and the juice is thus transformed into wine) through the action of yeasts.

firm: A descriptor for red wines that are not soft but are not harsh and tough; generally relates to the tannin content of a red wine.

finish: The final impressions that a wine gives after you swallow it or spit it out.

flavor compounds: Organic substances in grapes that are responsible for many of the aromas and flavors of wines.

flavor intensity: The degree to which a wine's flavors are pronounced and easily observable.

flavors: A wine's volatile aromatic compounds as you sense them in your mouth through your rear nasal passage.

fortified wine: A wine to which alcohol has been added.

French oak: Oak wood from the forests of France, considered the finest type of oak for aging most red wines; also the barrels made from such wood.

garrafeira: A Portuguese term for a reserva wine with specific aging requirements — for red wines, at least three years of aging in oak and in bottle before release. See also *reserva*.

gran reserva: On Spanish red wines, a wine that ages for at least five years in oak and in bottle before being released from the winery.

grand cru: An official rank bestowed on some French vineyards and on the wine made from the grapes of those vineyards, seen most frequently on the wines of Burgundy and Alsace; in the St.-Emilion district of Bordeaux, a classification awarded to specific properties.

grand cru classé: A term that appears on labels of Bordeaux wines that are made by châteaux recognized as classified growths in 1855; translates as "great classified growth;" in the St.-Emilion district of Bordeaux, a classification awarded to specific properties that is higher than grand cru.

grape tannin: Those tannins in a red wine that are attributable to the grapes from which the wine is made.

grape variety: A genetically individual type of grape.

length: A characteristic of fine wines that give a sustained sensory impression across the tongue.

maceration: The process of soaking the skins of red grapes in their grape juice to dissolve some of the skins' color, tannin, and other substances in the juice. The term is often used to describe the entire period during which the skins and juice are in contact, including the period of fermentation.

malolactic fermentation: A natural conversion of malic acid into lactic acid, which softens the total acidity of a wine; most red wines undergo this process.

maturation: The aging period at the winery during which a red wine evolves to a state of readiness for bottling; the process of development and evolution that fine red wines undergo after they are bottled.

new oak: An imprecise term to indicate both oak barrels that are brand new (also called *first year oak*) and barrels that have been used one to four times.

New World: Collective term for those winemaking countries of the world that are situated outside Europe.

oak: The type of wood used to make containers for wine in most parts of the world.

oaky: Having characteristics such as aromas, flavors, or tannin that are attributable to oak.

old oak: Oak barrels or casks that are old enough to have lost most of their oaky character, generally five years old and older.

old vines: An unregulated term for grape vines whose fruit quality presumably is quite good because the vines are old — generally 40 years old or older — and therefore produce very little crop.

Old World: Collective term for the winemaking countries of Europe.

palate: A term used by wine-tasters as a synonym for *mouth,* or to refer to the characteristics of a wine that become manifest in a taster's mouth.

phylloxera: An insect parasite that feeds on the roots of vitis vinifera grape vines, resulting in the vines' premature death.

premier cru: An official rank, lower than grand cru, bestowed on some French vineyards and on the wine made from the grapes of those vineyards; seen most frequently on the wines of Burgundy.

primary aroma: Fresh aromas in a wine that derive from the grapes used to make that wine.

red grapes: Wine grapes that have a reddish or blue pigmentation in their skins; also called *black grapes.*

region: A geographical entity less specific than a district but more specific than a country. When speaking of Italian wines, the term *region* applies to the political entity as well as to the wine zones within that area.

reserva: On a Spanish wine, a wine that has aged longer at the winery (usually in some specified combination of oak aging and bottle aging) than a non-reserva version of the same type of wine; red reserva wines must age at least three years before release. On a Portuguese wine, a wine of superior quality from one vintage.

reserve: A designation for wines that are presumably finer than the non-reserve, or normal, version of the same wine; use of the term is unregulated in the U.S. and in France.

residual sugar: Sugar remaining in a wine after fermentation.

rich: A descriptor of wines that offer an abundance of flavor, texture, or other sensory perceptions.

riserva: Italian word for "reserve," indicating a wine that has aged longer before release from the winery than a nonreserve version of the same type of wine and suggesting higher quality. The time a wine must age before the winery is entitled to use the term *riserva* (and sometimes the conditions of that aging) is defined by individual DOC regulations for each wine.

second-label wine: A less expensive wine or a second brand of wine made by a winery from grapes or wine not considered worthy of the winery's primary label.

sediment: The solid residue in a bottle of red wine that forms as the wine matures.

serious: A metaphorical descriptor for a wine that is of high quality.

single-vineyard wine: A wine that is made from the grapes of a single (presumably exceptionally good) plot of land and bottled without being blended with wine from other vineyards, and that usually carries the name of the vineyard on its label; the term is unregulated in that the term *vineyard* is not defined as to size or ownership.

skin contact: The process during which the juice of grapes rests in contact with the grape skins; in red wine, the process by which wines absorb color, tannin, and other substances.

smooth: Descriptor for a wine whose texture is not rough or harsh.

soft: Textural descriptor for a wine whose alcohol and sugar (if any) dominate its acidity and tannin, resulting in a lack of hardness or roughness.

solid: Metaphorical descriptor for a wine that conveys qualities of strength, firmness, and durability.

stemmy: Descriptor for red wines that give the impression of having dry, raspy, woody tannins.

stems: The woody parts of a grape bunch, which are high in tannin. The stems are usually removed and discarded prior to fermentation.

structural components: Principally, a red wine's alcohol, acid, tannin, and sugar (if any).

structure: That part of the impression a wine conveys that derives from the perception of the wine's structural elements (mainly alcohol, acid, tannin, and sugar).

style: The set of characteristics through which a wine manifests itself.

supple: A descriptor for wines that seem fluid in texture in the mouth, without roughness or sharpness.

sweetness: The impression of sweet taste in a wine, which can be due to the presence of residual sugar or other sweet-tasting substances in the wine, such as alcohol.

tannin: A substance that red wine derives from its grapes. Tannin is one of the most important constituents of red wine.

taste: A general term for the totality of impressions that a wine gives in the mouth; more specifically, the primary tastes found in wine: sweetness, sourness, and bitterness.

terroir: A French word that is a collective term for the growing conditions in a vineyard, such as climate, soil, drainage, slope, altitude, and topography.

texture: A wine's consistency or feel in the mouth.

varietal: A wine named for the sole or principal grape variety from which it is made.

varietal character: The characteristics of a specific grape variety; the characteristics of a wine that are attributable to the grape variety from which it is made.

vegetal: Aromas or flavors that suggest vegetation or vegetables.

vieilles vignes: French for "old vines."

vin de pays: French for "country wine;" legally, a category of French wine that holds lower status than AOC wines. See also *AOC.*

vinification: The activity of making grape juice into wine.

vintage: The year in which a wine's grapes grow and are harvested; sometimes used as a synonym for the grape harvest.

viticulture: The activity of growing grapes.

vitis vinifera: The species to which most of the world's wine grapes belong.

weight: The impression of a wine's volume in the mouth.

wood tannin: The tannin in a wine that is attributable to the barrels in which the wine ages.

yeasts: One-celled microorganisms that are responsible for transforming grape juice into wine.

yield: The quantity of grapes produced on a specific piece of land, usually expressed as tons (of grapes) per acre in the U.S. or as hectoliters (of wine) per hectare in much of Europe. Popular wisdom dictates that the lower the yield, the finer the quality of the grapes, and hence the wine from those grapes.

Appendix C

Contact Information for Wineries Whose Wines Are Available Only (Or Mainly) by Mailing List

• •

*S*ome wineries have such a tiny production, or their wines are so sought-after — or both — that obtaining their wines in any other way than being placed on the winery's mailing list is impossible. Even then, in some cases, there's no guarantee that you'll receive their wines in the near future. For instance, we know for sure that three of the wineries on our list, Grace Family Vineyards, Leonetti Cellar, and Williams & Selyem Winery, have waiting lists for their mail-order wines.

Also, check with your state alcohol regulatory board to make sure that it's legal for you to receive wine from another state through mail order.

The wineries listed here all have outstanding wines; ordering their wines by mail might be worth all the effort. Good luck!

California

Napa Valley's Grace Family Vineyards makes a Cabernet Sauvignon that is one of the world's most sought-after wines, with only 200 cases produced annually:

> ✔ Grace Family Vineyards
> 1210 Rockland Road
> St. Helena, CA 94574
> Telephone: 707-963-0808

Rafanelli's red Zinfandel has been consistently rated as one of the truly great ones — a classic Dry Creek Zin (well balanced with good acidity). His Cabernet Sauvignon is also pretty darn good. The winery is located in Dry Creek Valley, Sonoma:

> ✔ A. Rafanelli Winery
> 4685 Dry Creek Road
> Healdsburg, CA 95448
> Telephone: 707-433-1385

Joel Peterson, winemaker and co-owner of Ravenswood, is recognized as one of the finest winemakers in the U.S.; all of Ravenswood's single-vineyard red Zinfandels (Peterson makes about five of them) are superb, and they are available mainly through mail order. One vineyard (Dickerson Vineyard) is in Napa; the rest are in Sonoma, as is his winery:

> ✔ Ravenswood
> 18701 Gehricke Road
> Sonoma, CA 95476
> Telephone: 707-938-1960
> Fax: 707-938-9459

Helen Turley of Napa has been making some awesome wines lately. For all of Turley Cellars' single-vineyard red Zinfandels and Petite Sirahs, get on the mailing list:

> ✔ Turley Cellars
> 3358 St. Helena Highway
> St. Helena, CA 94574
> Telephone: 707-963-0940
> Fax: 707-963-8683

Williams & Selyem, in the Russian River Valley, Sonoma, are producing some of the best, highly sought-after Pinot Noirs in the U.S., as well as a very good Zinfandel. For their single-vineyard Pinot Noirs, especially Rochioli Vineyard and Allen Vineyard, and their Zinfandel, call to be placed on their mailing list:

> ✔ Williams & Selyem Winery
> 6575 Westside Road
> Healdsburg, CA 95448-9416
> Telephone: 707-433-6425

Washington State

DeLille Cellars, in the Puget Sound area near Seattle, is a new winery making some of Washington's most sought-after wines. Their Bordeaux-type blend, Chaleur Estate (Cabernet Sauvignon, Merlot, and Cabernet Franc), as well as a second red wine (called D 2), is made from Yakima Valley grapes. The surest way to buy them is to get on their mailing list:

> ✔ DeLille Cellars/Chaleur Estate
> P. O. Box 2233
> Woodinville, WA 98072
> Telephone: 206-489-0544
> Fax: 206-402-9295

Leonetti's Cabernet Sauvignons and Merlots are consistently among the highest-rated red wines in the U.S. They're probably Washington's rarest, most sought-after wines. Write to be placed on their mailing list. The winery is located in the Walla Walla Valley:

> ✔ Leonetti Cellar
> 1321 School Avenue
> Walla Walla, WA 99362
> The winery requests that you make all inquiries in writing; it is not equipped to handle telephone requests.

Quilceda Creek has one of the smallest wineries in Washington. They make mainly one wine — Cabernet Sauvignon. It's very special; get on their mailing list. The winery is in the Puget Sound area, near Seattle; the grapes are from the Columbia Valley:

> ✔ Quilceda Creek Vintners
> 5226 Old Machias Road
> Snohomish, WA 98290
> Telephone and Fax: 360-568-2389

Andrew Will Cellars, in the Puget Sound area, is even smaller than Quilceda Creek, with less than 1,000 cases produced annually. For all of Andrew Will's Cabernet Sauvignons and Merlots, get on the mailing list:

> ✔ Andrew Will Cellars
> 1526 SW Bank Road
> Vashon, WA 98070
> Telephone: 206-463-3290
> Fax: 206-463-3524

Red Wine Vintage Chart: 1975 – 1995

*A*ny vintage wine chart must be considered only a rough guide — a general, average rating of the vintage year in a particular wine region. There will always be some wines that are exceptions to the vintage's rating. For example, a few exceptional wine producers may find a way to make a decent — or even fine — wine in a so-called *poor* vintage.

The letter ratings (regarding when to drink the various vintages) are also general, or average, ratings. For example, you can find some tired 1987 Bordeaux from the Médoc and Graves and some tired 1985 red Burgundies, but the average rating for both vintages must be a "c" (ready to drink), always with the proviso, of course, that the wines have been stored well. This provision applies to all the ratings.

Wine Region	1975	1976	1977	1978	1979	1980	1981	1982	1983	1984	1985
Bordeaux:											
Médoc, Graves	85b	75c	70d	80c	80c	75d	80c	95b	85b	70d	90c
Pomerol, St.-Emilion	90c	80c	65d	80c	80c	70d	80c	95b	85b	65d	85c
Red Burgundy:											
Côte de Nuits	50d	85c	60d	90c	80c	85c	65d	75c	85b	75c	85c
Côte de Beaune	50d	85d	55d	85c	80d	80c	70d	75d	80c	70d	85c
Northern Rhône	70d	80c	70c	100b	85c	80c	75d	85c	90b	75c	90c
Southern Rhône	60d	70d	65d	95b	85c	75d	85c	70d	85c	70d	80c
Rioja (Spain)	85c	80c	70d	85c	75c	75c	85c	90c	80c	70c	80c
Piedmont	65d	65d	65d	90a	80c	75c	70c	90b	75c	65d	95b
Tuscany	85c	60d	85c	75d	80c	70d	80d	80c	85c	60d	95c
California North Coast:											
Cabernet Sauvignon	85c	85b	85c	85b	80c	80c	75c	75c	70d	85c	90b

Wine Region	1986	1987	1988	1989	1990	1991	1992	1993	1994	1995
Bordeaux:										
Médoc, Graves	90a	75c	85a	90b	95a	75b	75b	80a	85a	90a
Pomerol, St.-Emilion	85a	75d	85a	90b	95a	65c	75b	80a	85a	90a
Red Burgundy:										
Côte de Nuits	75d	85c	85b	85b	95a	85b	75b	85a	80a	85a
Côte de Beaune	70d	80d	85b	85b	90b	70c	80b	85a	80a	85a
Northern Rhône	80b	75c	90c	95b	90a	90b	75c	65c	85a	90a
Southern Rhône	75c	60d	85c	95a	95b	70c	75c	80b	85a	90a
Rioja (Spain)	80c	80c	85b	90b	85b	75c	85b	85b	90a	85a
Piedmont	85c	80c	90a	95a	95a	80c	70c	85b	80a	90a
Tuscany	85c	75c	90a	70c	90b	75c	70c	75c	85a	90a
California North Coast:										
Cabernet Sauvignon	80c	85c	75c	80b	95b	95a	90b	85a	95a	90a

Key:

100	=	Outstanding
95	=	Excellent
90	=	Very good
85	=	Good
80	=	Fairly good
75	=	Average
70	=	Below average
65	=	Poor
50-60	=	Very poor
a	=	Too young to drink
b	=	May be consumed now, but will improve with time
c	=	Ready to drink
d	=	May be too old

Good Older Vintages of Red Wines

Wine Region	Vintage(s)
Bordeaux:	
Médoc, Graves	1959, 1961, 1970
Pomerol, St.-Emilion	1961, 1964, 1970
Burgundy:	
Côte de Nuits	1959, 1964, 1969, 1972
Côte de Beaune	1959, 1969
Northern Rhône	1959, 1961, 1966, 1969, 1970, 1972 (Hermitage)
Southern Rhône	1961, 1967, 1971
Rioja (Spain)	1964, 1970
Piedmont	1964, 1971
Tuscany	1967, 1970 (Brunello di Montalcino), 1971
California North Coast:	
Cabernet Sauvignon	1951, 1958, 1968, 1970, 1974

Index

● ●

IDG BOOKS WORLDWIDE REGISTRATION CARD

RETURN THIS REGISTRATION CARD FOR FREE CATALOG

Title of this book: **Red Wine For Dummies**™

My overall rating of this book: ❏ Very good [1] ❏ Good [2] ❏ Satisfactory [3] ❏ Fair [4] ❏ Poor [5]

How I first heard about this book:

❏ Found in bookstore; name: [6] _____ ❏ Book review: [7] _____

❏ Advertisement: [8] _____ ❏ Catalog: [9] _____

❏ Word of mouth; heard about book from friend, co-worker, etc.: [10] ❏ Other: [11] _____

What I liked most about this book:

_____

_____

What I would change, add, delete, etc., in future editions of this book:

_____

_____

Other comments:

_____

_____

Number of computer books I purchase in a year: ❏ 1 [12] ❏ 2-5 [13] ❏ 6-10 [14] ❏ More than 10 [15]

I would characterize my computer skills as: ❏ Beginner [16] ❏ Intermediate [17] ❏ Advanced [18] ❏ Professional [19]

I use ❏ DOS [20] ❏ Windows [21] ❏ OS/2 [22] ❏ Unix [23] ❏ Macintosh [24] ❏ Other: [25] _____
(please specify)

I would be interested in new books on the following subjects:
(please check all that apply, and use the spaces provided to identify specific software)

❏ Word processing: [26] _____ ❏ Spreadsheets: [27] _____

❏ Data bases: [28] _____ ❏ Desktop publishing: [29] _____

❏ File Utilities: [30] _____ ❏ Money management: [31] _____

❏ Networking: [32] _____ ❏ Programming languages: [33] _____

❏ Other: [34] _____

I use a PC at (please check all that apply): ❏ home [35] ❏ work [36] ❏ school [37]
❏ other: [38] _____

The disks I prefer to use are ❏ 5.25 [39] ❏ 3.5 [40] ❏ other: [41] _____

I have a CD ROM: ❏ yes [42] ❏ no [43]

I plan to buy or upgrade computer hardware this year: ❏ yes [44] ❏ no [45]

I plan to buy or upgrade computer software this year: ❏ yes [46] ❏ no [47]

Name: _____ Business title: [48] _____

Type of Business: [49] _____

Address (❏ home [50] ❏ work [51]/Company name: _____)

Street/Suite# _____

City [52]/State [53]/Zipcode [54]: _____ Country [55] _____

❏ **I liked this book!**
You may quote me by name in future IDG Books Worldwide promotional materials.

My daytime phone number is _____

IDG BOOKS

THE WORLD OF
COMPUTER
KNOWLEDGE

❏ YES!
Please keep me informed about IDG's World of Computer Knowledge. Send me the latest IDG Books catalog.